D0931381

CAMBRIDGE CLASSICAL STUDIES

General Editors

M. I FINLEY   E. J. KENNEY   G. E. L. OWEN

PERSIUS AND
THE PROGRAMMATIC SATIRE

PERSIUS AND THE PROGRAMMATIC SATIRE

A STUDY IN FORM AND IMAGERY

BY

J. C. BRAMBLE

Fellow of Corpus Christi College
Oxford

CAMBRIDGE
AT THE UNIVERSITY PRESS
1974

Published by the Syndics of the Cambridge University Press
Bentley House, 200 Euston Road, London NW1 2DB
American Branch: 32 East 57th Street, New York, N.Y.10022

© Faculty of Classics, University of Cambridge 1974

Library of Congress Catalogue Card Number: 72–83579

ISBN: 0 521 08703 1

Printed in Great Britain
at the University Printing House, Cambridge
(Brooke Crutchley, University Printer)

CONTENTS

CONTENTS

PARENTIBUS OPTIMIS

PREFACE

I wish here simply to record my debts, which are many. I should like to thank Messrs R. G. G. Coleman and A. G. Lee, Dr A. J. Woodman, and Professors C. O. Brink and W. J. N. Rudd for their comments on parts or the whole of earlier drafts, Miss R. S. Padel for helpful suggestions about pruning at a later stage, Dr R. O. A. M. Lyne for reading the proofs, and, above all, Professor E. J. Kenney for his encouragement and patience as he was presented with this study in one amended version after another. A further debt to Professor Rudd is in respect of his – and his publishers' – permission to print an adapted version of his recent translation of Persius' first satire from *The Satires of Horace and Persius* (Penguin Books 1973). My gratitude is also due to the staff of the Cambridge University Press for the care and expertise applied by them to the process of publication. Finally, I wish to thank the Master and Fellows of Peterhouse, Cambridge, for their award of a Stone Research Fellowship for the period 1967–70, during which time the ideas for this book were first formulated.

Corpus Christi College   J.C.B.
Oxford
November 1973

ABBREVIATIONS

(A) *Books and articles*

After first mention, the following abbreviations are used:

Anderson 1960   W. S. Anderson, 'Imagery in the Satires of Horace and Juvenal', *AJPh* LXXXI (1960), 225–60.

Assfahl   G. Assfahl, *Vergleich und Metapher bei Quintilian* (Stuttgart 1932).

Brink, *Prolegomena*   C. O. Brink, *Horace on Poetry, Prolegomena to the Literary Epistles* (Cambridge 1963).

Buscaroli   C. Buscaroli, *Persio Studiato in Rapporto a Orazio e a Giovenale*, parte prima (Imola 1924).

Commager   S. Commager, *The Odes of Horace: A Critical Study* (New Haven and London 1962).

Curtius   E. R. Curtius, *European Literature and the Latin Middle Ages*, translated by Willard R. Trask (New York 1953).

D'Alton   J. F. D'Alton, *Roman Literary Theory and Criticism* (London 1931 and New York 1962).

Dessen   C. S. Dessen, *Iunctura Callidus Acri: a Study of Persius' Satires*, Illinois Studies in Language and Literature LIX (Urbana, Chicago, and London 1968).

Fiske   G. C. Fiske, *Lucilius and Horace*, University of Wisconsin Studies in Language and Literature 7 (Madison 1920).

Fraenkel   E. Fraenkel, *Horace* (Oxford 1957).

Gerhard   G. A. Gerhard, *Phoinix von Kolophon* (Leipzig and Berlin 1909).

Highet   G. Highet, *Juvenal the Satirist* (Oxford 1954).

Korzeniewski	D. Korzeniewski, 'Die erste Satire des Persius' (Originalbeitrag 1968), in *Die Römische Satire*, Wege der Forschung 238, edited by D. Korzeniewski (Wissenschaftliche Buchgesellschaft, Darmstadt 1970)
Lilja	Saara Lilja, *Terms of Abuse in Roman Comedy* (Helsinki 1965).
Marmorale	E. Marmorale, *Persio*, second edition (Florence 1965).
Otto	A. Otto, *Die Sprichwörter und sprichwörtlichen Redensarten der Römer* (Leipzig 1890; reprinted Hildesheim 1962).
Rudd	Niall Rudd, *The Satires of Horace* (Cambridge 1966).
Taillardat	J. Taillardat, *Les Images d'Aristophane* (Paris 1965).
Van Hook	Larue Van Hook, *The Metaphorical Terminology of Greek Rhetoric and Literary Criticism* (Chicago, diss. 1905).
Villeneuve, *Essai*	F. Villeneuve, *Essai sur Perse* (Paris 1918).
Wimmel	W. Wimmel, *Kallimachos in Rom, die Nachfolge seines apologetischen Dichtens in der Augusteerzeit*, *Hermes* Einzelschrift 16 (Wiesbaden 1960).

References to the authors of other books and articles, in addition to those listed above, will be found in the index of modern authors.

(B) *Editions of Persius are cited as follows:*

Bo	Domenicus Bo, *A. Persi Flacci Saturarum Liber* (Paravia, Turin 1969).
Casaubon	*A. Persii Flacci Saturarum Liber cum eius vita, vetere scholiaste et I. Casauboni notis cura et opera M. Casauboni ... Typis repetendum curavit et recentiorum interpretum observationibus selectis auxit Fridericus Duebner* (Leipzig 1833).

Clausen	W. V. Clausen, *A. Persi Flacci Saturarum Liber*, *accedit vita* (Oxford 1956).
Conington	*The Satires of A. Persius Flaccus, with a translation and commentary by John Conington, edited by H. Nettleship*, third edition (Oxford 1893; reprinted Hildesheim 1967).
Heinrich	*Des A. Persius Flaccus Satiren berichtigt und erklärt von* C. F. Heinrich (Leipzig 1844).
Hermann	C. F. Hermann, *A. Persi Flacci Saturarum Liber*, Bibliotheca scriptorum Graec. et Roman. Teubneriana (Leipzig 1854).
Jahn	O. Jahn, *A. Persi Flacci Saturarum Liber; cum scholiis antiquis* (Leipzig 1843).
Koenig	*A. Persi Flacci Saturae VI ad optimorum exemplarium fidem recensitae atque proemio et indice rerum instructae a* G. L. Koenig (Göttingen 1803).
Macleane	A. J. Macleane, *Juvenalis et Persii Satirae, with a Commentary* (London 1857).
Némethy	*A. Persii Flacci Satirae, ed. adnot. exeg. et indice verborum instruxit* Geyza Némethy (Budapest 1903).
Owen	*A. Persii Flacci et D. Juni Juvenalis Saturae, ed.* S. G. Owen, second edition (Oxford 1949).
Ramorino	*Le Satire di A. Persio Fl. illustrate con note italiane da* Felice Ramorino, second edition (Turin 1920).
Scivoletto	*A. Persii Flacci Satirae, testo critico e commento a cura di* Nino Scivoletto, Bibl. di studi superiori, vol. 36 (Florence 1956; second edition 1961).
Villeneuve	*A. Persii Flacci Satirae, Les satires de Perse, texte latin publié avec un commentaire critique et explicatif par* F. Villeneuve (Paris 1918).

(C) *Extensive use has been made of the following editions of authors other than Persius:*

Austin	R. G. Austin, *Quintiliani Institutionis Oratoriae Liber XII* (Oxford 1948; reprinted Oxford 1954).

Brink   C. O. Brink, *Horace on Poetry, the 'Ars Poetica'* (Cambridge 1971).

Friedländer   L. Friedländer, *D. Junii Juvenalis Saturarum Libri V, mit erklärenden Anmerkungen* (Leipzig 1895).

Gow–Page   A. S. F. Gow and D. L. Page, *The Greek Anthology, Hellenistic Epigrams* (Cambridge 1965).

Gow–Page, *Garland*   A. S. F. Gow and D. L. Page, *The Greek Anthology: The Garland of Philip and some contemporary epigrams* (Cambridge 1968).

Knox   A. D. Knox, *Herodes, Cercidas and the Greek Choliambic Poets*, The Loeb Classical Library (London and Cambridge, Massachusetts 1961).

Lejay   Paul Lejay, *Œuvres d'Horace, Satires* (Paris 1911).

Marx   F. Marx, *C. Lucili Carminum Reliquiae*, 2 vols. (Leipzig 1904 and 1905).

Mayor   J. E. B. Mayor, *Thirteen Satires of Juvenal with a Commentary*, second edition (London 1872 and 1878).

Nisbet and Hubbard   R. G. M. Nisbet and Margaret Hubbard, *A Commentary on Horace: Odes Book I* (Oxford 1970).

Russell   D. A. Russell, *'Longinus' on the Sublime* (Oxford 1964).

Summers   W. C. Summers, *Select Letters of Seneca* (London 1910; reprinted London 1952).

Wickham   E. C. Wickham, *Quinti Horatii Flacci opera omnia, The Works of Horace, with a Commentary*, vol. II, *The Satires, Epistles, and de Arte Poetica* (Oxford 1891).

For further bibliography on Persius the reader is recommended to consult the works of Bo and Dessen mentioned above.

INTRODUCTION

At the end of the *Satyricon*, by means of a simple play on the verb *comedere*, Petronius creates an horrific scene in which a dying man requests that his body be eaten by his legatees. All that Petronius has done is remind his reader of the literal sense of a verb frequently used as a metaphor for squandering an inheritance. Concrete embodiment of commonplace metaphor is likewise found at the opening of Persius' third satire, where the vocabulary of philosophical enlightenment, signalised by *clarum mane* and *lumine*, is interwoven with more mundane detail concerning windows and chinks in the shutters: metaphor is translated into the fabric of a realistic situation.

Most of the following pages are devoted to an examination of Persius' employment of a similar technique in his first satire – to a study of the way that he takes the concepts and metaphors of literary criticism back to their physical origins, so concretely dramatising an analysis of the causes of decadence in contemporary letters. I have attempted to find out why the composition has this particular form rather than any other, an enquiry which has involved speculation about the conceptual stage prior to actual composition. I have also dealt with the expressivist implications of the prelude to the fifth satire, and with Juvenal's adoption of the high style. Additional material relevant to, or arising from, my main concerns appears in excursuses or appendixes.

CHAPTER I

STYLE AND EXPRESSION IN PERSIUS' FIFTH SATIRE

Persius was not a wanton obscurantist. He wrote as he did for a reason; discontented with the state of literature, he required something other than the traditional poetic idiom for the expression of his ideas. Conventional literary language had, in his opinion, become too bland and voluble to have any true reserve of meaning. From the first satire we see that he regarded contemporary literature as utterly decadent and meaningless.[1] This work will occupy my attention for most of this study, but for the moment I should like to consider two passages which occur towards the beginning of the fifth satire. One of these is openly programmatic, the other only obliquely so, but both are more informative guides to Persius' stylistic aims than anything in the predominantly negative first satire. Here we are allowed insight into the reasons for his adoption of a difficult and complex manner as an antidote to triviality.[2] The first passage, v. 14–16, is commonly adduced with reference to Persius' methods. After a scornful repudiation of the high style, represented here by the hundred voices[3] of the

---

[1] The verdict belongs to P. We need not accept it ourselves; much less should we add it to other complaints, and apply them cumulatively to the period. Roman discontent, normally couched in metaphoric or moral terminology, has sometimes wrongly influenced our estimate of first-century literature.

[2] Of course the prologue also informs us of his conception of poetry. Rejecting the traditional imagery of inspiration, it advances a picture of a half-member of the fraternity of poets, his self-sufficiency tacitly contrasted with the materialistic incentives of other writers. Its programmatic implications have been discussed in recent years by e.g. K. J. Reckford, 'Studies in Persius', *Hermes* xc (1962), 476–504; E. C. Witke, 'The function of Persius' choliambics', *Mnem.* xv ser. 4 (1962), 153–8, *idem*, *Latin Satire* (Leiden 1970), pp. 79–82, and n. 3 with bibliography, and E. Paratore, 'I "choliambi", la prima e la quinta satira di Persio', *Studi in onore di Enrica Malcovati, Athenaeum* (1964), reprinted in *Biografia e Poetica di Persio* (Florence 1968); also C. S. Dessen, *Iunctura Callidus Acri*, Illinois Studies in Language and Literature LIX (1968), ch. 2 (*v. CR* ns XXI (1971), 46–7).

[3] *V.* P. Courcelle, *REL* XXXIII (1955), 231–40, A. Cameron, *Philologus* CXI (1967), 308–9 and A. S. Hollis on Ov. *Met.* VIII. 533–4.

inspired bard, he advises himself, through the medium of an interlocutor, of the procedure to be adopted:

> 'verba togae sequeris iunctura callidus acri,
> ore teres modico, pallentis radere mores
> doctus et ingenuo culpam defigere ludo.'

His language is to be that of everyday existence, *verba togae*. The toga signifies a modest lack of pretensions; at the furthest possible remove from senseless tragic bombast, it aligns him with the normalities, and more important, with the actualities, of life.[1] To follow the *verba togae* is to profess realism, an insistence on life in contrast to the irrelevances of epic, tragedy and mythology: but that life is presented to the reader as an inner quality, not as mundane or superficial fact. As we shall see, *verba togae* are set to explore the complexities of mind and spirit, after rejecting the attractions of the external world.

Telling himself to follow the language of ordinary life, Persius adds a further injunction about method: he must be skilled in making striking combinations of words. Of course, *iunctura callidus acri* can be retraced to Hor. *A.P.* 47–8, as also *verba togae*, a concrete counterpart to *notum ... verbum*:

> dixeris egregie, notum si callida verbum
> reddiderit iunctura novum.

But imitation is by no means the same as mindless repetition: Horace is chosen because his precept still holds good. By following ordinary Roman diction, and by deploying that diction in striking conjunctions, Persius hoped to avoid the triviality and bombast of the other genres. His adoption of the *os modicum* involved rejection of the gaping mouth of tragedy, and conscious choice of controlled and modulated utterance. But the end of his pursuit of linguistic dexterity is ethical, not formal: the satirist surgeon uses his training as a social corrective, to remove the infection on the surface of morality.[2]

---

[1] As D. Henss, 'Die Imitationstechnik des Persius', *Philologus* XCIX (1955), 287, notes, 'das Symbol des römischen Alltagslebens', and as Professor Rudd observes in a private communication, the dress of free citizens – hence a prelude to the satire's main theme.

[2] V. Jahn on v. 15, '*pallentes* morbo vitioque'. With *radere* Conington compares Pers. I. 107, *teneras ... radere ... auriculas*, and III. 114, *tenero ...*

In the second passage of the fifth satire, lines 19–29, we see Persius in the midst of the urge to expression, struggling to give verbal form to feelings lodged deep within himself – feelings which could not be materialised in the easy idiom of conventional language. The passage has a transitional function, acting as a bridge between the literary theme of lines 1–18, and the moral themes of the body of the satire, which begin at line 30 with the education of Persius by Cornutus. In this position it looks like an attempt at reconciling literature with morality; having ceased to be the vacant, ornamental servant of tragedy, language is to find a new meaning as the vehicle of philosophy. Although Persius narrows his focus from literature in general to the specific occasion of expressing his debt to Cornutus (*nunc*, 21; *hic*, 26), the lines provide incidental, but significant, illustration of his concept of the function of letters. Within the compass of eleven lines a Roman poet refuses to acquiesce in the limited expressive possibilities of traditional poetic diction – no ordinary phenomenon:

> non equidem hoc studeo, pullatis ut mihi nugis
> pagina turgescat dare pondus idonea fumo.
> secrete loquimur. tibi nunc hortante Camena
> excutienda damus praecordia, quantaque nostrae
> pars tua sit, Cornute, animae, tibi, dulcis amice,
> ostendisse iuvat. pulsa, dinoscere cautus
> quid solidum crepet et pictae tectoria linguae.
> hic ego centenas ausim deposcere fauces,
> ut quantum mihi te sinuoso in pectore fixi
> voce traham pura, totumque hoc verba resignent
> quod latet arcana non enarrabile fibra.

Persius begins with a negative definition of intent: he has no wish to become embroiled in the dark but trivial involutions of the tragic style, an objection shared with other writers, but personally expressed. A contrast between elaborate melodramatic language and insubstantiality of content is initiated by *pullatis . . . nugis*, a collocation based on such metaphors as *vestire oratione*. Persius has no time for trifling subject matter dressed in the

ulcus in ore . . . radere; with *pallentis* it suggests a scraping operation done with a surgical instrument.

4

impressive but completely superficial style of tragedy. The contrast is continued in *dare pondus idonea fumo*, where the heavy-weight style is applied to insignificant content. Hor. *Ep.* I. 19.42, *nugis addere pondus*, has been divided into two parts, the specific *fumo* substituted for the abstract *nugis*, which is moved back to assume a new aspect in conjunction with its 'dress' in *pullatis*. The same idea appears twice in different guise, *nugis* taken up by *fumo*, and *pullatis* by *pondus*, so subjecting immaterial content to a dark and weighty style. For all its obtrusive stylistic devices, tragedy cannot conceal its poverty of subject matter.

Persius then begins a positive definition of method. The two simple words – *secrete loquimur*, their directness an immediate contrast with the meaningless ornament of *pullatis . . . nugis . . . turgescat*, and, further back, with the pompous ambitions of *grande locuturi*, line 7 – tell us a great deal. He is exclusive – *secrete*, and uses the ordinary speaking voice – *loquimur*: although the primary meaning of *secrete loquimur* may be 'we (Persius and Cornutus) are talking on our own', the words also ask to be construed in the light of literary apologetics. Persius has here converted to his own purpose the distinction between public bombast and esoteric refinement. The distinction was in itself conventional: to say that one spoke only to the discerning few, spurning the common crowd, was to employ a literary common-place.[1] But context could disguise or transmute a commonplace, as here, where the reader cannot dismiss Persius' claims as merely conventional. A writer cannot invent something out of nothing: his medium is already biased and coloured by previous usage, and that bias and colour inevitably appear on inspection. This is

---

[1] It seems as though Lucilius bequeathed the themes of exclusiveness and rejection of the crowd to his successors: with 588–9 M, *nunc itidem populo* ⟨*placere nolo*⟩ *his cum scriptoribus:|voluimus capere animum illorum*, cf. Hor. *Sat.* I. 4.71–2, *nulla taberna meos habeat neque pila libellos,|quis manus insudet volgi Hermogenisque Tigelli*; *Ep.* I. 20.4–5, where his book, about to be publicised, deserts its prior refinement: *paucis ostendi gemis et communia laudas,|non ita nutritus*; *Sat.* I. 10.81 ff., admitting as readers only a few privileged friends. Further, *Carm.* III. 1.1, *odi profanum vulgus et arceo* (a literary, as well as a ritualistic claim: cf. Petron. 118.4), II. 16.39–40, *malignum|spernere vulgus*: cf. I. 1.29 ff., Prop. II. 13.13–14, and Mart. II. 86.11–12.

not to say that a neat genetic stemma can be constructed: just that there is no such thing as complete freedom. An observable process of transmission, however haphazard, necessarily exists, given that a writer's language belongs in the first instance to his predecessors. Originality only exists in relationship to tradition: depending on his personal gifts, the individual writer can reshape, modify, and reintegrate his transmitted medium in such a way that conventional elements begin to take on a new appearance. The private voice of Persius – *secrete loquimur* – is a case in point. Taken as an advertisement for what follows, the privacy ceases to maintain a merely retrospective connexion with the contrast between esotericism and banality in literature, and begins to look forward to a new definition of poetry's function. Assertion of privacy becomes a claim to knowledge of internal values, to be witness to hidden secrets. Persius is no longer esoteric and exclusive in the purely literary sense, his privacy and separation from the crowd now being qualifications for personal insight into man's moral existence. In practice the theoretical principle behind *secrete loquimur* is consistently substantiated.

The next sentence also transmutes a commonplace, imparting moral colour to its normal literary signification:

> tibi nunc hortante Camena
> excutienda damus praecordia, quantaque nostrae
> pars tua sit, Cornute, animae, tibi, dulcis amice,
> ostendisse iuvat.

His Muse may be the Italian, and perhaps Horatian *Camena* (he uses the word ten times), rather than the Greek *Musa*, but she still epitomises the conventions of inspiration. In the prologue, she and her sisters were dismissed out of hand, 4 ff.:

> Heliconidasque pallidamque Pirenen
> illis remitto, quorum imagines lambunt
> hederae sequaces.

Here *Camena* is retained for the purpose of metamorphosis, her dictates – that Persius should surrender his innermost being to inspection by Cornutus (with *excutienda* cf. I. 49) – at a far remove from the themes she usually recommends. A traditional motif in a novel context helps to redefine the nature and mission

6

of poetry, somewhat as at *prol.* 7, *ad sacra vatum carmen adfero nostrum*, where the conventional *sacra vatum* – compare Prop. III. 1.1, IV. 6.1, Hor. *Carm.* III. 1.3, IV. 9.28, Ov. *Tr.* IV. 10.19, Manil. I. 6 – is ironically juxtaposed to the personal *carmen nostrum*, the combination amounting to a vindication of the individual's claim to innovate within tradition. Like the elegists,[1] Persius has an interest in claiming a distinctive type of poetry: though *nunc* at 21 refers to the present moment of relation to Cornutus, the reader is indirectly informed of the satirist's reinterpretation of the communal Muse. Then, through the intricate syntax of line 21, suggestive of the inextricable union of his own and Cornutus' souls, Persius exhibits something of the complexity involved in her exhortations.

Requesting Cornutus to test him – what rings true, what is empty decoration? – he succeeds in identifying moral falsehood with 'poetic' diction:

> pulsa, dinoscere cautus
> quid solidum crepet et pictae tectoria linguae.

On reading 'the coverings of a painted tongue', *pictae tectoria linguae*,[2] we realise that the object of *pulsa* is not only his soul as regarded by Cornutus, but also the verbal formulation which is the vehicle for expressing their relationship. If Persius' language is superficial and opaque, no more than an ornamental veneer, then it will be non-expressive, hiding the truths of the reality with which it purports to deal: if style is to express unconventional ideas, then it must dispense with commonplace incrustation. The

---

[1] S. Commager, *The Odes of Horace, A Critical Study* (Yale 1962), pp. 2 ff., has some interesting observations on 'The Descent of the Muses'. The elegists in particular advocate love as the proper subject of poetry by substituting their mistress for the Muse of inspiration. Propertius denies the influence of Apollo and the Muses in favour of Cynthia, II. 1.3–4 (C. p. 5 n. 5, compares Prop. II. 30.37–40, Ov. *Am.* I. 3.19, II. 17.34, III. 12.16, *Tr.* IV. 10.59); Ovid dismisses the whole apparatus of inspiration, to claim *usus* – experience – as the moving factor behind his work, *A.A.* I. 25–30.

[2] Commentators refer *tectoria* to stucco or plaster used to decorate walls, noting that the metaphor is 'from striking a wall to see whether it is solid stone or not' (Conington); cf. Gell. XIII. 27.3, *quodam quasi ferumine immisso fucatior*. Taken with 27 ff., it acquires the abstract sense inherent in its etymological derivation from *tego*; cf. the metaphor of covering at Hor. *Sat.* I. 3.56, of an uncharitable refusal to award credit where due: *sincerum cupimus vas incrustare*.

painted tongue conceals, while the unaffected voice has the power
of revelation: compare Hor. *Sat.* II. 7.41–2, quoted below, p. 153.[1]

The process of redefinition is continued by the usurpation of the
outworn hundred voices for the causes of friendship, philosophy,
and self-realisation:

> hic ego centenas ausim deposcere fauces,
> ut quantum mihi te sinuoso in pectore fixi
> voce traham pura, totumque hoc verba resignent
> quod latet arcana non enarrabile fibra.

The first word, *hic*, is emphatic: 'this, if any, is the place for your
hundred voices'. Persius has robbed the devotees of high inspiration of their pompous convention:

> Vatibus hic mos est, centum sibi poscere voces,
> centum ora et linguas optare in carmina centum.

That was how the satire began. But there he wrote of *voces*, *ora*,
and *linguas*, relatively colourless terms, but nonetheless conveying
a tone of mock elevation. Now he writes of *fauces*.[2] The more
realistic word,[3] employed in a less than traditional manner, like
gutture at 6, deliberately contracts towards physical emphasis on
the mouth, simultaneously parodying the convention, and claiming it for satire: after the bombast of the opening two lines, a
conscious element of descent, aimed at ridiculing the pretensions
of the high style. As in the case of the rehabilitated Muse at 21 ff.,
so now the hundred voices of poetry – an old motif enlivened by
transposition to a new context – tell us what poetry ought to be
doing: immediately, there is the mission of writing about Persius'
relationship to Cornutus:

> ut quantum mihi te sinuoso in pectore fixi
> voce traham pura.

The union of souls found at 23 has now been replaced by the idea

---

[1] With less correspondence between theory and practice, Manilius tells the
reader not to expect ornament in his poetry, *nec dulcia carmina quaeras./
ornari res ipsa negat contenta doceri*, III. 38–9.

[2] The variation *fauces* (*PA²*) is more likely than the repetition *voces* (αVΦS):
as Clausen (*ed. mai.*) notes on v. 64, *voce*, 28, would follow *voces*. It would
also repeat the initial *voces* carefully varied through *ora*, *linguas*, and *gutture*, 2 and 6.

[3] From *ThLL* it appears that *faux* is relatively frequent in all poetic genres,
but is commonly used of animals, also by technical writers.

of internality in *sinuoso* and permanence in *fixi*. Cornutus – and his teachings, for above all Cornutus is a preceptor, an embodiment and paradigm of the Stoic way of life[1] – has been lodged deep within the heart of his pupil. The poetry which that pupil writes is the result of intense personal probing, and the struggle to realise those probings in a clear undecorated voice: to speak with a *vox pura*, and undergo the effort involved in *traham*, descriptive of the struggle to elicit internal feelings,[2] is the only way of bringing forth that which is normally hidden from view. Contrasting with *pictae*, *pura* introduces the ideas of *Latinitas*, terseness, and lack of corruption: but not necessarily the notion of simplicity.[3] The other way of speaking, the *pictae tectoria linguae*, is so ostentatious, so concerned with appearances, as to be devoid of all expressive capacities.

[1] *V.* W. Wimmel, *Kallimachos in Rom*, *Hermes* Einzelschrift, Heft 16 (Wiesbaden 1960), p. 312, who, while discussing Pers. v. 30 ff., points out the analogy between the rôle of Cornutus and that of Horace's father at *Sat.* I. 4.105 ff.: both act as preceptors of the aspiring satirist. Cf. p. 19, on Pers. v. 21 ff.: 'Persius ordnet sich ganz dem Cornutus unter (vgl. Properz und Mäzenas in Prop. 3.9). Bei Persius kommt hinzu, dass Cornutus auch insgeheim den freigewordenen Platz der berufenden Instanz (früher meist Apoll) einzunehmen beginnt . . . So sind auch v. 30 ff. *vita* des Persius und Berufungsimpulse miteinander verbunden wie ursprunglich im kallimachischen Aitienprolog. Unmittelbar hängt diese rechtfertigende "Berufungs-*vita*" zusammen mit Properz 4. 1.131 ff. und Horaz epist. 2. 2.41 ff.'

[2] With *sinuoso* (and *fixi*) cf. P.'s offering at II. 73–4, *sanctosque recessus mentis*.

[3] See L & S sv I. 2, '*free* or *clear* from any admixture or obstruction', also B. I, '*plain, natural, naked, unadorned, unwrought, unmixed, unadulterated, unsophisticated*', Wickham on *puris . . . verbis* at Hor. *Sat.* I. 4.54, 'plain, unadorned', referring to ψιλός at Ar. *Poet.* I. 7. Kiessling–Heinze, *ibid.*, 'καθαροῖς i.e. sine ornamentis', was perhaps thinking of Callimachean refinement, e.g. *Epigr.* VII. I, ἦλθε Θεαίτητος καθαρὴν ὁδόν; *Hymn. Ap.* III f., καθαρή τε καὶ ἀχράαντος . . . / . . . λιβάς. (Mr R. A. Harvey brings to my attention *Anth. Pal.* IV. 2.5 f. by Philippus, dated by Cichorius to *ca* A.D. 40, ἀλλὰ παλαιοτέρων εἰδὼς κλέος, ἐσθλὲ Κάμιλλε,/γνῶθι καὶ ὁπλοτέρων τὴν ὀλιγοστιχίην, which, preceded by a mention of Helicon, amounts to saying 'we are the new Callimacheans'. This might be taken as evidence for the perpetuation of an atmosphere in which the stylistic debate could continue.) Cf. Cic. *de Or.* II. 8.29, *oratio Catuli sic pura est, ut Latine loqui paene solus videatur, Brut.* 261, *pura et incorrupta consuetudo dicendi*, 262, *pura et illustris brevitas*, Quint. X. 1.94 (of Horace) *multo est tersior ac magis purus*, Plin. *Ep.* VII. 9.8, *pressus sermo purusque.*

Then, in the space of one and a half lines, a compressed account of stylistic aims:

> totumque hoc verba resignent
> quod latet arcana non enarrabile fibra.

Persius has progressed from the specific *te*, which also contains the wider notion of 'you and your philosophy', to a more general definition of the proper subject matter of poetry, namely the secret and difficult feelings of the heart:

> quod latet arcana non enarrabile fibra.

Picking up *sinuoso*, *latet* and *arcana* show that truth cannot be found near the surface, while *fibra*, looking back to *pectore* and *praecordia* continues emphasis on the heart as the seat of feeling.[1] The implication of *non enarrabile* is that he will deal with values of a kind not easily conveyed in the expansive idiom of orthodox poetry. The languid and elevated nature of the word in itself precludes expressive potential: anything which is *enarrabile*, capable of facile demonstration, will be trivial and vacuous.[2] Through *traham* he has already told us that there must be a battle to drag out the truth. Now through *verba resignent* he tells us that the heart is a tablet locked by a seal, a seal which is to be broken by words. The conception of the operation is almost

---

[1] There is possibly an allusion to extispicy: '*Fibrae*, teste Varrone (*L.L.* 5.29), et Servio (ad Virg. *Aen.* VI. 599. X. 176. *Georg.* 1.120), iecoris eminentiae sunt, et in auspiciis capiendis summae auctoritatis, unde in sacrificiis eae potissimum nominantur' (Jahn on Pers. II. 26). Admittedly *pectore* is not especially colourful, but *praecordia* is physically detailed: cf. Plin. *N.H.* XI. 37.77, *exta homini ab inferiore viscerum parte separantur membrana, quae praecordia appellant, quia cordi praetenditur, quod Graeci appellaverunt* φρένας.

[2] *V.* Austin on Quint. XII. 10.76, 'this (rare) adjective is always used with a negative or quasi-negative: so vi. 3.6 (with *nescio an*). Thes. L.L. quotes besides only Virg. *Aen.* viii. 625 (with *non*), Sen. *Epp.* 121.10 (with *vix*), Persius v. 29 (with *non*).' Persius possibly had Virgil in mind, who, as *ThLL* notes, was rendering the Homeric ἄσπετος. The prefix *e-* is emphatic (cf. *enarratio*, *enarrare*), referring to the fullness and ease of the operation: cf. *emirabitur* at Hor. *Carm.* I. 5.8, possibly expressive of the youth's open mouth. While making an ironic bow to the 'Inexpressibility Topos' (*v.* E. R. Curtius, *European Literature and the Latin Middle Ages*, tr. W. R. Trask (New York 1953), pp. 159 ff.), P. denies interest in subjects which admit of fully detailed exposition.

impersonal: it is words which break the seal, words which disclose the secrets of the heart. Persius' insistence on expression is that of the formalist who is fully aware of the power of language, of the necessity for careful arrangement of diction as the means of any worthwhile communication. He asks for a change in the mechanics of composition; for if the superimposed bombast of the high style is replaced by the unadulterated idiom of ordinary life, the *verba togae*, then a change of tone will accompany the change of style. Authenticity and seriousness will at last find a place in literature.

To recapitulate: after the negative dismissal of tragedy, which serves as a backcloth for his assertions of realism and serious intent, Persius accommodates time-honoured commonplaces of the Roman poetic to the cause of philosophy; first the motif of exclusiveness, then the Muse of inspiration, finally the hundred voices of the bard. The conversion is effected by constant moral emphasis on the inner man and his feelings, beginning with the personal *excutienda damus praecordia*, and ending with the more comprehensive *quod latet arcana non enarrabile fibra*. The simple *loquimur* and the unaffected *vox pura* contrast with the ornamentation of *pictae tectoria linguae*, accentuating the importance of honest diction, while the two active verbs, *traham* and *resignent*, both of them connected with the difficulty of hammering out a truly revelatory language, form an antithesis with the ideas of concealment contained in the static noun *tectoria*, and of easy, but meaningless diffuseness, contained in the equally static adjective *enarrabile*. If his writings are to be at all significant, the poet must avoid unintegrated mannerisms and idle fluency.

The result will not be simple. When he lays claim to the *verba togae* and to the *vox pura*, Persius does not mean that his poetry is to be easily and immediately understood; his work, manifestly complex and difficult, cannot be quoted as a case of practice falling short of intentions. We do him an injustice if we take the two phrases out of context and read them as assertions of over-all simplicity. For when he adopts the *verba togae* he also becomes *iunctura callidus acri*: conjunction will now complicate the simplicity of ordinary words, juxtaposed as they will be in more than ordinary – even violent – combinations. The outcome of his claim will necessarily be difficult, not on account of his diction as such, but because of its arrangement within the larger structural collocations. Likewise, his adoption of the *vox pura* is qualified by context: it is accompanied by the strenuous probing of the writer – *traham*, and directed at the formulation of things beyond the domain of linguistic facility – *non enarrabile*. Given these conditions, we cannot accuse Persius of producing obscurity after professing simplicity. Complexity and difficulty are the inevitable results of his methods when those methods are seen as a whole. What some critics have regarded as whimsical obscurity is an attempt to escape from the oppressive weight of convention, and to mould an instrument for careful and compact expression.

There is, however, an ultimate irony. No completely new idiom was readily available for linguistic experimentalism of the type which he wished to pursue; instead of making a departure from the *satura* tradition, he went back to Horace's hexameter poetry. Full of complexities in itself, it becomes yet more complex when remodelled by Persius: phrases and images are packed with connotations which reach far beyond surface meaning. The elder Seneca justly criticised Ovid for not knowing when to leave well alone;[1] Persius probably harboured similar feelings about the brilliant, but sometimes brittle, prolixity of the great rhetorician-poet who left such a deep imprint on the literature of the first century. But in his recreation of the Horatian idiom he went to the opposite extreme. Dependent on Horace in the first instance, his manner becomes more involved, more elliptical, and less humane; as a result, we are sometimes given the impression that Persius was writing specimens of satire, rather than satire itself.

EXCURSUS I

The rejection of mythology

The middle and lower genres tend to assert their involvement in life as much by the dismissal of the 'unreal' mythology of epic and tragedy as by any actually realistic features of style. This is to say that realism has a positive and a negative aspect; the non-mythological poet claims

[1] *Contr.* IX. 5.17; cf. II. 2.12.

'life' as his subject, positively, by writing in a low or moderate style, and negatively, by rejecting the unrealities of the higher genres. In the fifth satire Persius dismisses the high style in preparation for the assertion of his own realism; Juvenal does the same in his first satire,[1] pretending to realism elsewhere, as at IV. 34–5, *incipe Calliope. licet et considere: non est/cantandum: res vera agitur*, and XV. 27, where *nuper consule Iunco* contrives the illusion of realistic corroboration of an actual *monstrum*, against the fictitious *monstra* of myth. This is more an indication of intention – to do down epic in favour of satire – than a real date. The *Apocolocyntosis* begins with a similar specification of time, and procedes, *haec ita vera*. Yet nobody takes this as 'the truth'. For Lucilius' dismissal of epic and tragedy, *v.* p. 174 n. 1, and e.g. 587 M, *nisi portenta anguesque volucres ac pinnatos scribitis*.[2] At X. 4, Martial abjures mythological monsters, *non hic Centauros, non Gorgonas Harpyiasque/invenies*, before claiming realism, *hominem pagina nostra sapit*; cf. VIII. 3. The elegists reject the high style to vindicate love as the proper subject of poetry: *v.* e.g. Ov. *Am.* I. 1, II. 1, II. 18, and, with the concluding III. 15 in mind, and therefore less aggressively elegiac, III. 1; also Prop. I. 7, II. 34 and III. 3. Likewise, didactic poetry denigrates 'hackneyed' mythology in favour of a more relevant and exact subject matter; *v.*, e.g., Virg. *Georg.* III. 3ff., Manil. III. 5ff., *Aetna* 9ff., and Nemes. *Cyneg.* 15ff.

EXCURSUS 2

'Pullatis' and 'bullatis' at Persius V. 19

The reading *bullatis*[3] is manifestly inferior. If interpreted as meaning 'inflated' (from *bulla* = 'bubble'), then it merely repeats the idea contained in *turgescat*. If interpreted as meaning 'childish' (from *bulla* the ornament of childhood[4]), then it adds little to *nugis*. Moreover *bulla* occurs only a few lines later, at 31: if we read *bullatis* this would be an inelegant, and pointless repetition, even given Roman carelessness about verbal recurrence.

---

[1] *V.* W. S. Anderson, 'Studies in Book I of Juvenal', *YCS* xv (1957), 36, 'Epic, become the refuge of the dilettantes from the reality of the present, now concerns itself with the imaginary, a heroic past of legendary miracles and superhuman people.'

[2] Cf. Hor. *A.P.* 11–13.

[3] *W Leid. Voss.* 13, '*legitur et* bullatis' Σ.

[4] Juv. XIII. 33, *senior bulla dignissime*.

The reading *pullatis*, on the other hand, has everything in its favour. Meaning 'dressed in black',[1] it looks to the lugubrious themes of tragedy (cf. 3, *maesto ... tradoedo*), and contributes to the overall contrast between superimposed ornament, and expression drawn from within – triviality wrapped in outer garments, the linguistic façade which covers, and submerges true substance (*pictae tectoria linguae*, 25), against Persius' own style, the inner voice which probes into hidden truth. The metaphor originates from the analogy with dress.

EXCURSUS 3

Connotation in ancient literary theory

It is strange that critics and scholars have followed lexicographers in attempting to stratify meaning according to mainly denotative criteria, given that the old rhetoric is akin to the new criticism in its realisation that literary statements can amount to more than the sum of their parts. Concern with literal sense should not outweigh ancient testimony about surface and association, such as, e.g., Sen. *Ep.* LIX. 5, *loqueris quantum vis et plus significas quam loqueris*. Similar evidence for awareness of scope transcending diction is found at Sen. *Contr.* III *praef.* 7, *non lentas nec vacuas explicationes sed plus sensuum quam verborum habentes* and Quint. VIII. 3.83, *vicina praedictae sed amplior virtus est* ἔμφασις, *altiorem praebens intellectum quam quem verba per se ipsa declarant*. An exposition of a theory touching on the weakness of paraphrase, which we might label *quot verba, tot significantia*, along with a sense of the emotive connotations of language, is implied by Quint. VIII. 3.67–8, introducing the stock details belonging to descriptions of the sacks of cities:[2] *sine dubio enim, qui dicit expugnatam esse civitatem, complectitur omnia quaecumque talis fortuna recipit, sed in adfectus minus penetrat brevis his velut nuntius. at si aperias haec quae verbo uno inclusa erant* ... the details follow. Whether *ad Her.* IV. 39.51, *nemo, iudices, est qui possit satis rem consequi verbis nec efferre oratione magnitudinem calamitatis*, is simple hyperbole, or evidence for concern about the expressive powers of language is more difficult to decide.[3] But it is in

[1] Juv. III. 213, *pullati proceres*, of the garments of mourning.
[2] Cf. *Iliad* XXIV. 239 ff., Polyb. II. 56.7, on Phylarchus; Sall. *Cat.* 51.9; Tac. *Hist.* III. 32 and 83; Dio Chrysost. *Or.* XI. 29; Caplan on *ad Her.* IV. 39.51.
[3] Likewise, Sen. *Ep.* CXIV. 1, *sensus audaces et fidem egressi.*

any case obvious that a writer of any period may in practice go beyond the limits of the necessarily theoretical critical vocabulary of his day. For instance, allegory, a term used by the ancients, and probably by Virgil himself, provides a less adequate framework for discussion of the *Aeneid* than symbolism, a more modern, and more appropriate, concept.

CHAPTER 2

THE PROGRAMMATIC SATIRE AND THE METHOD OF PERSIUS I

It was common practice for the Roman satirist to give an account of his genre, arraigning public vice, perhaps ridiculing the insufficiencies of the other literary forms, and informing the reader of the tone which he himself intended to adopt. The vehicle for this account was the programmatic satire. It is quite clear that Horace *Satires* II. I, Persius I, and Juvenal I are related compositions. Their shared features have been duly discussed in the secondary literature. Noting that a scholiast entitles Juvenal's first satire *cur satiras scribat*, also the corresponding formal characteristics of the three programmes, L. R. Shero concludes:[1] 'Each of the satires is constructed upon a traditional framework; and we may reasonably conclude that a satire of this type, ostensibly justifying the writing of satire by means of conventional devices and stock arguments, came to be looked upon as an indispensable feature of the satirist's stock-in-trade.' More recently, E. J. Kenney has detected the following 'pattern of apology':[2] 'First, a pronouncement, lofty to the point of bombast, of the satirist's high purpose and mission. Second, a warning by a friend or the poet's *alter ego* or the voice of prudence – call it what you will. Third, an appeal by the satirist to the great example of Lucilius. Fourth, a renewed warning. Fifth and last, evasion, retraction and equivocation.'[3] But similarities apart, there is a marked degree of divergence in procedure. It is this – innovation within convention – which will occupy my attention.

First, we notice that Persius' programme deals with the blight which has invaded contemporary literature; secondly, that this blight is indicative of moral deficiency. Through criticism of style, the satirist effects another, more serious criticism – of morals. By

[1] 'The Satirist's Apologia', *Univ. Wisconsin Stud. Lang. Lit.* xv (1922), 148 ff., esp. 163.
[2] *PCPhS* ns viii (1962), 36.
[3] Cf. W. S. Anderson, quoted below, p. 164 n. 3.

way of contrast, he emerges with his chosen genre, and his exclusive audience, as one of the last ethically irreproachable Romans, and as the last adherent of sanity and health in style. The major part of the satire is composed of a subtle commerce between style and morals, which engineers an impression of total corruption. Previous critics have noted the presence of a moral dimension alongside the literary-critical, but there has been no analysis of the exact nature of their interaction. We are correctly guided by the comment of, for example, G. C. Fiske, 'His main concern is after all rather with literature as a social phenomenon than with literature as an art', also, 'Persius is, as usual, more concerned than Horace with the social conditions which breed poetry of this type';[1] compare Shero, 'It is important to remember that Persius' attack upon the literary tendencies of his day, with which the greater part of the satire is occupied, is in reality an attack upon the prevailing moral corruption of which these tendencies are the efflorescence. The underlying moral debasement is suggested especially in vss. 15–21,[2] 30–35, 83–87, 103–106',[3] and W. H. Semple, 'It is this change in literature, originating in the common luxury of the age, that Persius regrets in his first satire.'[4] The position is clarified by Kenney, who notes the all-important link between the programme of Persius and Seneca's one hundred and fourteenth *Epistle*: 'The body of the satire between vv. 12 and 120 is taken up with a dissertation on literature and morals at Rome, much of which recalls the 114th *Epistle* of Seneca and which is founded on the same text, *talis hominibus fuit oratio qualis vita*.'[5] Style reflects life.

[1] 'Lucilius, the *Ars Poetica* of Horace, and Persius', *HSCPh* XXIV (1913), 19–20.

[2] The 'debasement' extends past line 21.

[3] *Op. cit.* p. 159 n. 13, apparently appended as an afterthought. At least, it contradicts his option (p. 148) for a predominantly literary-critical theme: 'The greater part of Persius' satire is devoted to discussion of literary ideals and to detailed literary criticism; and Juvenal's satire is mainly a succession of vivid sketches of contemporary follies.' The antithesis is misleading.

[4] *The Bulletin of the John Rylands Library* XLIV (1961–2), 163; cf. G. L. Hendrickson, *CPh* XXIII (1928), 99–112, observing that vice explains incompetence of taste.

[5] *Op. cit.* p. 36. Contrast W. C. Korfmacher, *CJ* XXVIII (1932–3), 276 ff., and A. Cartault, *RPh* ns XLV (1921), 66 ff., who wrongly interpret the poem only as a criticism of literature.

Like Persius, Seneca attributes decline in literature to the decadence of the times. After the preliminary formulation of the principle, we find that style follows the proclivities of society – *genus dicendi aliquando imitatur publicos mores* ... ; and can be proof of moral decay – *argumentum est luxuriae publicae orationis lascivia* (§2) – that is, it can operate as a symbol of decadence. Maecenas is singled out to illustrate the proposition, *non oratio eius aeque soluta est quam ipse discinctus?*, §4; *soluta* and *discinctus* could be interchanged. Man and style are identical. His literary affiliations are paralleled by the outward display of his personal life, *non tam insignita illius verba sunt quam cultus, quam comitatus, quam domus, quam uxor*, §4. A list of the stages in luxury's progress which have prepared for the downfall of Roman literature occurs at §9, the catalogue including *cultus corporum, supellectilis, ipsae domus, cenae*, symptoms of decline similar to those of Persius, who inveighs against physical appearance – *cultus corporum* – at 1. 15 f., furniture – *supellectilis* – at 17 and 52–3, and banquets – *cenae* – at 30 ff. and 51 ff. Here, then, is a series of potential correlatives to the phenomenon of stylistic decay.

The history of the idea behind the Senecan *Epistle*, that literature is a guide to morals, is partly documented in the excursus at the end of this chapter. Adopting the concept, Persius in turn made morals mirror style, assisted in his dramatic development of the principle by the extensive possibilities inherent in the moralistic colour of literary-critical vocabulary. For rhetoricians and critics employed an idiom which was equally valid in matters of style and matters of morality: in particular, literary blemishes were chastised as if moral offences. Sometimes the analogy is only latent, or even inactive: witness Quint. VIII. 3.56, κακόζηλον, *id est mala affectatio, per omne dicendi genus* peccat, *nam et* tumida *et* pusilla *et* praedulcia *et abundantia et arcessita et* exultantia *sub idem nomen cadunt*, where *peccat* is the only unequivocally moral element, even though the various stylistic faults might have been developed into concrete representations of vice. For instance, turgidity – *tumida* – need not have been so closely confined to style: parallel images from those vices which swell the human body – gluttony, perhaps, or gout – could have expanded its area of reference. Likewise, *pusilla* might have been accompanied by a depiction of mental weakness, *praedulcia* and *exultantia* by images of effeminacy and sexual excess. A similar catalogue of defects occurs at Quint. XII. 10.73:

> falluntur enim plurimum qui *vitiosum* et *corruptum* dicendi genus, quod aut verborum *licentia exultat* aut puerilibus sententiolis *lascivit* aut inanibus locis *bacchatur* aut casuris si leviter excutiantur flosculis nitet aut praecipitia pro sublimibus habet aut specie libertatis *insanit*, magis existimant populare et plausibile.

Again, the terminology has latent moral import, but is metaphorically weary, tied by a merely tenuous thread to its place of origin in life.

But properly handled, it had distinct potential. Many terms drawn from human moral existence were at the satirist's disposal: for example, besides those already seen in Quintilian, *effeminatus*, *ebrius*, *pinguis*, and *meretricius*. So when Persius turned to the shortcomings of contemporary literature, he was not only equipped with a principle which directly correlated life and style, but he also had at hand a vocabulary predisposed to disapprobation. If he had used it as it stood, the first satire would have contained a moral dimension anyway, an inevitable circumstance of the terms. But his focus would have been centred on literature, since nobody acquainted with the metaphors of the schools would have been led by mere recurrence to the awareness of moral corruption required by Persius as satirist. In effect, he would have remained a literary critic. But in order to justify his choice of genre, evidence of moral concern must coincide with treatment of literature, so earning the title of satirist, as well as literary critic.[1] His solution is to rejuvenate the stylistic metaphors, by taking them back to their place of genesis in life, so reversing the process which gave them birth. Actual effeminacy now corresponds to stylistic effeminacy; gluttony to turgidity;

---

[1] It must be admitted that in the Roman context 'satire' and 'satirist' do not invariably have predominantly moral connotations. *Satura* included many types of composition (including literary-critical pieces), but its most pronounced tendency was towards the moral: hence I allow myself the antithesis 'literary critic' and 'satirist', though the two are in some ways complementary.

over-meticulous dress to fussy ornament in style; disease and distortion to disfigured composition. From the theoretical principle, *talis hominibus fuit oratio qualis vita*, and its ramifications in literary-critical terminology, Persius creates a class of images which refer simultaneously to life and letters. To these he adds several reminders of the now dishonoured past, and through the recurrent incidence of *auricula*, backed up by the repeated *euge* and *belle*, insinuates that Rome's ears are diseased and incapable of true judgement. My next chapter will be devoted to these various motifs and images, in an attempt to discover something of their history and background, before I go on to assess their function in the context of the first satire.

But first a few words on ancestry. It has been observed that the programmatic satire had its own conventions: can we find a Lucilian or Horatian precedent to the method of Persius – to the depiction of life and letters as interrelated entities? In the case of Lucilius exact conclusions are difficult. Ingredients of the later prescription can be discerned, in book twenty-six for instance, of which J. H. Waszink writes: 'His program ... presents a discussion of the poet with a friend who, like Trebatius in Horace, tries to persuade him out of his purpose of writing satires, but who finally – again like Trebatius – capitulates before Lucilius' argument, viz., that the poet has not only the right but also the duty towards his fellow-citizens to attack and blame anything detrimental to Roman society.'[1] Then there is book thirty, with its disclaimer of malicious intent. There are observations on the moral mission of satire, and on its style; but it is hard to say if there was anything which foreshadowed Persius' sustained identification between the two. Such evidence as remains is collected in the excursus.

There is something highly elusive in Horace's accounts of his genre – a lack of explicit comment, and a tendency to deceive the reader with ironic and elliptical half-truth: this is poetry, not methodical literary theory.[2] But amidst the subtleties and evasions two salient elements emerge – treatment of the satirist's

[1] *Mnem.* ser. 4, vol. XIII (1960), 30.
[2] For full bibliography, *v.* C. O. Brink, *Horace on Poetry, Prolegomena to the Literary Epistles* (Cambridge 1963), and *The 'Ars Poetica'* (1971).

moral mission to society, and of matters appertaining to style. However we find no prolonged correspondence or parallelism, owing, no doubt, to the special nature of Horace's concerns. Unlike Persius, he is not motivated to criticise literature which is downright corrupt: consequently there is no question of relating literary decadence to the prevalent morality. His stylistic pre-occupation is with the manner of satire and the position of Lucilius. The *fautores Lucili*,[1] ignorant of true Callimachean ideals, must be defeated, in a battle fought with their own metaphors. By calling Lucilius' verse careless and muddy, Horace worsts his opponents in the terms of their own pro-fessions.[2] But Lucilius the *inventor* must survive for reinterpreta-tion in the work of his only legitimate successor. Absorbed in this precarious task, Horace never had occasion to correlate style with the vices and follies which, as moralist, he felt moved to expose. But even though Lucilius' morals had to be preserved intact, he might have cast aspersions, pertinent to their peculiar stylistic aberrations, on the characters of his own literary oppo-nents: for example, Crispinus and Fannius, *Sat.* I. 4.14 f., 21–2, might have been indicted as criminals, to give a double edge to his criticisms. Likewise, the epithets *turgidus* and *pulcher*, used respectively of the bloated epicist Furius and the precious Hermogenes at *Sat.* I. 10.17 and 36, might have become full-scale evocations of gluttony and effeminacy. But as they stand, they are only the merest insinuation of the possibility that there may be some flaw in their characters. There is just conceivably a moral note at *Sat.* I. 10.60–1, *amet scripsisse ducentos/ante cibum versus, totidem cenatus*, where Horace directs attention to the dinner perhaps in order to condemn Lucilius' prolixity by association with the insensitive process of eating. In this case we would have an instance of the alimentary metaphor. But Lucilius composes before eating as well as after; and at *Sat.* II. 1.73–4 his food is the modestly respectable vegetable, which would hardly lead to an 'undigested' style. Of course there is the possibility that these

---

[1] *V.* Suet. *Gramm.* 2 and 14.

[2] On this type of water imagery, *v.* Wimmel pp. 222 ff., probably common-place by the time of, e.g., Sen. *Contr.* IV *praef.* 11, *multa erant quae repre-henderes, multa quae suspiceres, cum torrentis modo magnus quidem, sed turbidus flueret.*

times of day were particularly suitable for literary composition, in which case *cibus* would not in itself be especially significant. Apart from one occasion when he seems to be voicing moral objections to the epic – and these objections are rather playful[1] – the only time we see any kind of liaison between *vita* and *oratio* is during his treatment of the style appropriate to the satirist's βίος, or *persona*. And here he is very allusive: *Sat.* I. 4.13 f., *haec ego mecum/compressis agito labris; ubi quid datur oti,/illudo chartis*, implies that his virtuous self-questioning leaves a desirable mark on his style; again, II. 1.73–4, *nugari cum illo et discincti ludere, donec/decoqueretur holus, soliti* (if indeed the allusion is to composition), perhaps suggests that the virtues of vegetarianism are carried over into style. Finally, at II. 6.1 ff., the satirist's modest Callimachean professions are matched by similarly modest social and economic ambitions: *modus agri non ita magnus.*[2]

The method of Persius is distinctive, independent of anything in the literary-critical or programmatic satires of Horace. The types of metaphor deployed were not original creations; literary theory explains their pedigree. But what does appear to be original is the

---

[1] *V. Sat.* II. 1.7 ff., Trebatius' recommended cures for Horace's sleeplessness. A swim, or a bottle of wine, will produce deep sleep: if he must write, why not compose epic? Ideas of mental sluggishness (*somno . . . alto*) and drunkenness (*irriguum . . . mero . . . corpus*: cf. *irriguo . . . somno* at Pers. v. 56, meaning 'drunken sleep'. Lucr. IV. 907 and Virg. *Aen.* III. 511, sometimes adduced, are not to the point) are related to epic. The association of the three adds up to a Callimachean objection to the unwieldy higher genre. Horace's sleeplessness could be interpreted as a literary virtue: cf. Callimachus' tribute to the 'slender' Aratus at *Epigr.* XXIX. 4, Ἀρήτου σύμβολον ἀγρυπνίης. Deep sleep could result from the *pingue ingenium* of the uninitiated; and 'wine-drinking' is the pursuit of the careless. Trebatius is implicitly disqualified by his vulgar character from recognising Callimachean *bona carmina*, his crassness having led him to recommend epic, the genre of the *turgidi*, the moral status of which suffers by association with wine-drinking and sleep.

[2] Cf. Virgil's incorporation of stylistic professions into the situations of his *Eclogues*: *v.* W. V. Clausen, 'Callimachus and Roman Poetry', *GRBS* V (1964), 194–5, on the oblique assertion of Callimachean aims at *Ecl.* I. 2 and VI. 8 with the adjective *tenuis*, to which add X. 70–1, where *gracilis* transforms the weaving of the basket into a symbol for 'slender' composition (Serv. *ad loc.*, 'allegoricos . . . tenuissimo stilo'; cf. T. E. V. Pearce, *CQ* ns XX (1970), 336 on the rarity of *gracilis* as a critical term), so creating ring composition with *tenuis avena* of I. 2.

way in which he consistently accommodated these metaphors to moralistic ends.

EXCURSUS

Literature as a revelation of life

M. Puelma Piwonka, *Lucilius und Kallimachos*,[1] and M. H. Abrams, *The Mirror and the Lamp*,[2] have discussed ancient and modern manifestations of the fundamental concept behind Seneca's one hundred and fourteenth letter and Persius' first satire. Plato presents us with a version of the idea that literature reflects life at *Rep.* III. 11, 400 d: τί δ' ὁ τρόπος τῆς λέξεως καὶ ὁ λόγος; οὐ τῷ τῆς ψυχῆς ἤθει ἕπεται; Taken over by New Comedy – Menander, fr. 143 K, ἀνδρὸς χαρακτὴρ ἐκ λόγου γνωρίζεται, and Terence, *Heaut.* 384, *nam mihi quale ingenium haberes fuit indicio oratio*: pointers to some form of characterisation through style, albeit at a typical level – the concept is transmitted to Cicero, who writes of the Gracchan orator Q. Aelius Tubero, *Brut.* 117, *sed ut vita sic oratione durus incultus horridus*, expressing the analogy in more formulaic form at *T.D.* V. 47, *qualis ... ipse homo esset talem esse eius orationem*, and recoursing to the personal level at *Rep.* II. 1, of the elder Cato, *orationi vita admodum congruens*. Other biographical instances of the idea appear at, e.g., Plut. *Dem. et Cic.* 1, ἔστι δέ τις καὶ τοῦ ἤθους ἐν τοῖς λόγοις ἑκατέρου δίοψις, and *Cat. Mai.* 7, τοιαύτην δέ τινα φαίνεται καὶ ὁ λόγος τοῦ ἀνδρὸς ἰδέαν ἔχειν, while Juv. IV. 82 employs it in a sinister fashion: *cuius erant mores qualis facundia*.

Returning to the theorists we find Demetrius *de Eloc.* 114, and several Senecan variations on the subject: *Ep.* XL. 6, *quid de eorum animo iudicet quorum oratio perturbata et immissa est nec potest reprimi*; XL. 2, *pronuntiatio sicut vita debet esse composita*; LXXV. 4, *haec sit propositi nostri summa: quod sentimus loquamur, quod loquimur sentiamus: concordet sermo cum vita*; CVII. 12, *sic vivamus sic loquimur*; CXV. 2, *cuiuscumque orationem videris sollicitam et politam, scito animum quoque non minus esse pusillis occupatam*. A close parallel to the wording of the hundred and fourteenth letter – *talis hominibus fuit oratio qualis vita* – is found at Aristides *Or.* 45, vol. II. 133 Dind., οἷος ὁ τρόπος

---

[1] Frankfurt 1947, pp. 28 ff., 'Die Einheit der Kriterien für die Formen des Sprach- und Lebensstils'.

[2] Oxford 1953, ch. ix, 'Literature as a revelation of personality'.

τοιοῦτον εἶναι τὸν λόγον, a later instance of the formula advanced at
Quint. XI. 1.30, *profert enim mores oratio et animi secreta detegit. nec
sine causa Graeci prodiderunt, ut vivat, quemque etiam dicere.*[1] From the
written or spoken word we can come to large conclusions about
character. Exterior mirrors interior. Similarly, clothes can signify a
mental state,[2] as the face reveals thoughts.[3]

But in the defence of epigram or elegy, literature ceases to reflect
life: e.g. Cat. XVI. 5–6, Ov. *Tr.* II. 353–60, Mart. I. 4.8,[4]Plin. *Ep.* VII.
9 (cf. Mart. VIII, *praef.*), Apul. *Apol.* 11, Auson. *Eidyll.* 360 f. The
poet's reputation stands intact, his compositions dissociated from
personal life, and therefore no evidence against him. Strato's disclaimer
of sincerity, *Anth. Pal.* XII. 258, warns future generations against finding autobiography in his poetry. Allied to this convention is Callim.
Aet. praef. 21 ff.,

> καὶ γὰρ ὅτε πρώτιστον ἐμοῖς ἐπὶ δέλτον ἔθηκα
> γούνασιν, 'Απόλλων εἶπεν ὅ μοι Λύκιος·
> ' . . .] ἀοιδέ, τὸ μὲν θύος ὅττι πάχιστον
> θρέψαι, τὴν Μοῦσαν δ' ὠγαθὲ λεπταλέην.'

Implied here, and in its Latin counterparts, Virg. *Ecl.* VI. 1–5 (*pingues
. . . oves,/deductum . . . carmen*), and Hor. *Sat.* II. 6.14–15 (*pingue pecus
domino facias et cetera praeter/ingenium*), is a denial of the principle of
reflection: letters and life must be kept far apart. Literary style is one
thing, *modus vivendi* quite another. Callimachus' humorous rejection
of the rule of correspondence indicates its commonplace status:
Virgilian and Horatian reminiscence show that it had become nationalised – and a little banal.

In Lucilius, mainly in the first satire, we catch an occasional glimpse
of what seem to be correlations between literature and life: e.g. 84–5 M,
*quam lepide lexis conpostae ut tesserulae omnes/arte pavimento atque
emblemate vermiculato*, where pedantic style is associated with a complicated mosaic.[5] Similarly, at 15–16, '*porro "clinopodas" "lychnos"*-

---

[1] Some of the above are cited by Summers on Sen. *Ep.* CXIV. 1. I thank Dr
A. J. Woodman for the references to Plutarch.

[2] Cf. Quint. VIII *pr.* 20, quoted below, p. 40.

[3] *V.* R. G. M. Nisbet on Cic. *in Pisonem* I. 20, *voltus denique totus, qui sermo
quidam tacitus mentis est*, with references.

[4] But Mart. VII. 84 is a counter-example: epigram reflects life, like a picture.

[5] A symbol of luxury: cf. *pavimentum tesselatum* in Fabianus *ap.* Sen. *Contr.*
II. 1.12, and *lacunaria pavimentorum* at Sen. *Ep.* CXIV. 9; perhaps also Hor.
Carm. II. 14.27, and Cic. *Phil.* II. 41, *natabant pavimenta, madebant
parietes.*

que ut diximus semnos/anti "pedes lecti" atque "lucernas"', the pretensions of a ponderous style are criticised not only by the formal ridicule of the Graecisms, but also perhaps by the luxurious connotations of *clinopodas lychnosque*. The demand for simple *Latinitas* may contain another demand – for directness in our ethical outlook. Other possible examples of parallelism are 12, *praetextae ac tunicae Lydorum opus sordidulum omne*; 13, *psilae atque amphitaphi villis ingentibus molles*; and 17, *chirodyti aurati, ricae, toracia, mitrae*, where allusion to luxuriant oriental dress and appurtenances may extend to criticism of Asianic bombast.

CHAPTER 3

THE NATURE AND SOURCES OF PERSIUS' IMAGERY

The most important, and most complex aspect of the metaphoric background to the first satire is that category of images and motifs which has simultaneous moral and literary force. For it is mainly from this that Persius elaborates his pose of satirist and critic of letters. But there are other, ancillary motifs, one moralistic, some literary-critical, which play a part in his programme. The various classes sometimes overlap, but in the majority of cases the divisions have a good degree of validity.

LITERARY-CRITICAL MOTIFS

Firstly, three complementary motifs which are predominantly relevant to the literary part of the campaign against mid-century Rome. Though in the first instance aimed directly at lack of taste, during the course of the satire they gather moral force.

EARS

Most prominent are the allusions to ears,[1] their function one of indicting insensibility. Hendrickson has remarked that the ear is the medium for the reception of literature, and that Persius' question, *nam Romae quis non*, line 8, answered finally by *auriculas asini quis non habet?*, line 121, implies 'who is a competent reader?' To quote at length:

> It is not enough to say, with Casaubon and the commentators, that this [*sc.* 121] is but a way of saying that all at Rome are *asini*, that is *stulti*, or as a mere variant of πᾶς ἄφρων μαίνεται . . . the *auriculae asini* stand in direct relation to the question *quis leget haec?* For to the ancients . . . the ear was the medium of reception of the written

[1] In addition to 8 and 121, at 22, *auriculis alienis colligis escas*; 59, *auriculas imitari mobilis albas* 107–8, *sed quid opus teneras mordaci radere vero/auriculas?*; 126, *inde vaporata lector mihi ferveat aure*.

word, so that the ear, the hearer, and hearing are all essential syno-
nyms with reading and the reader, a usage which we still retain in
the word 'audience'. Thus the ... affected boldness of speech upon
which the whole satire is suspended at verse 8 resolves itself into
the poet's answer to the hostile query *quis leget haec?* 'Who will
read me you ask? Well, I care not if none: for who in Rome is there
whose ears are not asinine? Who is a competent reader? But if any
read me let it be those whose judgement has been formed on the
reading of the masters of truth and plain-speaking, Lucilius, Horace,
and the great trio of the Attic comedians.'[1]

K. J. Reckford[2] rightly maintains that the diminutive *auricula* is
contemptuous, suggestive of disease and corruption: note the
dirty ears in a medical simile at Hor. *Ep.* I. 2.53, *auriculas ... collecta sorde dolentes*, and the image of purgation at Pers. v. 63–4,
cultor enim iuvenum purgatas inseris aures/fruge Cleanthea, from
Hor. *Ep.* I. 1.7, *purgatam crebro qui personat aurem*. It should be
added that in conjunction with the ass motif, which defines the
size of the ears, *auricula* further implies stupidity and garrulity,
apt qualities for Persius' opponents: Pliny records this symbolism
at *N.H.* XI. 114.276, *auricularum magnitudo loquacitatis et
stultitiae nota est*.[3] Again, as with *asinus*, and *euge* and *belle*, there
is yet another overtone – of smugness and self-congratulation.[4]
Its associations clearly shade away from the purely literary-critical: the ears of Persius' compatriots prefer to be deaf to any kind
of moral incrimination.

'ASINUS'

Connotations from the word *asinus* accompany the references to
ears. The stupidity of the animal was proverbial,[5] allowing, for

[1] 'The first Satire of Persius', *CPh* XXIII (1928), 101. For ancient etymological links between *auricula* and *audire*, cf. Vel. *Gramm.* VII. 71.23 *pro
audiculis ab audiendo auriculas dicimus*, and Isid. *Orig.* XVII. 7.2, *in auriculis,
quae initio audiculae dictae sunt*.

[2] 'Studies in Persius', *Hermes* XC (1962), 476 ff.

[3] Cf. Ar. *H.A.* I. 11, 492 b, 2–3; E. S. McCartney, 'Big ears and loquacity',
CW XXIII (1929–30), 93. Fat ears are suitable for the reception of rustic
poetry at Calp. Sic. IV. 147 f., *rustica credebam nemorales carmina vobis/con-
cessisse deos et obesis auribus apta*.

[4] Cf. *molles auriculae*, Hor. *Sat.* II. 5.32, of ears open to flattery.

[5] A. Otto, *Die Sprichwörter und sprichwörtlichen Redensarten der Römer*
(Leipzig 1890; repr. Hildesheim 1962), sv *asinus* 1; *ThLL* sv II. 36 ff.

example, a joke on the proper name *Asina* at Hor. *Ep.* I. 13.8 f.
We might compare the Greek equivalent, ὄνος λύρας, 'of a dunce
who can make nothing of music'.[1] Distaste for the banal seems
to be the point of the image at Callimachus *Aet. Praef.* 30–2:

> 'θ]όρυβον δ' οὐκ ἐφίλησαν ὄνων.'
> θηρὶ μὲν οὐατόεντι πανείκελον ὀγκήσαιτο
> ἄλλος.

As we shall see in the case of the catalogue of animal signs at
Pers. I. 58 ff., the ass recurs in the second *Iambus*. Pollianus,
Anth. Pal. XI. 130.5–6, follows Callimachus, applying the image
to tasteless piracy:

> θηρὶ μὲν οὐατόεντι γενοίμην, εἴ ποτε γράψω,
> εἴκελος, ἐκ ποταμῶν χλωρὰ χελιδόνια.

Besides stupidity, imitation, and, as we have seen from Pliny's
auricularum magnitudo, garrulity – the attributes of Persius'
moderns – the ass image may symbolise the collusive relationship
between writer and audience portrayed in the first satire. The
Roman proverb, *mutua muli*,[2] specifying mule rather than ass, is
not so apt as Strato's κνήθειν οἶδεν ὄνος τὸν ὄνον:[3] but perhaps we
can take the two together as referring to back-scratching, a mutual
conspiracy of author and audience which underlies most of the
satire, especially the final question.[4]

'EUGE' AND 'BELLE'

As in the case of the reiterated *auricula*, the repetition[5] of these
exclamations of empty enthusiasm and approval bewails the
degeneration of Roman taste. Both words were favourites with
the audiences at recitations; as S. F. Bonner writes:[6] 'The adverb

---

[1] LSJ sv ὄνος, citing *Paroem.* ὄνος λύρας ἤκουσε καὶ σάλπιγγος ὗς.

[2] Papinius (Pompilius, Bergk) *ap.* Varro *L.L.* VII. 28, Morel p. 42, Otto,
p. 232.

[3] *Anth. Pal.* XII. 238.8.

[4] For *asinus* in the vocabulary of invective, *v.* Nisbet (p. 196) on Cic. *in Pis.*
73, referring to J. B. Hofmann, *Lateinische Umgangssprache* (Heidelberg
1962), p. 98.   [5] At 49; 75; 87, and 111: cf. *decenter*, 84.

[6] *Roman Declamation in the Late Republic and Early Empire* (Liverpool
1949), p. 79, citing Mart. II. 7, where *bellus* or *belle* are used 13 times in 7
lines, and IV. 80. Add I. 49.37, II. 27.3, II. 7.1, Hor. *A.P.* 428 (with Brink's
note); Plut. *de rect. rat. aud.* 45 f., for excessive exclamations of θείως,
θεοφορήτως, and ἀπροσίτως at public readings.

belle was extremely fashionable among declamatory audiences, both as a favourable criticism and as a delighted ejaculation. A recent critic ... [H. Bardon] has counted twenty-one instances in the elder Seneca alone.'

THE HEROIC PAST

Evocations of Rome's innocent youth – an ever receding quantity – held up to view healthy standards now abandoned, so increasing awareness of present corruption, whose extent was diagnosed by images of disease and decay. Conventional ideas of virtue, in the form of a rustic moral primitivism rooted in stereotyped adulation of the past, provided lessons from Rome's earliest days for the edification of an equally stereotyped decadence. In particular, the period before the Punic wars was regarded as a Golden Age of military prowess or agricultural innocence.[1]

Satire adopted this simple schema as a foundation for its sermons: *traditum ab antiquis morem* (Hor. *Sat.* I. 4.117). Horace's ethical resort to his *rus Sabinum* was a serious attempt to activate the rural values of a revivalistic Augustan ideology – that peripheral 'ruralism' which surrounded a harder core of specifically political themes, the *proelia Caesaris*. But the primitivism of a Tibullus,[2] the obtrusively Italianate tone of the *Georgics*, and language such as *Aen.* VI. 811, *Curibus parvis et paupere terra*, easily lent themselves to parody: by, for instance, an earlier Horace, in the second *Epode*, proving the hackneyed nature of

---

[1] Note Cato *de agr. cult.* 1–2, *maiores nostri ... virum bonum quom laudabant, ita laudabant, bonum agricolam bonumque colonum.* In general *v.* D. C. Earl, *The Political Thought of Sallust* (Cambridge 1961); A. O. Lovejoy and G. Boas, *Primitivism and Related Ideas in Antiquity* (Baltimore 1935); A. C. Van Geytenbeek, *Musonius Rufus and Greek Diatribe* (Assen 1963), tr. B. L. Hijmans, ch. VII §2, 'The philosopher as farmer'; A. Oltramare, *Les Origines de la Diatribe Romaine* (Geneva 1926). The pattern of innocence and decline was schematic: e.g. Vell. Pat. II. 1, following Sallust's and Livy's date of 146 B.C., *potentiae Romanorum prior Scipio viam aperuerat, luxuriae posterior aperuit: quippe remoto Carthaginis metu, sublataque imperii aemula non gradu, sed praecipiti cursu a virtute descitum, ad vitia transcursum; vetus disciplina deserta, nova inducta; in somnum a vigiliis, ab armis ad voluptates, a negotiis ad otium conversa civitas.*

[2] *V.* F. Solmsen, 'Tibullus as an Augustan poet', *Hermes* XC (1962), 295–325.

this material even before its official adoption, or by the glibly disrespectful modernism of Ovid, at *A.A.* III. 113 ff.:

> simplicitas rudis ante fuit; nunc aurea Roma est
> et domiti magnas possidet orbis opes.
> aspice, quae nunc sunt, Capitolia, quaeque fuerunt:
> alterius dices illa fuisse Iovis.
> Curia consilio nunc est dignissima tanto,
> de stipula Tatio regna tenente fuit;
> quae nunc sub Phoebo ducibusque Palatia fulgent,
> quid nisi araturis pascua bubus erat?
> prisca iuvent alios, ego me nunc denique natum
> gratulor: haec aetas moribus apta meis.

Even if ironically, Juvenal makes more of bygone days than Horace, enlisting parody of epic, or recognisably poetic touches to mourn, or pretend to mourn, the irretrievable dissociation of present from past.[1] Perhaps following Lucilian precedent, who parodied a *concilium deorum* in book I, and, more important, rendered a cynical version of the theme of Ulysses and Penelope in XVII, Horace employed an epic framework to illustrate descent from heroic behaviour in *Satires* II. 5, where he adapted the *Odyssey* to show how 'the Homeric Ulysses, whose heroic values became defined through the high ethical goal implicit in his arts, has degenerated into the artful *captator*, merely unscrupulous in his devices'.[2] A Juvenalian analogue is the transposition of κίναιδος for σίδηρος at IX. 37, in a travesty of Homer's αὐτὸς γὰρ ἐφέλκεται ἄνδρα σίδηρος from *Od.* XVI. 294, suggesting that sturdy military qualities have degenerated into effeminacy. Again, in the same satire, there is the concluding Homeric verdict, transmitted through the vehicle of Prop. III. 12.34, *Sirenum surdo remige adisse lacus*, to the effect that Naevolus is a dangerous, though pathetic figure, like the Sirens attempting to seduce a Fortune

---

[1] The antithesis, *nunc ... olim*, is common: e.g. X. 77–88, XI. 77–120, XIV. 180–9; *quondam ... nunc*, VI. 288–92, XIII. 38–60; cf. *quondam*, III. 313, XI. 83. The present is often indicted by a derogatory *nunc*: cf. I. 39, II. 37, III. 13, 36, 49, V. 113, VI, 659, VII. 94, 140, X. 225, XI. 79, XII. 48, XIV. 29, 172, XV. 70. In many cases there is an implied or explicit contrast with bygone days.

[2] W. S. Anderson, 'Imagery in the Satires of Horace and Juvenal', *AJPh* LXXXI (1960), 229.

which is uncooperative, probably in the interests of self-preservation. Similarly, after mockery of the paraphernalia of the underworld (which need be interpreted as no more negative than the sausages of x. 355 – *exta et candiduli divina tomacula porci*: Juvenal has no time for the meaningless exterior), there is, at the end of the second satire, an appeal to the exemplary, quasi-mythological heroes of an earlier, more virile age. Persius joins the company of the three other satirists when he intrudes an epic cliché, *adsensere viri*, I. 36, into his description of an effete recitation, so eliciting nostalgia for an almost forgotten world.

Analogous to epic comment is the use of demonstrably poetic diction in incongruous contexts, in appeal to a recognised external standard of 'beauty', a moral quality inherent in literary formulation. From relatively amoral examples like Catullus LXXX:

> quid dicam, Gelli, quare rosea ista labella
> hiberna fiant candidiora nive . . .

where the attractive detail, comprised of the favoured contrast between red and white in *rosea* and *candidiora*, and reminiscence of Homer's λευκότεροι χιόνος, *Iliad* x. 437, belies our later realisation that Gellius is a *fellator*, we pass by the tantalising contrast between setting and action in Petronius' treatment of Circe, 126 and 131, to arrive once more at Juvenal's ninth satire, where poetic diction, as well as epic commentary, undermine Naevolus, and even more, Virro. The former's poetic idea of himself, though somewhat too benign, nonetheless contains Anacreontic pathos, 126–9:

> festinat enim decurrere velox
> flosculus angustae miseraeque brevissima vitae
> portio, dum bibimus, dum serta unguenta puellas
> poscimus, obrepit non intellecta senectus.

Old age creeps upon us while we drink and ask for garlands, perfumes, girls. Juvenal's prior apostrophe, *o Corydon, Corydon*, 102, displayed Naevolus' tendency to inflate himself to sadly poetic proportions: mainly an allusion to an ideal pastoral world in contrast to sordid realities, the reminiscence of the second *Eclogue* can hardly be pressed to yield 'a further criticism of . . . homosexual love among literary shepherds, and a Johnsonian distaste for the mode'.[1] Pastoral is not so much at issue, as the element of *la ronde*, Juvenal's insinuation being that Naevolus will find another patron, as did Corydon after Alexis. Virro, on the other hand, is sinister: complacently suffering from the delusion that he is Ganymede (46 f.), he is reproached by his hired companion's use of the poetic image, *madidum ver*, 51. Persius employs these techniques at 1. 38–40:

> nunc non e manibus illis,
> nunc non e tumulo fortunataque favilla
> nascentur *violae?*

where the incongruously poetic reference to flowers is a means of exposing the falsehood of the purportedly laudatory funerary epigram.

Of Juvenalian epic allusions F. J. Lelièvre observes that they have a moral as well as a literary-critical function, pointing to 'the gap between the spiritual level at which man should live, and the actual level at which he does live,[2] in this followed by P. Green, who notes that Juvenal applies reminiscence of earlier writers 'as touchstones to intensify the sense of moral decadence'.[3] But we must beware of over-simplification, since Juvenal tends to combine the serious with the sardonic. Witness his reminders of lost glory at I. 100, VIII. 181, XI. 95 – *Troiugenas*, and VIII. 56 – *Teucrorum prolem*, similar in kind to the Trojan and Roman allusions in Persius' first satire, which tend to appear in low or shocking contexts, the tension which results from incongruous juxtaposition forcing us into recognition of the dishonour now clouding once glorious origins.[4] Besides the apparent seriousness

---

[1] H. A. Mason, 'Is Juvenal a Classic?' in *Critical Essays on Roman Literature* (*Satire*), ed. J. P. Sullivan (London 1963), p. 105.

[2] *CPh* LIII (1958), 22–5, comparing Juvenal's method to that of T. S. Eliot, but perhaps not allowing enough room for purely literary disillusionment on Juvenal's part: *omnia iam vulgata.*

[3] *Juvenal* (Harmondsworth 1967), p. 51.

[4] Note 4, *Troades*; 20, *ingentes trepidare* Titos; 31, *Romulidae* saturi; 36, *adsensere viri*; 51–2, crudi/ ... *proceres*; 69, *heroas*; 73, *unde Remus sulcoque terens dentalia, Quinti*; 82, *trossulus* exultat ... *levis*; 87, *an, Romule,* ceves?; 96, *arma virum.* I have not italicised words which clash with the elevation of the allusions: cf. Juv. II. 20–1, *de virtute locuti/* clunem *agitant.*

of Juvenal's vision of the other side of the epic coin, as in his description of Priam's fall at x. 268 ff., where the heroic *ante aram summi Iovis ut vetulus bos* (cf. Virg. *Aen.* v. 481, *procumbit humi bos*; Hom. *Od.* iv. 535, βοῦν ἐπὶ φάτνῃ) clashes with the pitiable realism of *qui domini cultris tenue et miserabile collum/ praebet*, there is the sick and gratuitously amoral importation of poetic colour, *umbriferos ubi pandit Thabraca saltus*, 194, and *ceu pullus hirundinis*, 231, into the earlier part of his treatment of old age.

With regard to present escapist refreshment, at hand in the possibility of retreat to the country, his attitude smacks of disappointed idealism and literary self-consciousness. In the closing lines of the third satire, he tells us that he is a poet of Rome, a man tied to the city and its ways. On occasions, he will take moral refuge in the country; but his satires are too sophisticated to adopt the simple solution offered by the rural myth. Umbricius will wear rough country boots – *caligatus* – a sign of his total conversion: but Juvenal's satires will continue to find something facile and amusing in such conversion. *ni pudet illas* places his moral intelligence at too high a level: he is unable to accept the usual categories of virtue and vice, and in particular, their outworn literary vehicles. His sophistication may make him an agnostic – but not a nihilist.

As for the debatably amoral obtrusion of cynicism into his representations of the past, I would argue, *pace* H. A. Mason, that there is little by way of gratuitous literary sarcasm: the eleventh satire is the most anarchic. Juvenal's usual technique, of attributing realistic vestiges of modern vice to a distant Golden Age, or ridiculing the normal concept of virtue, shows a pessimistic, but not necessarily negative, view of human nature. We have proved unworthy of the morality we vaunt, so the satirist in parodistic vein tarnishes its earlier manifestations with the vices which were later its destruction. But insufficient though that morality has proved, it is still active in reminding us, however faintly, of how far we fall short of our promise. As F. R. Leavis writes of Swift:[1] 'But even here, even in the *Argument*, where Swift's ironic

---

[1] In *The Common Pursuit*, Chatto and Windus 1952, and Peregrine Books 1962, pp. 74–5.

intensity undeniably directs itself to the defence of something that he is intensely concerned to defend, the effect is essentially negative. *The positive itself appears only negatively – a kind of skeletal presence, rigid enough, but without life or body; a necessary pre-condition, as it were, of directed negation'* [1]. Likewise, Juvenal's cynicism has purpose and direction: by mocking positive values, he shows that we, more than he, are the anarchists. Any discomfiture caused by uncovering the loopholes in our moral system shocks the real villain, the reader, into assuming the guilt of the pretended villain, the satirist, who, as moral and literary malcontent, has offered himself as a scapegoat to offend conventional values.

MOTIFS SIMULTANEOUSLY SATIRIC AND LITERARY-CRITICAL

The metaphoric terminology of literary criticism, drawn from man's physical and social existence, has direct bearing on the type of imagery which I now intend to study – a class constituted by cases where metaphors have assumed a novel aspect as a result of human embodiment. The writers themselves – the propensities of their characters, their physical appearance, their care for their stomachs – are presented in terms which relate to style. Through the incarnation of literature in life, a double end is achieved: the chosen motifs, with their moralistic tone and literary-critical potential, are combined in an objective materialisation which presents us with a satirist who has joined forces with a literary critic. I deal with disease, dress and appearance, homosexuality and effeminacy,[2] and food and drink.[3]

[1] My italics. Defence of Juvenal along the lines of D. Wiesen's appeal to prior verdicts (*Latomus* XXII (1963), 440 ff.) is as unconvincing as Mason's absolutist charges of amorality.

[2] Briefly discussed by W. S. Anderson in the preface to W. S. Merwin's translation of Persius (Indiana, 1961).

[3] After a preliminary draft of this chapter I noticed Anderson's comments, *Wissenschaftliche Zeitschrift der Universität Rostock* XV (1966), 409 ff.: 'He is perhaps most telling in likening the whole art of poetry practised by "others" to the process of eating and drinking. There is a liquid quality, a tastiness in contemporary poetry which the satirist must entirely reject ... He wished to suggest that the "sickness" of the mind or soul is caused

DISEASE

The imagery of disease, and closely related to disease, of physical deformity, has a place in the first satire.[1] One of the most common satiric metaphors, its symbolism is explained by a fragment of Lucilius, 638 M:

animo qui aegrotat, videmus corpore hunc signum dare.

Bodily sickness mirrors spiritual sickness: internal vice leaves its mark on the frame, to be cured by the philosopher or satirist in his guise as physician. Plato made frequent use of medical imagery, and the Stoics and Cynics followed his precedent.[2] From them, it passed into diatribe and satire, to provide one of the mainstays of the moralist's metaphoric repertoire.[3] In the rôle of satirist,

by the "eating" or "drinking" through the ears of the wrong "food".' Dessen p. 33 notes 'patterns of imagery which either relate poetry to parts of the anatomy or describe it as food or sexual stimulus', without discussion of origins. Her instances of the relationship between poetry and anatomy are not very significant: *pulmo*, 14; *guttur*, 17; *ocello*, 18; *lumbum*, 20; *iecore*, 25; *nare*, 33; *palato*, 35; *linguas*, 81; *cervice*, 98; and *labris*, 105. None of these is related to the bodily analogy, and some should be redistributed into other classes of imagery: e.g., *palato*, *linguas*, and *labris* belong with food; *ocello*, *lumbum*, *iecore*, and *cervice* with homosexuality.

[1] Note 26, *pallor* (with stronger homosexual overtones); 57, *pinguis aqualiculus*; 51, *ebria veratro* (madness); 76, *venosus liber Acci*; 77–8, *verrucosa ...Antiopa*; 79, *patres...lippos*; 107, *mordaci radere vero* (cf. 126, *vaporata...aure*); 124, *palles* (true whiteness); 128, *lusco...dicere* '*lusce*'; also possibly 16, *albus* and 33, *rancidulum*.

[2] E.g. Plato *Gorg.* 36, the Cynic Antisthenes *ap.* D.L. VI. 4, and Epicurus fr. 221 Us. (Summers on Sen. *Ep.* VII. 1); P. Louis, *Les métaphores de Platon* (Paris 1945), R. Joly, 'Platon et la médecine', *BAGB* suppl. 'Lettres d'Humanité' XX (1961), 435–51, and R. Heinze, 'Ariston von Chios bei Plutarch u. Horaz', *Rh.Mus.* XLV (1890), 497 ff. For technical observations on the difference between *morbus* and *vitium*, *v.* Gell. IV. 2.

[3] Cf. e.g. Hor. *Sat.* I. 4.125 f.; πολυπραγμοσύνη as a disease at *Sat.* II. 3.37, *avaritia* at *Ep.* I. 1.35 and II. 2.146 ff.; from *Ep.* I alone, 1.7, 30–1, 32–40, 61 and 101 ff.; 2.33–4, 37–9, 47–9, 52 ff.; 3.26; 6.28–31; 7.2–9; 8.7 ff.; 12.14; 15.4 ff.; 16.21 ff. Typical Stoic vices are represented as diseases at Pers. III. 107 ff. Allied is the metaphor of defective vision, *lippitudo*: *v.* Hor. *Sat.* I. 1.120, 3.25; *Ep.* I. 1.28–9, 2.52, 17.4; Pers. II. 72, *v.* 77; Juv. IV. 114 ff., transforming real blindness; Sen. *Ep.* CXV. 6, an analogy between physical sight and spiritual blindness, illustrates its rationale: *sed, si quemadmodum visus oculorum acui solet et repurgari, sic nos aciem animi liberare impedimentis voluerimus, poterimus perspicere virtutem.* It was so established as to be capable of inversion: *v.* Cic. *Tusc.* V. 111 ff., especially

3-2

Persius uses the imagery to strike at corruption, directing it, like the *sermo* envisaged by Cicero at *de Off.* 1. 136, *ad urendum et secandum*,[1] to diagnose, and perhaps heal, the vices of society.[2]

Armed with a weapon from rhetorical theory, which frequently drew analogies between style and the human body, as literary critic he gave concrete form to metaphors which subjected the body of a composition – *corpus orationis* – to the same afflictions as beset the human frame, so imaging a disfigured literary manner.[3] The phrase, *corpus orationis*, is common enough: at Petron. 2.2, the teachers of rhetoric have brought it about that the 'body' is now enervated and moribund, *ut corpus orationis enervaretur et caderet*; at *ad Her.* IV. 45.58 it has 'limbs' and 'blood', *huic* [*sc.* the figure *commoratio*] *exemplum satis idoneum subici non potuit, propterea quod hic locus non est a tota causa separatus sicuti membrum aliquod, sed tanquam sanguis perfusus est*

114, *Democritus luminibus amissis alba scilicet discernere et atra non poterat: at vero bona mala, aequa iniqua, honesta turpia, utilia inutilia, magna parva poterat*... *atque hic vir impediri etiam animi aciem aspectu oculorum arbitrabatur, et cum alii saepe quod ante pedes esset non viderent, ille in infinitatem omnem peregrinabatur, ut nulla in extremitate consisteret*; cf. Lucr. I. 66 ff., *primum Graius homo mortales tollere contra/est oculos ausus primusque obsistere contra*...; 72 ff., *ergo vivida vis* animi *pervicit, et extra/processit longe flammantia moenia mundi/atque omne immensum peragravit mente animoque*, also Hor. *Carm* I. 28, with Nisbet and Hubbard on *animoque*... *percurrisse*, line 6, Russell on Longinus 35.2–36. Cicero soon introduces the archetypal Tiresias, *augurem Tiresiam, quem sapientem fingunt poetae, numquam inducunt deplorantem caecitatem suam*, 115.

[1] Of vituperation: *sed ut ad urendum et secandum, sic et ad hoc genus castigandi raro invitique veniemus, nec unquam, nisi necessario, si nulla reperietur alia medicina.*

[2] For details in Persius, *v.* H. Lackenbacher, 'Persius u. die Heilkunde', *WS* LV (1937), 130–41.

[3] *V.* F. Quadlbauer, 'Die *genera dicendi* bis Plinius d. J.', *WS* LXXI (1958), 55–111 (the 'Soma-Vergleich') citing Longin. 3.4, *ad Her.* IV. 10.15, and 11.16, where the vice of the *genus dissolutum* is that it lacks physical fibre, *quod est sine nervis et articulis*: the vice of the *genus exile* is that it is in danger of becoming an *aridum et exsangue genus orationis. V.* La Rue Van Hook, *The Metaphorical Terminology of Greek Rhetoric and Literary Criticism* (diss. Chicago, 1905), 18 ff., for metaphors from 'The Human Body: its condition, appearance, dress, care etc.'; G. Assfahl, *Vergleich und Metapher bei Quintilian* (Stuttgart 1932), pp. 4 ff., 'Der Körper und seine Funktionen', noting the metaphoric uses of, e.g., *caput, oculus, facies, vultus, lacerti* and *nervi*; also the brief abstract of A. Desmouliez *REL* XXXIII (1955), 59–60, 'La signification esthétique des comparaisons entre le style et le corps humain dans la rhétorique antique'.

per totum corpus orationis.[1] Health then becomes an object of care.[2] The pursuit of stylistic *sanitas* was so keen that Tacitus was forced to condemn the zealous: archaists are like hypochondriacs whose very concern with health is akin to disease, *Dial.* 23.3, *adeo maesti et inculti illam ipsam quam iactant sanitatem non firmitate sed ieiunio consequuntur* . . . (§4) *prope abest ab infirmitate in quo sola sanitas laudatur.*[3] Disease has various manifestations – at Sen. *Suas.* II. 17, magnitude of style is a *morbus* as is the passion for writing at Sen. *Ep.* LXXIX[4] – and can strike at any time – as at Sen. *Contr.* VII. 5. 12, *gravis scholasticos morbus invasit,* and Petron. 2, where bloated Asianist rhetoric, unlike the truly grand style, which is neither *maculosa* nor *turgida,* permeates youthful minds *veluti pestilenti quodam sidere.* Corrupt literature is also infectious: Fronto II, p. 112, *scabies, porrigo ex eiusmodi libris concipitur.* His advice is to avoid Seneca and his like as models, in case of contagion.

The body can be marred or spoilt by other types of deformity,

---

[1] *V.* H. Caplan *ad loc.* for further exx.; Assfahl, 'Körper der Rede', citing *inter alia* Quint. I. 5.65, III. 11.23, VII. 10.16, VIII *pr.* 22, IX. 4.61, Cic. *Or.* 126, *Brut.* 208, and Petron. 118.5. For *sanguis* of style, as above in *ad Her.,* cf. Cic. *Brut.* 36, 283, Quint. VIII. 3.6, X. 1.60, X. 1.115, X. 2.12, XI. 1.34, Tac. *Dial.* 26.4.

[2] Usually compared to Pers. I. 76 ff., Tac. *Dial.* 21.7 indicts the bony withered style of the archaists, giving the prescription for true *sanitas*: *Pacuvium certe et Accium non solum tragoediis sed etiam orationibus expressit; adeo durus et siccus est.* (§8) *oratio autem, sicut corpus hominis, ea demum pulchra est in qua non eminent venae, nec ossa numerantur, sed temperatus ac bonus sanguis implet membra et exsurgit toris, ipsosque nervos rubor tegit et decor commendat.* With the anatomical details cf. Plin. *Ep.* V. 8.10, *hanc* [history] *saepius ossa musculi nervi, illam* [oratory] *tori quidam et quasi iubae decent*; on health and sanity in style (*bona valetudo, sanitas, salubritas, integritas*), Quint. X. 1.44, XII. 10.15, II. 4.9, Cic. *Brut.* 51, 284, 278, *de Opt. Gen. Or.* 8, 11, 12, Tac. *Dial.* 25.4, 26.6 (Van Hook); on proportion within the 'body' of the speech, Quint. VIII. 5.34, discussing the function of epigrams within the composition as a whole, *ego haec lumina orationis velut oculos quosdam esse eloquentiae credo. sed neque oculos esse toto corpore velim, ne cetera membra officium suum perdant,* where the ambiguity of *lumen* (from 'figure of speech' (so *ad Her.* IV. 23.32, and often in Cicero; Tac. *Dial.* 22.3) it becomes 'eye') allows the full *corpus*-comparison.

[3] Cf. Quint. II. 3.9, *non virium, sed infirmitatis vitio laborare, ut corpora non robore, sed valetudine inflantur.*

[4] Cf. *Anth. Pal.* XI. 340, νόσος, of a passion for writing epigrams, and Mayor on Juv. VII. 52.

by scars for instance, a metaphor for the unsightly mark left on a composition by too much revision or alteration, Quint. x. 4.4: *accidit itaque ut cicatricosa sint et exsanguia et cura peiora.*[1] Or the body can be misshapen and subjected to all sorts of bizarre and unnatural defacements, Quint. II. 5.11:

> illa vero, quae utcunque deflexa sunt [*sc.* in sermone], tanquam exquisitiora miramur, non aliter quam distortis et quocunque modo prodigiosis corporibus apud quosdam maius est pretium iis, quae nihil ex communis habitus bonis perdiderunt, atque etiam qui specie capiuntur, vulsis levatisque et inustas comas acu comentibus et non suo colore nitidis plus esse formae putant, quam possit tribuere incorrupta natura, ut pulchritudo corporis venire videatur ex malis morum.[2]

Like Quintilian, Persius conducts a battle against *distorta et prodigiosa corpora*, and against those whose perverted sense of beauty is *ex malis morum*. Given the double potential of metaphoric disease and distortion, we must consider the possibility that he is incriminating style as well as morals, when he says of the poet-patron that he has a misshapen and monstrous stomach, *pinguis aqualiculus propenso sesquipede extet*, 57, or that the taste for archaic literature involves countenancing varicose veins and warts, *venosus liber Acci . . . | . . . verrucosa . . . | . . . Antiopa*, 76–8.[3]

DRESS AND APPEARANCE

Clothing and physical appearance – the *cultus corporum* of Seneca's one hundred and fourteenth *Epistle* – frequently provoked the satirist's wrath. They were also in constant use as stylistic metaphors, form being the garment in which content is

---

[1] Cf. IV. 1.61, *cum possit prooemium videri cicatricosa facies* (Assfahl pp. 6–7).
[2] Cf. the contrast between real health and false effeminate beauty at VIII pr. 19, *corpora sana et integri sanguinis et exercitatione firmata ex isdem his speciem accipiunt, ex quibus vires, namque et colorata et adstricta et lacertis expressa sunt; sed eadem si quis volsa atque fucata muliebriter comat, foedissima sunt ipso formae labore*; Lucian *quom. Hist. Conscr.* 8–9, and Sen. *Ep.* CXV. 2 (Assfahl p. 8 n. 1). Ovid thought moles an enhancement of natural stylistic beauty: Sen. *Contr.* II. 2.12, *aiebat interim decentiorem faciem esse, in qua aliquis naevus esset.*
[3] 57 is normally treated without reference to literature, 76–8 solely in literary terms.

clothed. The motif is not prominent in the first satire,[1] but again we must be open to argument from dual capacity.

Ornament and luxury incurred the moralist's distaste, as simple clothing elicited his approval. From the transparent garment of Eubulus, fr. 67 K, 3 ff.:

> ἐξὸν θεωρήσαντι . . .
> γυμνὰς . . .
> ἐν λεπτοπήνοις ὕφεσιν ἑστώσας . . .
> μικροῦ πρίασθαι κέρματος τὴν ἡδονήν

we come across the expensive Coan silks of Roman times. Passing from the morally neutral Hor. *Sat.* I. 2.101, *Cois tibi paene videre est/ut nudam, ne crure malo, ne sit pede turpi* – rather different in tone from the disapproval of *Carm.* IV. 13.13[2] – and Ovid's *sive erit in Cois, Coa decere puta*, *A.A.* II. 298, we arrive at Seneca's tired fulminations, *Ben.* VII. 9.5, *video sericas vestes, si vestes vocandae sunt, in quibus nihil est, quo defendi aut corpus aut denique pudor possit, quibus sumptis parum liquido nudam se non esse iurabit.* His father, on the other hand, can be quoted on the topic of the chaste matron's dress, *Contr.* II. 7.3, *prodeat in tantum ornata, quantum ne immunda sit*, and can at the same time be invoked to illustrate criticism's moral inheritance, approving or condemnatory as that may be, II. 7.4, *cum tot argumentis impudicitiam praescripseritis, cultu, incessu, sermone, facie.* The definition of *impudicitia* in terms of *cultus* or *sermo* implies a parallelism of the two attributes, both dress and speech being outward signs of a character trait.

Style, clothed in various vestments, often serves in critical vocabulary as a guide to a writer's personality. From simple formulations, such as *sententias vestiebat oratio*, Cic. *Brut.* 274, or *vestire atque ornare oratione*, *de Or.* I. 142,[3] there was no long

---

[1] 15, *pexusque togaque recenti*; 16, *natalicia . . . cum sardonyche albus*; 32, *cui circum umeros hyacinthina laena est*. Differently, 127, *qui in crepidas Graiorum ludere gestit*.

[2] *nec Coae referunt iam tibi purpurae . . . tempora.*

[3] Cf. Plat. *Ax.* 369 d, πομπὴ καὶ ῥημάτων ἀγλαϊσμός, Dion. Hal. *de Dem.* 18 p. 167, 4, ἔστιν ὥσπερ σώμασι πρέπουσά τις ἐσθής, οὕτως καὶ νοήμασιν ἁρμόττουσά τις ὀνομασία, Quint. II. 8.9, Fronto II p. 38, *sententiae . . . verbis vestiuntur*; Sandys on Cic. *Or.* 42, *de Or.* II. 94, III. 177; Plut. *de Rect. Rat. Aud.* 42 d, objecting to the man who insists on style above content, ἀλλ' ὥσπερ ἐν τρίβωνι Λυσιακοῦ λόγου λεπτῷ καὶ ψιλῷ καθήμενος.

distance to more moralistic phrasings, such as Tac. *Dial.* 26.1, *adeo melius est orationem vel hirta toga induere quam fucatis et meretriciis vestibus insignire*, and thence to passages where the nature of stylistic dress is expressive of the author's moral constitution, like Quint. VIII *pr.* 20,

> et cultus concessus atque magnificus addit hominibus, ut Graeco versu testatum est, auctoritatem; at muliebris et luxuriosus non corpus exornat, sed detegit mentem, similiter illa translucida et versicolor[1] quorundam elocutio res ipsas effeminat, quae illo verborum habitu vestiantur

which expressly states that effeminate ornament does not enhance, but symbolises – *detegit mentem* – mental character: care must be taken not to enervate style with the wrong kind of decoration.[2] Likewise Seneca employs literary dress as a clue to inner mentality – and as an indication of personal appearance. At *Ep.* CXV. 2, *si (oratio) circumtonsa est et fucata et manu facta, ostendit illum quoque non esse sincerum et habere aliquid fracti*, an over-elaborate style signifies flaws in an individual's character; while at *Ep.* CXIV. 6 we are told that a reading of one of Maecenas' compositions will remind us of the way he dressed: *non statim cum haec legeris hoc tibi occurret: hunc esse qui solutis tunicis in urbe semper incesserit?* Working by way of inference from loose stylistic dress, we are meant to conjure up an image of a slovenly Maecenas, whose style appears to have been particularly prone to criticism on grounds of extravagant ornamentation, likened to curls or curling irons.[3]

So far we have been concerned with style as an exterior reflection of personal peculiarities. What of personality, and personal appearance as a guide to the nature of style? To some extent reciprocity is inherent in the passages above: if style provides a commentary on character, then character potentially provides a

---

[1] Cf. X. 1.33, *versicolorem . . . vestem*, of Demetrius of Phalerum.

[2] Cf. XI. 1.3, for a simile taken from the dress appropriate to one's sex.

[3] Tac. *Dial.* 26.1, *calamistros Maecenatis* (cf. Cic. *Brut.* 262, *qui illa volunt calamistris inurere*), or Suet. *Aug.* 86, *exagitabat . . . Maecenatem suum cuius myrobrecheis, ut ait, cincinnos usque quaque persequitur*; *v.* further Macrob. II. 4.12. Cosmetics – *fucus* – are also a critical favourite, as at Quint. VII. 3.6 and Sen. *Ep.* CXV. 2.

commentary on style. But speculation apart, Sen *Ep.* cxx. 2 can be adduced, where dress and appearance – personal attributes – act as clues, not admittedly to style, but at least to ethics: *nosti comptulos*[1] *iuvenes, barba et coma nitidos, de capsula totos, nihil ab illis speraveris forte, nihil solidum*. It is not difficult to conceive of an analogous passage where such externals would act as a guide not only to ethics, but also to style. So when Persius describes the appearance of his two reciters, at I. 15 ff., and 32, we must be alert for implied criticism of style through the medium of apparently literal, but potentially symbolic, details of dress.

Ridicule of the habit of wearing rings[2] is found in literary contexts at Juv. VII. 139–40, *fidimus eloquio? Ciceroni nemo ducentos/nunc dederit nummos, nisi fulserit anulus ingens*, and VII. 143–4, *conducta...agebat/sardonyche*.[3] Admittedly, none of these examples reflects directly on style: but we should note *ornatus margaritarum* at Cic. *Or.* 78, Mart. V. 11, where, with the normal movement from style to man, *gemmae* in verse are likened to those on the poet's fingers, Quint. XI. 1.3, and the *aurum* and *gemmae* which, acting as correlatives for stylistic devices, form part of the orator's 'furniture', at Tac. *Dial.* 22.4:

> oratorem . . . non eo tantum volo tecto tegi quod imbrem ac ventum arceat, sed etiam quod visum et oculos delectet; non ea solum instrui supellectile quae necessariis usibus sufficiat, sed sit in apparatu eius et aurum et gemmae, ut sumere in manus, ut aspicere saepius libeat.[4]

HOMOSEXUALITY AND EFFEMINACY

The first satire is full of allusions to effeminacy and homo-sexuality[5] (already treated to some extent above in the section 'The Heroic Past'), also to the hypocritical severity which was the

---

[1] Buecheler.

[2] E.g. Mart. II. 29.2, of a sardonyx ring, Juv. I. 28 f., *aestivum aurum* and *maioris pondera gemmae*.

[3] Cf. VI. 382, a musical context, VII. 135–6, *purpura vendit causidicum, vendunt amethystina*, Quint. XI. 3.142, a ban on excess in wearing such ornaments.

[4] For *supellex* signifying stock of invention, cf. Quint. II. 4.29.

[5] At 4, *Troades*; 17–18, *liquido cum plasmate guttur/mobile conlueris, patranti fractus ocello*; 20–1, *ingentes trepidare Titos, cum carmina lumbum/intrant et tremulo scalpuntur ubi intima versu*; 23, *articulis ... et cute perditus*; 29, *cirratorum*; possibly 33, *balba de nare locutus*; 35, *tenero ... palato*; 63–4,

traditional mask of the pervert.[1] Persius considers it his mission to impugn the grave airs of old men[2] engaged in literary pursuits for which they are no longer suited, who lead the youth astray. But besides being matter for moral reproof, homosexuality and effeminacy also supply metaphors to the language of criticism. Once more Persius has the opportunity for combining stylistic and moral protest, in a declamation against the vice of which the literary trait is indicative. The beginning of Juvenal's second satire, merging the themes of homosexuality and hypocrisy, is typical in its contrast:

> ultra Sauromatas fugere hinc libet et glacialem
> Oceanum, quotiens aliquid de moribus audent
> qui Curios simulant et Bacchanalia vivunt.

The opposition between *Curios* and *Bacchanalia* symbolises the death of genuine Republican traditions; the simple virtues of an earlier age have surrendered to perversion, camouflaged in a thin disguise of pretended gravity.[3] The old traditions are perpetuated, but now they are a name without substance, 39 ff.:

> habeat iam Roma pudorem:
> tertius e caelo cecidit Cato. sed tamen unde
> haec emis, hirsuto spirant opobalsama collo
> quae tibi?

---

molli| ... numero ... leve; 82, *trossulus exultat ... levis*; 87, *an, Romule, ceves?*; 98, *tenerum ... laxa cervice*; 103–4, *haec fierent si testiculi vena ulla paterni/viveret in nobis? summa delumbe saliva ...* ; 105, *Maenas et Attis* (cf. 93 and 99–102); 107–8, *teneras ... /auriculas.*

[1] Esp. 9, *canitiem et nostrum istud vivere triste*, and 11, *cum sapimus patruos*; also 83, *cano*. Jahn rightly dismisses literal interpretation of *canitiem*, 'non de aetate intelligendum est, sed de corporis animique eorum statu, qui omni luxuriae genere dissoluti ante tempus senes facti sunt'. But luxury and premature old age miss the point: *canities* is the disguise of the homosexual moralist, for which *v.* the works cited by G. Highet, *Juvenal the Satirist* (Oxford 1954), p. 249; for Cynic opposition to paederasty, G. A. Gerhard, *Phoenix von Kolophon* (Leipzig 1909), pp. 140–56; for false Stoics, K. Praechter, *Hierocles der Stoiker* (Leipzig 1901), pp. 148–50, and Austin on Quint. XII. 3.12; also H. I. Marrou, *A History of Education in Antiquity*, tr. G. Lamb (London 1956), p. 209, 'the pupil became attached – often passionately – to his master, and the master felt a corresponding affection for the pupil: it was in philosophic circles that the great archaic tradition of educative *eros*, the source of all virtue, survived longest'. On such *eros*, *v. ibid.* pp. 26 ff.   [2] Note 22, *vetule*; 56, *calve*; 79, *patres*.

[3] Cf. Mart. VII. 58.7 ff., *quaere aliquem Curios semper Fabiosque loquentem/ hirsutum et dura rusticitate trucem;/ invenies: sed habet tristis quoque turba*

This third Cato is an insult to his predecessors. The proper name recalls the standard from which he has deviated, simultaneously informing the reader of his method of deviation: the first and second Catos pass judgement on their false successor, condemnation made the more certain by the formal clash of *hirsuto* with the unexpected *opobalsama*. Throughout, Juvenal's technique is one of unveiling the false *tristitia* of these subversive adherents of an archaic morality.[1] The only valid standards lie in the irrecoverable past, long dead, along with the real Curius and the real Camillus. These *exempla*[2] of true *virtus* are brought on stage at the end of the satire, 153 ff., and asked for their verdict on their nominal usurpers. The movement is circular: first, the false Curii, with their counterfeit moral stance and pseudo-military exploits;[3] then, in accusation, the real Curii, along with their virile compatriots, the *bellorum animae*, 156, who fought the battles on which Rome's reputation rested.[4] Persius, like

cinaedos, IX. 27.6 ff., *Curios Camillos Quintios Numas Ancos/et quidquid usquam legimus pilosorum/loqueris sonasque grandibus minax verbis . . .*, I. 24.3, *qui loquitur Curios adsertoresque Camillos*, IX. 48; Quint. XII. 3.12, *in publico tristes, domi dissoluti.*

[1] E.g. II. 9, tristibus *obscaenis*; 11–12, hispida *membra quidem et* durae *per bracchia saetae/promittunt* atrocem *animum*; 36, *non tulit ex illis* torvum *Laronia quendam*; 62, *de nobis post haec* tristis *sententia fertur?*; cf. IX. 1, *tristis*, and perhaps 14–15.

[2] On the generic value of *exempla* v. A. Nordh, 'Historical *exempla* in Martial', *Eranos* LII (1954), 224–38, esp. 229 ff., 'as fixed patterns, the principal characters of the high national tradition were organised into an easily manageable system of symbols . . . How well this suits the satirical poet, who, seeking the typical and the broadly human, needs some absolute points to which he can place his personages in relation, characterising them by similarity, dissimilarity and contrast' (citing Quint. V. 11.5, *omnia igitur ex hoc genere sumpta necesse est aut similia esse aut dissimilia aut contraria*). The *tertius Cato* of Juv. II. 40 is an example of identification, *similia, and* contrast, *contraria*. N.'s 'absolute point' is briefly one of similarity; then, the usurper's hypocrisy once revealed through identification, similarity fades into contrast, leaving a sense of contrast alone, 'Cato' operating as the antithetical moral norm.

[3] For the condemnation of Otho at 100 through Virgilian reminiscence, *v.* Lelièvre, *CP* LIII (1958), 22–5; cf. the disgrace of the noble gladiator Gracchus, 143 ff.

[4] I suspect intended ring-composition. J. wishes to flee to distant lands (*ultra Sauromatas*): yet distant lands (*Artaxata*) are becoming infected by contact with Rome (*praetextatos . . . mores*). Easy refuge in the primitivistic τόπος of barbarian innocence is refused.

Juvenal, notes the pretence of spurious *tristitia* to retention of the exacting code of earlier days; similarly, he sees homosexuality behind the solemn façade.

These faults also contaminate literature; whence no doubt the idea of representing the writers themselves as effeminate profligates. Seneca's one hundred and fourteenth *Epistle* displays at §6 the expected process of inference from style to man: a perusal of the work of Maecenas reminds the reader that his constant companions were two eunuchs, *spadones duo, magis tamen viri quam ipse*. Effeminate style suggests effeminate *modus vivendi*, *oratio* finding its parallel in *vita*, as again at §20, where *oratio tenera et fluxa* is the attribute of the *delicatus homo*. Then there is Seneca the Elder's complaint about the decay of oratory, relating literary decline to the evanescence of manliness, *Contr.* I *praef.* 9–10, *quis aequalium vestrorum . . . satis vir est? . . . ite nunc et in istis vulsis atque nusquam nisi in libidine viris quaerite oratores.*

Sexual overtones load the vocabulary of the critics: *tener, mollis, fractus, effeminatus, enervis,*[1] their opposites epithets like *fortis* or *virilis.*[2] This patently moralistic terminology often acted as a substitute for rational criticism, as at Quint. XII. 10.12, where we hear that in his own day, Cicero was taxed with being *in compositione fractum, exultantem, ac paene, quod procul absit, viro molliorem.* The reader, browbeaten by fervid appeal to his more

---

[1] Cf. Quint. VIII. 3.57, *corrupta oratio in verbis maxime impropriis, redundantibus . . . compositione fracta . . . consistit*, I. 10.31, *effeminata et impudicis modis fracta* (of music), Sen. *Suas.* II. 23, *nimius cultus et fracta compositio*, Dion. Hal. *de Comp.* 18 p. 83, 17, ὑπὸ γυναικῶν ἢ κατεαγότων ἀνθρώπων λέγοιτ' ἄν, and Philo Jud. I. 262, ἄνανδροι καὶ κατεαγότες καὶ θηλυδρίαι τὰ φρονήματα (Austin on Quint. XII. 10.12). Add Tac. *Dial.* 39.2, *frangitur eloquentia*, Cic. *T.D.* IV. 38, *enervata oratio*, Dion. Hal. *de Dem.* 20 p. 171, 4, τὸ . . . τῆς λέξεως λεῖον καὶ μαλακόν, Quint. IX. 4.142, (*compositionem*) *effeminatam et enervem, qualis apud multos . . . lascivissimis syntonorum modis saltat*, where *saltare*, like *exultare*, has pejorative, and implicitly sexual, overtones: cf. Cic. *Or.* 226, *Hegesias . . . saltat incidens particulas*, Quint. IX. 4.28, *quae in hoc ipsum petuntur, ut exultent atque lasciviant*, II. 2.9, *at nunc proni atque succincti ad omnem clausulam non exsurgunt modo verum etiam excurrunt, et cum indecora exultatione conclamant*, Hor. *A.P.* 430, *tundet pede terram*, with Brink's note, Pers. I. 20–1 and 82.

[2] E.g. Pers. VI. 4, *marem strepitum* (of Bassus), Sen. *Ep.* CXIV. 15, *virilem putant et fortem quae aurem inaequalitate percutiat*, 22, *illo* [*sc. animo*] *sano ac valente oratio quoque robusta fortis virilis est.*

conservative instincts, is forced into repugnance. The imagery can become so vehement that the composition which it pretends to criticise is almost forgotten, as at Quint. v. 12.17–18:

> declamationes, quibus ad pugnam forensem velut praepilatis exerceri solebamus, olim iam ab illa vera imagine orandi recesserunt atque ad solam compositae voluptatem nervis carent, non alio medius fidius vitio dicentium, quam quo mancipiorum negotiatores formae puerorum virilitate excisa lenocinantur. nam ut illi robur ac lacertos barbamque ante omnia et alia, quae natura proprie maribus dedit, parum existimant decora, quaeque fortia, si licerent, forent ut dura molliunt: ita nos habitum ipsum orationis virilem et illam vim stricte robusteque dicendi tenera quadam elocutionis cute operimus et, dum levia sunt et nitida, quantum valeant, nihil interesse arbitramur.

Rather than criticism, we find a conflict between hardy virility and the horrors of castration. There is no question of proof – only of coercion. Like Quintilian, Persius relies on foreseeable emotional response to an imagery which, though not conducive to reasoned analysis, was a powerful weapon in satire.

FOOD AND DRINK

Literary-critical metaphors from food and drink are more complex than those studied so far.[1] But food and drink as material for satire present less difficulty.[2] Again Persius has the opportunity to retrace metaphor to its place of origin in life, representing his opponents as drunkards or gluttons. The description of a *cena*

---

[1] Note 22, *escas*; 30–1, *inter pocula | ... saturi*; 33, *rancidulum*; 35, *eliquat ... palato*; 41–2, *an erit ... |os populi meruisse*; 50–2, *Ilias Atti|ebria veratro? ... crudi|dictarunt proceres? ... lectis|scribitur in citreis*; 53, *calidum scis ponere sumen* (cf. 70, *ponere lucum*); 57, *pinguis aqualiculus propenso sesqui-pede extet*; 67, *prandia regum*; 76, *Brisaei ... Acci*; 80, *sartago loquendi*; 104–5, *summa delumbe saliva|hoc natat in labris et in udo est Maenas et Attis*; 106, *sapit*.

[2] As early as Hipponax the glutton is punished by public stoning, fr. 89 Knox; at Eur. fr. 892 N², a contrast of the later diatribe is used: ἐπεὶ τί δεῖ βροτοῖσι, πλὴν δυοῖν μόνον,/Δήμητρος ἀκτῆς, πώματος θ' ὑδρηχόου,/ ἅπερ πάρεστι καὶ πέφυχ' ἡμᾶς τρέφειν; /ὧν οὐκ ἀπαρκεῖ πλησμονή. τρυφῇ δέ τοι/ἄλλων ἐδεστῶν μηχανὰς θηρεύομεν. Cf. Gell. vi. 16, preserving the lines to exemplify the depradations of *peragrans gula*, and noting Varro's antipathy, in περὶ ἐδεσμάτων, to the *helluones* who search for food *terra marique*; also Manil. iv. 387 ff., where the stomach gloats on plunder.

is a favourite in Roman satire: Lucilius treats it in books V
(193 ff. M), XIII (439 ff. M), XX (568 ff. M) and XXX (1060 ff. M);
there is Horace's *cena Nasidieni*, *Sat.* II. 8, while *Satires* II. 2 and
II. 4[1] are also based on the theme of food; then Juvenal devotes
Satires V and XI to the topic of the dinner-party.[2] But full-scale
cena apart, satire is full of references to food, many of which rely
on a received public symbolism: e.g. the admonitory motif of
the glutton's punishment, which twice takes the form of seizure
and death while bathing after an excessive undigested meal. From
Juv. I. 142 f.:

> poena tamen praesens, cum tu deponis amictus
> turgidus et crudum pavonem in balnea portas,

in which self-indulgence results in death, we work back to Pers.
III. 98:

> turgidus hic epulis atque albo ventre lavatur

where *albo* further implies the disease of the profligate who ignores
the satirist's prescription for health, heedless of the practical
medicinal value of ethics. From Persius we return to the Horatian
source, *Ep.* I. 6.61–2:

> crudi tumidique lavemur
> quid deceat, quid non, obliti.

Over-eating causes not only sickness and death, as in the first
two cases, but also moral impercipience and blindness to the
precepts of philosophy.[3] We are warned of this again in the
opening lines of Hor. *Sat.* II. 2, where true insight into the virtues

---

[1] *V*. Anderson 1960, p. 229: 'As Catius starts retailing his precepts, it
becomes clear that he is treating culinary recipes as equivalent to philosophic principles.' It might be added that the philosophic principles
constitute the criterion by which he is judged: real Epicureanism, in the
form of Lucretian parody, indicts the false.

[2] In general, *v*. N. J. Rudd, *The Satires of Horace* (Cambridge 1966),
pp. 161 ff., for *Sat.* II. 2; pp. 202 ff., for *Sat.* II. 4 and 8; Highet, ch. xi and
xx, for Juv. v and xi; L. R. Shero, *CPh* XVIII (1923), 126–43, on the *cena*;
C. Witke, *Latin Satire*, p. 41, on Crates; F. Fuhrmann, *Les Images de
Plutarque* (Paris 1964), pp. 43 ff., and 228 ff. J. André, *L'Alimentation et
la Cuisine à Rome* (Paris 1961), is a historical survey.

[3] Cf. Petron. *Cena* 72.2–3, with irony; Mayor on Juv. I. 142 f., citing material
indicative of the theme's firm entrenchment in diatribe.

of the simple life, and the pleasures of the table are shown to be mutually exclusive:

> quae virtus et quanta, boni, sit vivere parvo ...
> discite, non inter lances mensasque nitentes,   4
> cum stupet insanis acies fulgoribus et cum
> acclinis falsis animus meliora recusat,
> verum hic impransi mecum disquirite.

An ethical dimension is present throughout: *virtus* announces a philosophic theme, *discite* a didactic element; *nitentes*, at first apparently referring to the actual glitter of an extravagantly laden table, is transformed by the insinuation of *stupet insanis acies fulgoribus* – to the effect that dulled sight has no power of discrimination – into the unhealthy glitter of deception; *acies* then reaches a yet more philosophical level when it becomes *animus*. Moral and literal dimensions now meet, integrated in the image *acclinis falsis*, where the mind is seated at the table of falsehood, an identification of high living and delusion, the victim of which cannot see the better course. When we reach *impransi*, we know that Horace is not only talking about empty stomachs: *vivere parvo* has become a moral as well as a material concept. Intemperate gourmandise and vain ostentation are now so intertwined with downright corruption that at line 21 of *Sat.* II. 2, the two steps in the argument ' "fat with food" equals "riddled with vice" ' have become telescoped into a single image, *pinguem vitiis albumque*, where 'fat with food' has shifted to 'fat with vice'.[1]

Simple food, a symbol of worthy *paupertas* and *humilitas*, leads to health[2] and virtue. In the ordinary course of events Ofellus only ate vegetables and smoked ham, *holus fumosae cum pede pernae*, Hor. *Sat.* II. 2.117. It is his simple way of life which gives him the right to criticise luxury, and his immunity from the shocks of fortune. Likewise, Lucilius and his powerful friends enjoyed their leisure while the vegetables were on the boil, *donec/decoqueretur holus*, *Sat.* II. 1.73–4; and Horace's own meal is a dish of vegetables, *ad porri et ciceris refero laganique catinum*, *Sat.* I. 6.115. As Juvenal remarks, such was the food of earlier, more

---

[1] Pers. III. 32–3, *sed stupet hic vitio et fibris increvit opimum/pingue* is perhaps indebted to Hor. *Sat.* II. 2, *stupet, vitio,* and *pingue* recalling lines 5 and 21.

[2] Cf. Hor. *Sat.* II. 2.71, *imprimis valeas bene.*

virtuous days: *Curius parvo quae legerat horto/ipse focis brevibus ponebat holuscula*, XI. 77–8. The diminutive *holuscula*, together with *parvo* and *brevibus*, recommends the unassuming modesty of this innocent way of life.[1]

Style was related to drink through description in terms such as *sobrius, ebrius, vinolentus*, and *siccus*. Just as *tener* and *mollis* allowed easy metamorphosis into objective representation of effeminacy, so the vocabulary of sobriety, a virtue of style, and of drunkenness, its opposite vice – and, as we shall see, the meta-phorics of food, which coloured style with an ethical complexion – permitted dramatic development. Before the Romans used the imagery of sobriety and inebriation, it had gained currency in Greece. The comic poet Cratinus, later adopted as hero by the adherents of intoxicated inspiration, dismissed the sober water-drinkers as inferior poets.[2] Isocrates drew a distinction between drunkenness and temperance in literature;[3] then, in Hellenistic times, came the great debate, between the 'water-drinkers' and the 'wine-drinkers'. Callimachus called Archilochus a drunkard,[4]

---

[1] *holus* and *holusculum* commonly symbolise the simple life: e.g. Hor. *Sat.* II. 6.63, with some irony II. 7.30, Virg. *Georg.* IV. 130 ff., a contrast to the *macellum*. Vegetarianism, with its bearing on the Golden Age and Nature's original beneficence to man, is a common topic in diatribe: *v.* A. Oltramare (above, p. 29 n. 1), J. Haussleiter, *Der Vegetarismus in der Antike* (Berlin 1935), and e.g. Sen. *Ep.* CVIII, Ov. *Met.* XV. 75 ff. The theme occurs early, Hes. *W.D.* 41 praising mallow and asphodel, food of the simple man. On *fraga* and *glandes*, Golden-Age fruits of the earth, *v.* Mayor on Juv. XIII. 57 and XIV. 182–4. The story of Philemon and Baucis, Ov. *Met.* VIII. 616 ff., has a range of representative motifs: e.g. 630, *parva ... canna tecta palustri*, 633, *casa paupertatemque*, 637, *parvos ... Penates*, 647, *holus*, 648, *sordida terga suis nigro pendentia tigno*, 664, *bicolor sincerae baca Minervae*, 665, *corna autumnalia*, 666, *intibaque et radix et lactis massa coacti*, 668, *omnia fictilibus*, 671, *epulasque foci misere calentes*; cf. Ov. *Fast.* V. 505 ff., and the *Moretum*. Like Baucis and Philemon, Horace's father is *macro pauper agello*. Sen. *Ep.* XVIII. 5, recommending the simple life, associates it immediately with an image of cheap food: *contentus minimo ac vilissimo cibo*. Cf. Hor. *Ep.* I. 14.35, *cena brevis*, I. 10.11.

[2] Cratinus fr. 199.2, ὕδωρ δὲ πίνων οὐδὲν ἂν τέκοι σοφόν; *v.* Ar. *Pax* 700 ff. At Pind. *Ol.* VI. 91, γλυκὺς κρατὴρ ἀγαφθέγτων ἀοιδᾶν, the poet is a mixing-bowl of song; *Pyth.* IX. 111–12, ἐμὲ δ' ὧν τις ἀοιδᾶν/δίψαν ἀκειόμενον πράσσει χρέος, he quenches his thirst for song.

[3] Isocr. VIII. 13, καὶ νομίζετε δημοτικωτέρους εἶναι τοὺς μεθύοντας τῶν νηφόντων, Van Hook p. 32.

[4] Callim. fr. 544, μεθυπλῆγος φροίμιον Ἀρχιλόχου. Commager p. 28 notes that in addition to Cratinus and Archilochus, Anacreon, Alcaeus, Aristophanes,

while Callimachus and his followers, the water-drinkers, met
with hostile reception from their Dionysiac opponents.[1] The
debate is continued in Augustan Rome, perhaps only formally,
by Ovid, Propertius, and above all, by Horace.[2]

Not limited to the poets, the images became a favourite of the
rhetoricians and theorists, drunkenness the metaphor for irra-
tionally inspired composition. Of the orator who is all passion
and no moderation, so that he seems like a madman in the company of the sane, and like a drunkard among the sober, Cicero
writes, *Or.* 99:

> qui enim nihil potest tranquille, nihil leniter, nihil partite, definite,
> distincte, facete dicere, praesertim cum causae partim totae sint eo
> modo partim aliqua ex parte tractandae, si is non praeparatis auribus
> inflammare rem coepit, furere apud sanos et quasi inter sobrios
> bacchari vinolentus videtur.[3]

The metaphors reappear in Quintilian in a slightly different form
– a comparison between chanting delivery and the utterances of
drunkards – XI. 3.57, *quid enim minus oratori convenit quam
modulatio scaenica et nonnumquam ebriorum aut comissantium
licentiae similis?*; also in Seneca's one hundred and fourteenth
Epistle, where the style of Maecenas is likened to that of a drunken
man, *videbis itaque eloquentiam ebrii hominis involutam et errantem
et licentiae plenam* (§4), then later in more detail, *quomodo in vino
non ante lingua titubat quam mens cessit oneri et inclinata vel
prodita est: ita ista orationis quid aliud quam ebrietas nulli molesta
est nisi animus labat* (§22).[4] There is no need to multiply

and Aeschylus were styled as wine-drinkers; *v.* his references in n. 56, and
add Plut. *Quaest. Convival.* 622 e for Aeschylus.

[1] *V.* Gow–Page, *Philip*, vol. II, pp. 17, 37–8 and 48, on *Anth. Pal.* IX. 305,
406, XI. 20 and 31; also p. 114 on *Anth. Pal.* XI. 322, for the *Garland*
epigrammatists' antipathy to the pedantry of Callimachus and Aristarchus.

[2] Cf. Ov. *Met.* VII. 432, Prop. IV. 6.75, Hor. *Ep.* I. 19 (Commager p. 29
and n. 59). In general Wimmel p. 225, H. Lewy, *Sobria Ebrietas* (Giessen
1929), and A. Kambylis, *Die Dichterweihe und ihre Symbolik* (Heidelberg
1965), pp. 118 ff.

[3] Cf. *Brut.* 276. With the metaphor of madness, *furere apud sanos,* cf. e.g.
Quint. XII. 10.73, *corruptum dicendi genus, quod . . . specie libertatis insanit,*
also Brink on Hor. *A.P.* 296 and 453 ff.

[4] Further, Sen. *Ep.* XIX. 19, Longin. 3.5, Aristides XXXIV (51). 18, μεθύειν
περὶ τοὺς λόγους (Van Hook p. 32).

instances: what matters for Persius is that here, as with food, there was another metaphor applicable to the criticism of style, at the same time potentially incriminatory of the morality symptomised by that style.

More interesting, and more complex, is the relationship between food and literature, conflation of which allows the realisation of metaphor in dramatic situation. Greek criticism enlisted several terms originating from the notion that literature has a taste – sweet, sour, bitter – e.g. ἀγλευκής, δριμύς, πικρός, γλυκύτης, μελιχρός.[1] In Rome, the verb *sapere* is found at the more rudimentary level, as at Quint. VI. 3.107, *aliud oratio sapit nec vult nimium esse condita*.[2] If literature has a peculiar flavour, the reader or listener tastes or savours it, enjoying the physical sensation: in Greek, γεύειν and γεύεσθαι are used, as at Pind. *Isthm.* v. 20, γεύεσθαι ὕμνων, Plat. *Alc. I* 114 a, γεύεσθαι λόγου, and Men. *Georg.* 45, γεύειν τινὰ ἀγαθῶν λόγων. In Latin the corresponding verbs are *gustare* and *degustare*, used at e.g. Plaut. *Most.* 1063, *gustare ego sermonem eius volo*, Quint. XII. 2.4, *qui litteras vel primis, ut aiunt, labris degustarit*, or again x. 1.104, during his review of Latin literature, *sed nos genera degustamus, non bibliothecas excutimus*.[3]

The flavour of literature is tasted at a feast of words. At *Eq.* 538 f., Aristophanes speaks of the comic repast prepared by Crates:

> ὃς ἀπὸ σμικρᾶς δαπάνης ὑμᾶς ἀριστίζων ἀπέπεμπεν,
> ἀπὸ κραμβοτάτου στόματος μάττων ἀστειοτάτας ἐπινοίας.

A fragment of Astydamas contains the same notion, 4 N² (= *Com. Adesp.* 1330 K):

> ἀλλ' ὥσπερ δείπνου γλαφυροῦ ποικίλην εὐωχίαν
> τὸν ποιητὴν δεῖ παρέχειν τοῖς θεαταῖς τὸν σοφόν.

---

[1] Cf. Van Hook pp. 28 ff.; Assfahl pp. 26 ff. ('Ernährung; Speisen; Nährungsmittel'); J. Taillardat, *Les Images d'Aristophane* (Paris 1965), pp. 439 ff. I am indebted to these works for many of the subsequent examples; I add others noted personally.

[2] Cf. Mart. x. 4.10, *hominem pagina nostra sapit*.

[3] For *degustare*, cf. Quint. IV. 1.14, Sen. *Ep.* XLVI. 1, and Gell. v. 16.5 (Assfahl). *gustus* is also used: e.g. Quint. VI. 3.17, *sermo prae se ferens . . . et sono et usu proprium quendam gustam urbis*.

The poet is a cook, catering for his audience.[1] The idea reappears in an epigram of Martial, IX. 81:

> lector et auditor nostros probat, Aule, libellos,
> sed quidam exactos esse poeta negat.
> non nimium curo: nam cenae fercula nostrae
> malim convivis quam placuisse cocis.

The epigrammatist writes for the consumer, not for the cook. Further, there is the philosophic feast of words.[2] Allied is the metaphor of literary diet, comparing reading and study to nourishment or the digestion of food, in which case emphasis is not so much on the writer/cook as on the reader/consumer. In Latin, *alere* is often used to describe the rearing of the orator, usually in conjunction with *ingenium*.[3] Out of nourishment is formulated a menu of studies: at Quint. II. 4.5, the first steps in education are compared to a milk diet, *quin ipsis quoque doctoribus hoc esse curae velim, ut teneras adhuc mentes more nutricum mollius alant et satiari velut quodam iucundioris disciplinae lacte patiantur*;[4] the study of history supplies the orator with a 'rich juice' at x. 1.31, *historia quoque alere oratorem quodam uberi iucundoque suco potest*; and at x. 1.58, the reading of the classics is the main course at a banquet, to be followed by the inferior, but attractive, food of the minor poets, *sed ad illos iam perfectis constitutisque*

---

[1] Further comic examples are Teleclides 39 K, Μνησίλοχός ἐστ' ἐκεῖνος ὃς φρύγει τι δρᾶμα καινὸν/Εὐριπίδῃ καὶ Σωκράτης τὰ φρύγαν' ὑποτίθησι (Dindorf's reconstitution), and Metagenes 14 K, ὡς ἂν/καιναῖσι παροψίσι καὶ πολλαῖς εὐωχήσω τὸ θέατρον; cf. Plaut. *Poen.* 6–10. At Athen. 347 e Aeschylean drama is made of 'slices from the banquet of Homer': τεμάχη τῶν Ὁμήρου μεγάλων δείπνων. Cf. also the comparison between cookery and rhetoric in Plato's *Gorgias*, e.g. 465 d: ὃ μὲν οὖν ἐγώ φημι τὴν ῥητορικὴν εἶναι, ἀκήκοας· ἀντίστροφον ὀψοποιίας ἐν ψυχῇ, ὡς ἐκεῖνο ἐν σώματι.

[2] Plat. *Rep.* IX. 571 d, ἑστιάσας λόγων καλῶν καὶ σκέψεων; Cic. *Topic.* 5.25, *quoniam avidum hominem ad has dicendi epulas recepi, sic accipiam ut reliquiarum sit potius aliquid quam ut te hinc patiar non satiatum discedere*; cf. *de Div.* I. 29.61, *saturataque bonarum cogitationum epulis. Or.* 83 is different, comparing avoidance of figures of speech to avoidance of display at a banquet, *nam sic ut in epularum apparatu a magnificentia recedens non se parcum solum sed etiam elegantem videri volet, ⟨et⟩ eliget quibus utatur: apparatus* refers to external trappings, not to food.

[3] Cf. Quint. I. 8.6, I. 8.8, II. 5.18, VIII *pr.* 2, XII. 6.6, Cic. *Brut.* 126, *de Off.* I. 105 (Assfahl).

[4] Cited by Curtius p. 134, along with other instances of the alimentary metaphor, biblical or mediaeval.

4-2

viribus revertemur; quod in cenis grandibus saepe facimus ut, cum optimis satiati sumus, varietas tamen nobis ex vilioribus grata sit. Then there is the representation of reading as digestion at Quint. XI. 2.41, in preparation for *memoria, quaecunque aetas operam iuvandae studio memoriae dabit, devoret initio taedium illud et scripta et lecta saepius revolvendi et quasi eundem cibum remandendi;* and X. 1.19, a comparison of the assimilation of one's reading with the completed process of absorption, *repetamus autem et retractemus et, ut cibos mansos ac prope liquefactos demittimus, quo facilius digerantur, ita lectio non cruda sed multa iteratione mollita et velut confecta memoriae imitationique tradatur.*[1]

A common identification is that between poetry, and nectar or honey. Nectar occurs at Pind. *Ol.* VII. 7 f., καὶ ἐγὼ νέκταρ χυτόν, Μοισᾶν δόσιν, ἀεθλοφόροις/ἀνδράσιν πέμπων, γλυκὺν καρπὸν φρενός,/ἱλάσκομαι; Theocr. VII. 82, οὕνεκά οἱ γλυκὺ Μοῖσα κατὰ στόματος χέε νέκταρ; and Pers. *prol.* 14, *Pegaseium nectar.* Perhaps more frequent is the honey metaphor: Taillardat[2] cites Ar. *Av.* 908, μελιγλώσσων ἐπέων . . . ἀοιδάν, Pind. *Ol.* XI. 4, μελιγάρυες ὕμνοι, *Nem.* XI. 18, μελιγδούποισι . . . ἀοιδαῖς, *Isthm.* II. 32, μελικόμπων ἀοιδᾶν, Alcman 41 D, μέλεα μελιπτέρωτα, Simon. 40 D, μελιαδέα γᾶρυν, and of Nestor, *Iliad* I. 249, μέλιτος γλυκίων . . . αὐδή. To these could be added e.g. Lucr. I. 947, *et quasi Musaeo dulci contingere melle,*[3] and Hor. *Ep.* I. 19.44, *fidis enim manare poetica mella/te solum.*

If the dish is to be tasty, it must be well seasoned. Quintilian summarises the precept at IX. 3.4, *velut adsperso quodam condimento, iucundior erit [sc. oratio];*[4] the more unattractive the

---

[1] Cf. Sen. *Ep.* LXXXIV. 5 f., *debemus . . . in unum saporem varia illa libamenta confundere . . . concoquamus illa,* and *Ep.* II. 3, also the diets at Quint. X. 5.14, where eloquence feeds on the exercise of declamation, *alitur enim atque enitescit velut pabulo laetiore facundia* (cf. Cic. *Cat. Mai.* 49, *Acad.* II. 127), and X. 5.15, comparing the composition of poetry to the leisurely feast of an athlete, *ne carmine quidem ludere contrarium fuerit, sicut athletae, remissa quibusdam temporibus ciborum atque exercitationem certa necessitate, otio et iucundioribus epulis reficiuntur.*

[2] P. 491 n. 9; cf. O. Goram, 'Pindari translationes et imagines', *Philologus* XIV (1859), 495–6, 'carminum cum melle comparatio'.

[3] Cf. I. 936–8 and Quint. III 1.5.

[4] For *condimentum*, cf. Lucian *Rhet. Praec.* 16, καὶ ἐν ἅπαντι λόγῳ καθάπερ τι ἥδυσμα ἐπίπαττε αὐτῶν (Assfahl); add Ar. *Poet.* 6, 1450 b, Dion. Hal. *de Thuc.* 23 p. 359, 24.

subject matter, the more need for seasoning, v. 14.35, *quoque quid est natura magis asperum, hoc pluribus condiendum est voluptatibus*;[1] for appetite is not aroused by cold uninteresting food, II. 4.29, *necesse vero iis, cum eadem iudiciis pluribus dicunt, aut fastidium moveant velut frigidi et repositi cibi.* The same type of composition delivered again and again destroys interest; sauce, salt, and vinegar must be liberally employed.[2] Salt is the most frequent image, an extended development of which we find at Quint. VI. 3.19:

> salsum igitur erit, quod non erit insulsum,[3] velut quoddam simplex orationis condimentum, quod sentitur latente iudicio velut palato, excitatque et a taedio defendit orationem. sales enim, ut ille in cibis paulo liberalius adspersus, si tamen non sit inmodicus, adfert aliquid propriae voluptatis, ita hi quoque in dicendo habent quiddam, quod nobis faciat audiendi sitim.[4]

Metaphors of sauce and vinegar are used by, amongst others, Aristophanes and Martial. At *Eq.* 343, the sausage-seller laces his compositions with sauce:

> ὁτιὴ λέγειν οἷός τε κἀγὼ καὶ καρυκοποιεῖν

and at fr. 151 vinegar, as well as salt, is needed to make the plays of Sthenelos the tragedian palatable:

> A. καὶ πῶς ἐγὼ Σθενέλου φάγοιμ' ἂν ῥήματα;
> B. εἰς ὄξος ἐμβαπτόμενος ἢ ξηροὺς ἅλας.[5]

---

[1] For *condire* cf. Quint. XII. 10.38, *verborum gratia . . . extrinsecus condienda est*; VI. 3.96, VI. 3.39, Cic. *Or.* 185, *de Or.* II. 227, *Cat. Mai.* 10 and Plin. *Ep.* III. 1.9 (Assfahl).

[2] Cf. Plat. *Alc. I* 114 a 13; Dion. Hal. *de Dem.* 15 p. 161, 7; Juv. VII. 154, *crambe repetita*; also Longin. τεχν. ῥητ. p. 307, 15 Sp., δεῖ δὲ ἐκ τῆς ἀκοῆς τὸν δικαστὴν λίχνοις τε καὶ ἡδείαις ὥσπερ καρυκείαις καὶ ὀψοποιίαις τε καὶ προαγωγαῖς ἐπισπᾶσθαι καὶ προάγεσθαι, ποιεῖσθαι δὲ τοῦτο χρὴ τοῖς θεραπευτικοῖς τε καὶ κολακευτικοῖς ὀνόμασι (Assfahl).

[3] Note the etymological pun.

[4] Assfahl compares Socrates *ap.* Stob. 34.18, τῷ γελοίῳ καθάπερ ἁλὶ πεφεισμένως δεῖ χρῆσθαι, and Dio Chrysost. 18.13, ὥσπερ γὰρ οὐδὲν ὄψον ἄνευ ἁλῶν γεύσει κεχαρισμένον, οὕτως οὐδὲν εἶδος ἔμοιγε δοκεῖ προσηνὲς ἂν γενέσθαι χάριτος Σωκρατικῆς ἄμοιρον. *V.* further Plut. *Mor.* 68 c, *Com. Adesp.* 12 a, Cic. *Or.* 87, *de Or.* I. 159, *ad Att.* I. 13.1, Mart. VII. 25.3.

[5] Cf. Ar. *Thesm.* 162, where the lyricists Ibycus, Anacreon, and Alcaeus season their works to make them tasty, οἷπερ ἁρμονίαν ἐχύμισαν, the preparation of literature at *Eq.* 215 f., τὸν δῆμον ἀεὶ προσποιοῦ/ὑπογλυ-

Martial insists, this time without derogatory intent, that vinegar be poured on the food of epigram, VII. 25.5:

> nec cibus ipse iuvat morsu fraudatus aceti

and at IX. 26.5–6 describes his work as the spicy olive adorning a more ambitious dish:

> sed tamen et parvae nonnulla est gratia Musae;
> appetitur posito vilis oliva lupo.[1]

It emerges quite clearly that literature was frequently conceived as some kind of foodstuff, to be seasoned before consumption.

Another property of this class of metaphors is the potential relationship of particular stylistic features to edible commodities: Aristotle notes the culinary aspect of Alcidamas' epithets, *Rhet.* III. 3.3, 1406 a, 18–19 οὐ γὰρ ἡδύσματι χρῆται ἀλλ' ὡς ἐδέσματι τοῖς ἐπιθέτοις; the epilogue is a sweetmeat at Dion. Hal. *Art. Rhet.* X. 18, p. 373, 3, ἡγοῦνται τοὺς ἐπιλόγους ὥσπερ ἐν δείπνῳ τραγήματα εἶναι τῶν λόγων;[2] and figures of speech cater for those with a taste for bitterness at Quint. IX. 3.27, *haec schemata ... habent quendam ex illa vitii similitudine gratiam, ut in cibis interim acor ipse iucundus est.* It is not a long distance from the border-line decadence of such modishness to Persius' denigratory analogy at the beginning of his fifth satire, where we find a continuous witty correlation between eating and composition. Part of a manifesto for satire is relayed solely in terms of food:

> Vatibus hic mos est, centum sibi poscere voces,
> centum *ora* et *linguas* optare in carmina centum,
> fabula seu maesto *ponatur hianda* tragoedo,
> volnera seu Parthi ducentis ab inguine ferrum.
> 'quorsum haec? aut quantas robusti carminis *offas*   5
> *ingeris, ut par sit centeno gutture niti?*
> grande locuturi nebulas Helicone legunto,

καίνων ῥηματίοις μαγειρικοῖς, *Av.* 462 f., καὶ προπεφύραται λόγος εἷς μοι,/ ὃν διαμάττειν οὐ κωλύει, and the description of Euripidean drama in terms of food, noted at D.L. IV. 18–19.

[1] But cf. x. 59, objecting to the reader who wants all flavour and no bread, 3 ff., *dives et ex omni posita est instructa macello/cena tibi, sed te mattea sola iuvat./non opus est nobis nimium lectore guloso;/hunc volo, non fiat qui sine pane satur.* Epigram needs body as well as point.

[2] Cf. Prisc. *Gramm.* III. 497.1 (cod. Leid. Voss.), *hinc et tragoediae sunt vilia carmina quasi bellaria,* comparing the τραγήματα of Dionysius.

si quibus aut Procnes, aut si quibus *olla* Thyestae
fervebit, saepe insulso *cenanda* Glyconi . . .   9
hinc trahe quae dicis *mensas*que relinque Mycenis   17
cum capite et pedibus *plebeiaque prandia* noris.'

The italicised words effect an interplay between two different media: the mouth delivers poetry, as well as consuming food. A change of emphasis, culinary in nature, accompanies the transformation of *centum voces* in the first line, with its dependence on the hundred-mouth conceit of epic, into *centum ora et linguas . . . centum* in the second, words which create a more realistic and physical impression: voice becomes mouth, then tongue. Followed by the ambiguous *ponatur*, a verb equally applicable to literary composition and serving food, followed again by the probably ambivalent *hianda* – the *mot juste* for description of tragic recitation and writing, but also opening the mouth into a gaping maw[1] – the earlier indications of a conflation between style and eating are confirmed by lines 5–6, which represent tragedy as coarse edible lumps crammed into the mouth of the reciting poet.[2] Persius elicits his reader's repugnance by using

---

[1] *hiare* = χάσκειν; cf. Juv. VI. 636, Prop. III. 3.4 (*hiscere*: cf. the neutral II. 31.6) and Hor. *A.P.* 138, where Fiske, *HSCPh* XXIV (1913), 28, notes similarity to Persius. The situations in both are parallel: expression of intention to write in the high style, succeeded by an image of a gaping mouth, so dissolving pretension by ridicule. *A.P.* 137 ff., '*fortunam Priami cantabo et nobile bellum.*/*quid dignum tanto feret hic promissor hiatu?*/*parturient montes, nascetur ridiculus mus*, does not develop *hiatus*: Horace immediately switches to a new image. As often Persius reads his predecessor with an eye to the elaboration of dormant imagery (cf. *A.P.* 186–7 and 91 for Procne and Thyestes).

[2] *ingeris*, 6, refers to the poet feasting himself on the raw edible material of tragedy, in preparation for regurgitated recitation. This is implied by the change to *gutture*, from *voces*, *ora*, and *linguas*: the poet has consumed great gobbets of tragedy, and now strains his throat during regurgitation. But there is some confusion in the imagery, arising from the presence of an actor, along with a poet-reciter. At 3 it looks as though the poet is setting a dish before the gaping mouth of an actor, and at 8–9 the poet certainly cooks the dish while the actor Glyco consumes it. Logically, the poet should only cook the tragedy, ready for consumption by the actor. But the poet becomes, 5–6, a consumer too, preparing for recitation. Hence we have two poetic deliveries, one by the poet, 5–6, and the second by the actor, 3 and 9. But it is probably wrong to work out such niceties when Persius' main concern was over-all vilification of the high style through identification with the crudity of eating.

the connotations of crass physical appetite to detract from the higher genre, identifying unrestrained voracity with turgid poetry.[1] He then proceeds to mock the two most horrific tragic banquets, which he dubs with the vulgar deflatory *olla*,[2] making Glyco the actor dine on them at every production. Returning to his original imagery at line 17, he associates tragedy with carnivorous banquets, reminding the reader of their menu: *mensasque relinque Mycenis/cum capite et pedibus*. The satirist eats the food of the people, plain, and therefore irreproachable: *plebeiaque prandia noris*.

On the basis of opportunities inherent in the sometimes rather neutral analogies between style and the alimentary processes, Persius has evolved a symbolism which allows criticism to operate solely in terms of food. Literature is not mentioned at lines 17–18: but the metaphors yield a rounded verdict on the nature of tragedy and satire. The high genre is questionable because of its crude luxury and tumid gravity. Satire, on the other hand, relies for its superiority on the humble virtues of the simple life: in eating the food of the people, Persius represents himself as an unassuming realist.[3] Evaluative criticism is enacted in a language which belongs to an entirely separate realm of activity. This is not a case of allegory, but of a novel symbolism with independent validity.

Finally, some observations on the metaphor of fatness and

---

[1] I disagree with Anderson, *Philol. Quarterly* XXXIX (1960), 70, 'The elderly philosopher [*sc.* Cornutus] has observed . . . that poets take such exaggerated delight in the heightened style of epic and tragedy as to savor, like a gourmet, the mellifluous words they utter.' This is a case of gluttony, not gourmandise.

[2] L & S cite no occurrences of the word in the higher genres; it has the same aggressively realistic tone as *offas*.

[3] The doctrine here is partly similar to that of Hor. *A.P.* 317–18, *respicere exemplar vitae morumque iubebo/doctum imitatorem et vivas hinc ducere voces*, but the method of expression is very different: the generalised *exemplar vitae morumque* is replaced by the concrete images of *plebeia . . . prandia*, and earlier, 14, *verba togae*. There is some inconsistency between the positive connotations of *plebeia* here (cf. *plebeia . . . beta* at III. 114, paralleled in tone by Lucr. II. 36, *quam si in plebeia veste cubandum est* and Hor. *Sat.* II. 2.38 *ieiunus raro stomachus volgaria temnit*), and Persius' usual scorn for the common people, probably occasioned by dependence on commonplace sentiment about modesty and humility.

corpulence, situated half-way between the alimentary and bodily images, and in the latter function potentially evocative of disease. When a composition is described as fat, we do not only visualise physical grossness. As R. E. H. Westendorp-Boerma observes on *pingui* at *Catalepton* v. 4, 'metaphora nimirum sumpta est de corpore quod adipatis cibis alitur':[1] we also envisage the engulfing greed – a topic of the moralists – which has inflated the human frame. In Greek, the adjective παχύς is used of bombast: perhaps its best known occurrence is in Callimachus' description of Antimachus' *Lyde* as a παχὺ γράμμα καὶ οὐ τορόν, fr. 398. Another instance is *de Dem.* 5 p. 137, 9, where Dionysius of Halicarnassus criticises the style of Plato at its more effusive as being ἀηδεστέρα [τῆς ἑτέρας] καὶ κάκιον ἑλληνίζουσα καὶ παχυ-τέρα.[2] Latin employs several related terms: *pinguis, opimus, adipes, adipatus, turgere* and its cognates. With Quint. II. 10.6, encouraging the declaimer to rid his compositions of excess fat, *ita sibi quoque tenuandas* adipes, *et quidquid humoris corrupti contraxerit, emittendum, si esse sanus ac robustus volet,* where the professor envisages a body encumbered with sickly obesity, we can compare XII. 10.35, with its allied doctrine that fat words are unsuitable for thin matter, *nec rerum nimiam* tenuitatem, *ut non dicam* pinguioribus, *fortioribus certe verbis miscebimus.* Again, Cic. *Or.* 25, opimum *quoddam et tamquam* adipale *dictionis genus,*[3] and *Brut.* 64, of the imitators of Lysias – *habet certos sui studiosos, qui non tam habitus corporis* opimos *quam* gracilitates consectentur, *quos valetudo modo bona sit,* tenuitas *ipsa delectat* – bear out the idea that a thin body symbolises one type of style, a fat body

---

[1] He goes on to note that *scholasticorum natio madens pingui* is not in fact an instance of the alimentary metaphor, but a comparison between style and greasy hair: 'ut grammaticorum capilli unguento madent, sic et oratio pinguis et adipata est'. *madens pingui,* a compressed identification between man and style in the manner of Persius, simultaneously indicts unpleasant physical appearance and turgid rhetoric.

[2] Cited by J. F. Lockwood, *CQ* XXXI (1937), 201, along with *de Dem.* 27 p. 188, 1, *de Isaeo* 19 p. 121, 25, Phot. bibl. cod. 225 p. 242 a, παχυτέραις ... λέξεσι, and Schol. Ar. *Ran.* 1445 d, ἀγροικότερον καὶ παχύτερον (in explanation of ἀμαθέστερον).

[3] Sandys here cites Cic. *Brut.* 64 and 271, *doctus Hermagorae praeceptis quibus etsi ornamenta non satis opima dicendi*; cf. Gell. XVII. 10.8, of Pindar, *qui nimis opima pinguique esse facundia existimatus est.*

another.[1] As for *turgere* and its cognates, we can adduce *loci* such as *ad Her.* IV. 10.15 (below, p. 158 n. 3), Petron. 2.6, *turgida oratio*, Persius' own *non equidem hoc studeo, pullatis ut mihi nugis/pagina turgescat* at v. 19–20, or Hor. *A.P.* 27, *professus grandia turget*, where it is the writer of the grand style, not his writings, who is swollen and inflated.[2]

To sum up: as the external correlative for his discontent with the voluble superficiality of Neronian literature, Persius adopts the time-sanctioned but weary metaphors of literary criticism, to realise their abusive capacities in a series of concrete, but partially fragmented dramatic situations. In qualification I should add that particularly in the second half of the satire, dramatisation is more spasmodic, individual physical images appearing at first sight to be somewhat randomly interwoven with an uneven texture of argument. Perhaps this results from awarding relatively prolonged and consistent status to the depictions of the recitation and dinner-party scenes in the first part of the satire: large-scale objectification is less necessary once typical settings have acquired a considerable degree of physical extension from the faded connotations of their parent metaphors. Especially after line 62, sequence is loose, one fragment succeeding another in an abstract, but nonetheless explicable continuity.

Given the static, deterministic Roman view of character, it follows that everything – from physique to literature – reflects fundamental traits of personality: as the man, so the style. But style can also reflect the man: hence Persius redeems derogatory critical metaphors from their moribund banality by causing them to coalesce in a succession of scenes which condemn his *dramatis personae*. Writers and audience are represented as suffering from the moral manifestations of the stylistic failings out of which the drama has been constructed. A hint of condemnatory homosexual imagery appears at line 4, to be continued by lines 9–11, finally receiving full dramatic form in the recitation scene of lines 15–21. Setting is not absolutely consistent, interspersed as it is with individual autonomous images; it disappears completely at 24–30,

---

[1] The polarity is also found at Ar. *Ran.* 939–41, τὴν τέχνην ... οἰδοῦσαν ... ἴσχνανα.

[2] *V.* Brink *ad loc.* for connexion with disease.

although metaphor – mainly sexual, but still mixed – is external-ised in the form of dialogue.

At line 30 dramatic form is resumed, food metaphors joining those of effeminacy to produce, in a *cena*, a material extension and reproachful counterpart of stylistic corruption. But the scene fades into the background once again, 36–40, Persius this time not sustaining the dominant metaphor, but giving us instead his personal commentary, answered by his interlocutor at 40–3. From 44 ff., dramatisation becomes more abrupt and piecemeal. But still the objects of Rome's applause – *euge* and *belle* – are denigrated through the correlative of another *cena*, represented in patchwork form by the three questions of 51–4, which amount to an associative, rather than fully objective, image of faults – turgidity and indigestion – which would normally receive meta-phoric description. Lines 55–62 serve partly to body forth the metaphor of fatness, as well as insinuating that the writer is a coarse and imitative hack. After a few formal criticisms at 63–8, Persius switches attention to education, 69 ff., now much less dramatic in his treatment, but still maintaining contact with substantiated metaphor, as in the case of *sartago* at line 80. Homo-sexual imagery is resumed at lines 81–2, and developed in the law-court episode at 83 ff., which is not completely dramatised, although certain metaphors – *cano*, *rasis*, *ceves* – receive physical embodiment. Stylistic vice is again corporealised at 103 ff., *testiculi*, *delumbe*, *Attis*. In these later passages the imagery has no stable congruence with scene, which consequently fluctuates elusively in its measure of materiality.

EXCURSUS I

Sexual imagery in Horace Epistles I. 20 and Callimachus
Epigram XXVIII Pf.

The imagery of homosexuality and effeminacy elucidates interpretation of Hor. *Ep.* I. 20, and Callim. *Epigr.* XXVIII, two compositions whose interrelationship has gone unnoticed. It has been recognised that *Ep.* I. 20 relies for much of its effect on a metaphorical conflation between the *liber* and a boy-prostitute: *prostes, pumice mundus, pudico, communia laudas, cum plenus languet amator, carus, donec te deserat aetas, contrectatus ubi manibus sordescere volgi, senectus.* All these words contribute to the *double-entendre*.[1] What is not normally noted is the derivation of the metaphors from literary-critical vocabulary, and Horace's probable dependence on Callimachus.[2]

Epigram XXVIII is not based on a conflation of sex and literature. Perhaps for this reason its relevance to Horace has been overlooked. Instead of using metaphor, Callimachus operates on a double level, juxtaposing two sets of disparate images:

> Ἐχθαίρω τὸ ποίημα τὸ κυκλικὸν οὐδὲ κελεύθῳ
> χαίρω τὶς πολλοὺς ὧδε καὶ ὧδε φέρει,
> μισέω καὶ περίφοιτον ἐρώμενον, οὐδ' ἀπὸ κρήνης
> πίνω· σικχαίνω πάντα τὰ δημόσια.
> Λυσανίη, σὺ δὲ ναίχι καλὸς καλός· ἀλλὰ πρὶν εἰπεῖν   5
> τοῦτο σαφῶς, Ἠχώ φησί τις· 'ἄλλος ἔχει'.

Like Horace, he is indebted to the language of the critics. But shared commonplace is not so likely as direct influence. Prop. II. 23.1–2, collocating individual items on a single erotic level,

> cui fugienda fuit indocti semita vulgi,
> ipsa petita lacu nunc mihi dulcis aqua est,

shows that the epigram was known in Rome before the composition of *Ep.* I. 20: Callimachus' juxtaposed parallelism has given way to subordination to a single erotic purpose.[3] Horace alters the prior manner of composition to sustained metaphoric equation, declaring through his borrowings that he has said farewell to a small côterie with shared theoretical views. Until the time of collected publication for a wider audience, the author's intentions have been pure and exclusive: but now he has an eye on posterity. He manages to get the best of both worlds, by pretending previous devotion to the most esoteric standards, while simultaneously prophesying, with expected false modesty, a popular future for his compositions.

Epigram XXVIII has caused distress amongst the commentators: Gow–Page write of the final couplet, and the problem of punctuating before or after Ἠχώ:[4]

[1] For a summary, *v.* D. West, *Reading Horace* (Edinburgh 1967), pp. 17 ff.

[2] *Epigr.* XXVIII is normally referred to Hor. *A.P.* 131–5, on imitation, but not to *Ep.* I. 20: *v.* Brink, *Prolegomena*, p. 109, and p. 210 of the commentary.

[3] Enk *ad loc.* quotes Callimachus, without comment on compositional mechanics.

[4] Vol. II, pp. 156–7. I adopt Pfeiffer's punctuation in the last line.

Whichever punctuation is preferred, the couplet as a whole presents difficulties. As it stands the epigram states the author's dislike of pleasures shared by the mob and leads up to his rejection of Lysanias because his favours are bestowed also on another. If therefore the περίφοιτος ἐρώμενος is to be mentioned at all before this point it should be at the end of the list, not sandwiched between the highway and the drinking place. The first four lines make in themselves a satisfactory epigram, and the proposal of Haupt (and others) to excise 5 f. as a later addition deserves serious consideration.

This misses the point: apart from the indisputably erotic περίφοιτος ἐρώμενος, which requires explanation even if the last couplet is abandoned, we can adduce literary-critical vocabulary, and Hor. *Ep.* I. 20, as parallels for the admixture of the literary and the sexual; we can also explain the relevance of the last couplet to the rest of the epigram. In the first four lines various prejudices are stated: (i) against the cyclic poem and the broad path; (ii) against the promiscuous lover; and (iii) against the common spring. Justification for these literary and erotic prejudices is found in the last couplet.

Working from the contention that the image of the περίφοιτος ἐρώμενος is a correlative for the loss of stylistic integrity – promiscuity being parallel to publicity and lack of quality – and that Lysanias is one and the same as the περίφοιτος ἐρώμενος, I would argue that in the last couplet Callimachus expresses distaste for the literary and erotic predilections of the mob. Firstly, the crowd, in its vulgar way, thinks the promiscuous Lysanias beautiful; secondly, it employs hackneyed formulaic language. Mair's note on σὺ . . . ναίχι καλὸς καλός makes it clear that the words are banal, the kind of thing which commends itself to the tasteless crowd.[1] Before a representative of that crowd can finish mouthing its formula, 'an echo' butts in, objecting to the completion of the accolade: with εἰπεῖν I understand τινα rather than με, and interpret the specification τις by reference to the fact that it is *Callimachus* who assents to the verdict of echo. Her objection consists of detraction from Lysanias, on the grounds that as a complement to his vaunted beauty he is promiscuous, and from the trite language used by the populace when awarding its worthless praise. The pun, ναίχι καλός and 'ἄλλος ἔχει' implies that just as the letters of the two

---

[1] A. W. Mair, Loeb Classical Library, pp. 156–7 (punctuating after Ἠχώ): 'The repeated καλός as part of the lover's language occurs as early as Pind. *P.* II. 72, καλός τοι πίθων . . . παρὰ παισὶν ἀεὶ καλός, and Attic vases frequently exhibit such forms as ὁ παῖς ναιχὶ καλός, καλός νεανίας, ὁ παῖς καλός, Δωρόθεος καλός.'

phrases are interchangeable, so are the ideas constituted by the letters: popular beauty necessarily involves promiscuity. That the beautiful Lysanias is now in the keep of a new master is conveyed by the description, through 'ἄλλος ἔχει', of the transference of his affections.

So much for the erotic level. As for the literary, besides the topics already adumbrated – the obvious indictment of the mundane formula, ναίχι καλὸς καλός and the contempt for popularity implied by the words of echo, 'ἄλλος ἔχει': 'beauty' is too easily discovered and applauded – there is scorn for the imitative and derivative in literature. Distaste for the way in which bad writers plunder the work of their second-rate predecessors is mirrored in the pun, 'ἄλλος ἔχει' alluding to the facile communication of mundane commonplace like ναίχι καλὸς καλός from one writer to another. Just as the physical beauty approved by the crowd has promiscuity as its complement, so in literature a thoughtless, imitative, and impersonal pastiche is the inevitable result of employing popular formulae. The prejudices of the first four lines, both erotic and literary, are now explained. Wherever it is found – cyclic epic, broad path, common spring, and promiscuous lover: the whole amounting to contempt for the derivative, the formulaic, and the popular – Callimachus shuns τὰ δημόσια in all its meretricious guises.

EXCURSUS 2

'Digentia' in Horace's Epistles

At *Ep.* I. 18.104 ff., Callimachean water-imagery takes on an ethical aspect:

> me quotiens reficit gelidus Digentia rivus,
> quem Mandela bibit, rugosus frigore pagus,
> quid sentire putas? quid credis, amice, precari?

A catalogue of modest requirements follows:

> sit mihi quod nunc est, etiam minus, et mihi vivam
> quod superest aevi, si quid superesse volunt di;
> sit bona librorum et provisae frugis in annum
> copia, neu fluitem dubiae spe pendulus horae.

Horace is here the healthy philosopher, in contrast to his ambitious addressee: the final autobiographical sketch is *ad hominem*, its emphatic *me* introducing a tone of needed advice.[1] He does not simply write about returning to the country, but about being refreshed by the cold stream of Digentia, landscape acting as a prelude to the morality of seclusion. We are in the presence of an ethical conversion of a commonplace from literary apologetics.[2] *Digentia* might be regarded as bearing the same relationship to the *Epistles* as Bandusia and the waters of Tibur to the *Odes*.[3] Instead of a conventional Greek fountain or stream, a transformation of Horace's own Italian landscape.

In the *Epistles* one of Horace's concerns is the creation of a symbol of moral sanity out of his country retreat. When Digentia first appears, during his description of the *Sabinum* at *Ep.* I. 16.12 ff., this preoccupation can be distinguished:

> fons etiam rivo dare nomen idoneus, ut nec
> frigidior Thracam nec purior ambiat Hebrus
> infirmo capiti fluit utilis, utilis alvo.

Comparison with the Hebrus takes the reader to the river of the poet Orpheus, or of the Bacchantes.[4] But most important, the medicinal value of the stream – *infirmo capiti fluit utilis, utilis alvo* – has, under a disguise of irony, the function of indicating that here in the country Horace possesses a degree of moral stability unknown to Quinctius his addressee.[5] Both *Epistles* I. 16 and I. 18 invite comparison with the more famous streams and fountains of Greece: Hippocrene has become a moralised Digentia, transplanted to a new realistic locality.

---

[1] Details aimed at Lollius are *etiam minus*, 107, insinuating that he wants too much; *mihi* in the same line, opposing H.'s αὐτάρκεια (cf. *Ep.* I. 14.1, mihi me *reddentis agelli*, and I. 18.101, *quid* te tibi *reddat amicum*) to L.'s career as a dependant; and aequum *mi* animum *ipse parabo*, suggesting the addressee's lack of αὐτάρκεια in contrast to H.'s claim to its possession.

[2] *V.* Wimmel pp. 222–3, and Kambylis pp. 23 ff., 66 ff., 98 ff., 108 f., 110 ff., 183 ff., for streams, fountains, and water.

[3] On *Bandusia*, *v.* E. Fraenkel, *Horace* (Oxford 1957), pp. 203, 423; also Commager p. 324. Cf. *Carm.* IV. 3.10 ff., *sed quae Tibur aquae fertile praefluunt/et spissae nemorum comae/fingent Aeolio carmine nobilem*, for a naturalised Roman Hippocrene; more briefly, *aquae* at III. 4.7–8, and *ripas*, III. 25.12–13, both in contexts of poetic inspiration.

[4] Virg. *Georg.* IV. 524; Hor. *Carm.* III. 25.10, in a context of poetic inspiration.

[5] On the tone adopted towards him, *v.* M. J. McGann, *CQ* ns X (1960), 205–12.

EXCURSUS 3

Furius at Horace Satires II. 5.40–1

In extension of my comments on alimentary imagery, a few observations on Horace's depiction of the poet Furius[1] at *Sat.* II. 5.40–1,
where a crass *ingenium* and a bombastic style are associated with a
peculiarly rich and nauseating type of food:

> seu pingui tentus omaso
> Furius hibernas cana nive conspuet Alpes.

Two factors contributed to the creation of *pingui tentus omaso*: the
adjective accompanying Furius' début in *Satires* I, and the verb from
the original line here parodied.[2]

At *Sat.* I. 10.36 Horace called him *turgidus – turgidus Alpinus iugulat
dum Memnona –* an adjective evocative of turgidity and indigestion.[3]
'Bloated with rich tripe'[4] is a concrete expansion of *turgidus*, transforming a fault in style into a fault in appetite. But besides *Sat.* I. 10.36,
Horace recalled a line from Furius himself, which with its offending
conspuit sparked off a witty train of ideas:

> Iuppiter hibernas cana nive conspuit Alpes.[5]

[1] For a summary of the arguments on his identity *v.* Rudd p. 289 n. 52, who
tentatively inclines to the view that he is distinct from the 'neoteric'
Bibaculus; Fraenkel p. 130 n. 1 asserts that the distinction has been settled
by Nipperdey, *Opuscula*, pp. 499 ff. The example of Varro Atacinus and
Cicero (also Virgil, for that matter), who used Alexandrian forms as well
as the more conventional epic, should warn against a hypothesis of two
Furii based on argument from genre.

[2] Interpretation has tended to ignore the growth of the tripe image from
turgidus at *Sat.* I. 10.36 and Furius' own *conspuit*. Wickham, 'as though the
coarseness of taste in his metaphors were connected with coarseness of
taste in his feeding', is on the right lines, but no food imagery is cited. Acro,
'Furius poeta immanis ventris', looks like a literal-minded shot in the dark.

[3] *turgidus* and *tumidus* are associated with indigestion at Hor. *Ep.* I. 6.61,
Pers. III. 98, and Juv. I. 143, quoted above, p. 46.

[4] *omasum*, which reappears at *Ep.* I. 15.34, is supposedly a Gallic word:
cf. *Corp. Gloss. Lat.* II p. 138, 29, Goetz. Lejay thinks Furius himself may
have used it in search of 'la couleur locale'. A more attractive interpretation,
suggested by Mr R. G. G. Coleman, is that the Gallic *omasum* connects
with Furius' Alpine origins (cf. *Alpinus* at *Sat.* I. 10.36, and *Alpes* here).
If so, H. has wickedly chosen F.'s local dish as the vehicle for his metaphor.
With *omasum* cf. the more abstract *sagina* at Quint. X. 5.17, of the rich
nourishment of declamation and versification; with moral disapproval,
II. 15.25.   [5] Cited at Quint. VIII. 6.17 as an example of harsh metaphor.

In Horace it is no longer Jupiter who spits upon the Alps, but Furius.[1] However there has been a change in meaning: the primal act of spitting has suggested the act of vomiting. A verb which brands Furius as a *pinguis poeta* becomes entangled with the alimentary metaphor. Horace seizes upon *conspuit*, associates it with the process of vomiting, and because literary-critical metaphorics allowed identification between style and food, finds a repulsive correlative for Furius' bombast in an image of rich tripe. His antagonist is now bloated in a way far more gross than suggested by the *turgidus* of his initial appearance. The new image, *pingui tentus omaso*, still has the same critical function as *turgidus*: Furius' poem is a παχὺ γράμμα καὶ οὐ τορόν. But now Furius is not only an incompetent, pompous writer: he is also a slave to his stomach. He has not digested his material properly, hence vomits it up as though it were a dish of tripe swallowed too quickly.

My contention that there has been a shift of meaning in *conspuet*, from spitting to vomiting, needs support. Superficially at least, closest to Horace is ἔπτυσας at D. L. Page, *Greek Literary Papyri*, Loeb Classical Library, 93a, lines 12 ff.,

> τὴν τ' ἀπὸ Μουσῶν ἄφθιτον αὐδὴν
> ἣν σὺ μερίμναις ταῖσιν ἀτρύτοις
> καθυφηνάμενος πόντος τις ὅπως
> ἔπτυσας ἄλ[λο]ις [ο]ὐ [μυθητοῖ]ς
> φωσὶν ἐπ' ἀκτάς,

where Homer is the sea 'spitting' upon the shore. Citing Aelian *V.H.* XIII. 22 Page remarks 'ἐμοῦντα is coarse, ἔπτυσας is not'. But this does not preclude the possibility that Furius' unfortunate metaphor became associated in Horace's mind with the process of vomiting. From the various allusions to writers and speakers being sick, the nearest to our parody is Epictet. *Ench.* 46, 'in philosophical discussions keep quiet, μέγας γὰρ ὁ κίνδυνος εὐθὺς ἐξεμέσαι ὁ οὐκ ἔπεψας'.[2] Likewise, indigestion causes Furius to vomit. What originally issued from the mouth of Jupiter, now with slight modification issues from the mouth of the poet. For literary indigestion – *turgida oratio* – leading to vomiting, we can adduce e.g. Hor. *A.P.* 457, of the *vaesanus poeta, dum sublimis versus ructatur*, and Mart. II. 90.6, *Accius et quidquid Pacuviusque vomunt.*[3]

---

[1] At *Sat.* I. 10.36 F. was similarly transposed to be the subject of the sentence, performing the actions of his characters.

[2] *V.* Summers on Sen. *Ep.* LXXXIV. 7.

[3] Also Cic. *Cat.* II. 10, *eructant sermonibus*; *Phil.* V. 20, *orationem ex ore*

Finally, a word on *cana nive*, the white snow which accompanies the rich literary tripe during the process of vomiting. Possibly this contributes to Furius' condemnation, though it could be argued that it is an inevitable survival from the original line. At any rate, Seneca makes Homer's ἔπεα νιφάδεσσιν ἐοικότα χειμερίῃσιν, of Odysseus,[1] a sign of elevated and unchecked verbosity: *itaque oratio illa apud Homerum concitata et sine intermissione in morem nivis superveniens oratori data est, Ep.* XL. 2. On reading *cana nive*, which is very close to νιφάδεσσιν ... χειμερίῃσιν, Horace may have been reminded of the fluency of Odysseus: the epithet is a certain example of unnecessary, almost formulaic, verbosity. Finding a line of 'fat' redundant epic containing a noun–epithet combination reminiscent of the unquenchable flow of Odyssean rhetoric, Horace, the writer of 'thin' polished verse, may have decided to put a stop to the noisy Furius. Given the epic setting of *Sat.* II. 5, an Homeric allusion would not be out of place.[2]

---

impurissimo evomuit; Callim. *Aet.* fr. 75 v. 7, ἤρυγες ἱστορίην. Mr J. Griffin kindly brings to my attention *Anth. Pal.* VII. 377, εἰ καὶ ὑπὸ χθονὶ κεῖται, ὅμως ἔτι καὶ κατὰ πίσσαν/τοῦ μιαρογλώσσου χεύατε Παρθενίου,/ οὕνεκα Πιερίδεσσιν ἐνήμεσε μυρία κεῖνα/ φλέγματα καὶ μυσαρῶν ἀπλυσίην ἐλέγων ..., and the article by F. Marx in *Rh. Mus.* LXXVI (1927), 446 ff. on the imagery of spitting and vomiting, starting from Aelian *V.H.* XIII. 22, Γαλάτων δὲ ὁ ζωγράφος ἔγραψε τὸν μὲν Ὅμηρον αὐτὸν ἐμοῦντα, τοὺς δὲ ἄλλους ποιητὰς τὰ ἐμημεσμένα ἀρυομένους. In some cases, the allusion is to vomit; others are merely extensions of the sea and water imagery so commonly found in literary criticism and apologetics: so Marx on the papyrus fragment above, and on the passage of Aelian. Cf. Brink on *A.P.* 457 for the relative coarseness of the verbs.

[1] *Il.* III. 222.

[2] Van Hook, 'Ψυχρότης ἢ τὸ ψυχρόν', *CPh* XII (1917), 74, citing also Athen. XIII. 430, Mart. III. 25, and Cat. XLIV, notes that *cana nive* may have struck H. as frigid in the technical rhetorical sense.

CHAPTER 4

PERSIUS' FIRST SATIRE: ANALYSIS

The first twelve lines tell us that the genre is unpopular, that the Romans have no taste, and that their apparent severity is suspect. Persius begins with a false start, quoting, or giving the illusion of quoting, a line from a supposedly inchoate work on κενο-σπουδία:[1]

> O curas hominum! o quantum est in rebus inane!

An interlocutor[2] immediately asks him if he will find an audience for such high-minded moralising, lines 2–3:

> 'quis leget haec?' min tu istud ais? nemo hercule. 'nemo?'
> vel duo vel nemo.

Persius knows that satire is unpopular.[3] But he is undeterred,

---

[1] Schol. on line 2 'hunc versum de Lucilii primo transtulit' surely refers to line 1. Hendrickson, *CPh* XXIII (1928), 99–112, dismisses the attribution, in favour of Lucretian origin, citing II. 14, 47, 1425, v. 45; also the tenfold occurrence of the formula *namque est in rebus inane*. L. uses themes from diatribe; but is it inherently likely that P. should make his début with an imitation of a writer who was not a member of the *satura* tradition? Although the vanity theme was common (e.g. Cic. *de Or.* III. 2.7, *o fallacem hominum spem fragilemque fortunam* [Scivoletto]), and P. quite capable of independent variation, I see no cogent reason for dismissing Lucilian imitation. Casaubon sums up the theme with 'per *curas hominum* intellegit τὰ πραττόμενα et actiones ac studia cuncta mortalium; *rerum* appellationem refer ad τὰ ὄντα'. His examples of *res*, 'non ab hominibus factas', namely jewels and silver, are not particularly apt, but his broad antithesis is correct.

[2] Hendrickson, above, observes that the satire is not a dialogue in any strict sense, but a 'mimetic monologue', noting that P. here uses a favourite device of diatribe, *contradictio*, or *occupatio* (= ἀνθυποφορά), to reflect in his own words objections of hostile criticism. There is no attempt at objective characterisation (*v.* 44 for proof), as the scholiast realised, e.g. on I. 24 f., 'in illius transit poetae vocem quem corripiebat; nec tamen recessit a sua persona'. For Dessen's misconceived attempts to give the interlocutor a life not his own, *v. CR* ns XXI (1971), 46–7; M. L. West's repunctuation of 1–3 (*CR* ns XI (1961), 204) seems likewise to result from needless anxiety about 'inconsistent characterization'.

[3] Cf. Hor. *Sat.* I. 4.22–3, *cum mea nemo/scripta legat*.

expressing surprise at the interruption of his thoughts, and remaining confident and nonchalant about the superiority of his tastes. Implied is the Stoic proposition that only the wise man is a good poet: μόνον δέ φασι τὸν σοφὸν καὶ μάντιν ἀγαθὸν εἶναι καὶ ποιητὴν καὶ ῥήτορα, Stob. *Ecl.* vol. II p. 67, Wachsmuth. It follows that the ἄσοφος is necessarily a bad poet. Persius' uncompromising attitude is paralleled by another Stoic text, Sen. *Ep.* VII. 9, which Summers rightly thinks he imitates:

> non est quod te gloria publicandi ingenii producat in medium, ut recitare istis velis aut disputare. quod facere te vellem si haberes isti populo idoneam mercem: nemo est qui intellegere te possit. aliquis fortasse, unus aut alter incidet, et hic ipse formandus tibi erit instituendusque ad intellectum tui.[1]

Besides the general similarity of situation, Persius' modification of *nemo* to *vel duo vel nemo* corresponds to Seneca's change, *nemo est qui . . .*, to *aliquis fortasse, unus aut alter*.[2] Persius refuses the sympathy offered by the interlocutor, and answers by lashing out at second-rate epic and at the habits of Rome, lines 3–5:

> 'turpe et miserabile.' quare?
> ne mihi Polydamas et Troiades Labeonem
> praetulerint? nugae.

He does not care if Polydamas and the Trojan ladies prefer Labeo's[3] shoddy translation of Homer. Satire is vindicated against

---

[1] Cf. *ibid.* § 10.

[2] As Summers notes, Sen.'s next statement, '*cui ergo ista didici?*' *non est quod timeas ne operam perdideris, si tibi didicisti*, is close to Pers. I. 24 ff. *V.* Casaubon on line 3 for examples of the Greek ἢ ὀλίγοι ἢ οὐδείς and ἢ τις ἢ οὐδείς, corresponding to *vel duo vel nemo*.

[3] Identified with Attius, 50, by Buecheler (*RhMus* XXXIX (1884), 289; LXIII (1908), 190), on the basis of Schol. on I. 4 and I. 49. Kroll's identification (*AJPh* LIX (1938), 479 ff.) is with the translator of Praxidicus, Plin. *NH* XVIII. 55.200. (There is an insane, and irrelevant, Labeo at Hor. *Sat.* I. 3.82.) E. Marmorale, *Persio*[2] (Florence 1956), pp. 187 f., suggests a veiled attack on Lucan: but turgid mythological epic is one thing, L.'s modernisation of the genre quite another. Such speculation is on a level with the futile attempts to find Statius lurking behind Martial's generalised attacks on epic, or the figure of Nero looming as efficient cause behind the literature of his reign.

popular epic. The assault on bad literature has begun. And so, almost imperceptibly, has the assault on morality. As the commentators note, *Polydamas et Troiades* owes something to the Roman adoption of Homer's Πουλυδάμας and Τρωάδας ἑλκεσιπέπλους (*Il.* XXII. 100 and 105) as proverbial types of a judgement which must be respected.[1] For the moment the words refer with scorn to the severity of the self-styled literary pundits, a severity which is further defined at lines 9 ff. But in the light of future developments we look back to *Polydamas et Troiades* to see that the words operate simultaneously as an evocation of the past, and, more important, as an insinuation of effeminacy. A glance at heroic Trojan origins accompanies an implication that the Romans no longer deserve to be called men. For *Troiades* is not only indebted to Hector's fears at *Iliad* XXII. 105: it also depends in part upon the rebuke of cowardice through imputation of womanliness at *Il.* II. 235, Ἀχαιΐδες, οὐκέτ' Ἀχαιοί, nationalised by Virgil as *o vere Phrygiae, neque enim Phryges* at *Aen.* IX. 617. In calling his pundits Trojan women, Persius uses this second set of epic associations to begin his questioning of his compatriots' virility. But the symptom discovered by *Troiades* has to wait until lines 13 ff. for full diagnosis, when the façade of proud respectability is finally stripped away.

In lines 5–7 Persius adopts a stance outside the vulgar preferences of his countrymen:

> non, si quid turbida Roma
> elevet, accedas examenve inprobum in illa
> castiges trutina nec te quaesiveris extra.

Rome's balance is defective, but he has no desire to correct it.[2] The verdict of the self-sufficient man is his only requirement, not

---

[1] Cf. Cic. *ad Att.* II. 5.1, VII. 1.4, VIII. 16.2.

[2] *elevet* introduces the metaphor ('levius existimet, obtrectet, damnet', sim., sc. 'in trutina' (Bo)): cf. Hor. *Sat.* I. 3.69 ff., *Ep.* II. 1.29 f., *Romani pensantur eadem/scriptores trutina*, Pers. IV. 10 f., with similarly derogatory overtones, III. 82, V. 100–1. C. Buscaroli, *Persio Studiato in Rapporto a Orazio e a Giovenale*, parte prima (Imola 1924), pp. 20–1, also notes Cic. *de Or.* II. 159, *ad ea probanda quae non aurificis statera, sed quadam populari trutina examinantur*, and Juv. VI. 436–7, *committit vates et comparat, inde Maronem/atque alia parte in trutina suspendit Homerum*.

mass adulation.[1] For the Romans have – *a, si fas dicere*. Bad taste
is the answer – the asses' ears. Or rather, bad taste is the first
answer. For by the time that Persius has answered his own
question, bad taste has become identified with delinquent morals.
But for the moment the reader is left in suspense with a tantalising
fragment – *nam Romae quis non?* – a device which allows the
satirist to develop his argument against the insufficiencies of
Polydamas and the Trojan ladies, rejecting them as unable to
appreciate the corrective of his writings, and as beyond redemp-
tion in their own literary proclivities.

Yet Rome has all the airs of respectable morality, pretending to
maintain the grand tradition. It is this hypocritical front which
drives Persius into completing the satire, lines 8–12:

> nam Romae quis non? – a, si fas dicere – sed fas
> tum cum ad canitiem et nostrum istud vivere triste
> aspexi ac nucibus facimus quaecumque relictis,
> cum sapimus patruos. tunc tunc – ignoscite (nolo,
> quid faciam?) – sed (sum petulanti splene) cachinno.

False gravity decides the issue: an answer to his question is
required.

The broken syntax – a grammatical necessity, not an editorial
superimposition – illustrates his ironic, stuttering diffidence.
Housman's punctuation,[2] demanding a second parenthesis, may

---

[1] With *nec te quaesiveris extra*, Stoic αὐτάρκεια, cf. Hor. *Ep.* I. 16.19, *vereor
ne cui de te plus quam tibi credas*, and Sen. *Ep.* XXIX. 12, *malis tibi placere
quam populo* (Ramorino); cf. F. Villeneuve, *Essai sur Perse* (Paris 1918),
p. 243 n. 4. The second part of Schol. on *turbida* 'ab aqua translatio; vel
quod multis gentibus repleatur' deserves consideration. Although its
immediate significance is 'confused' or 'disordered', play on its derivation
from *turba* makes sense preceding the injunction to αὐτάρκεια: self-
reliance and individuality are set against mass opinion. Cf. Hor. *Sat.* I.
10.73–4, *neque te ut miretur turba labores/contentus paucis lectoribus*.

[2] *CQ* VII (1913), 12–14. C. F. Hermann's alternative punctuation:

> tunc tunc – ignoscite (nolo,
> quid faciam?) sed sum petulanti splene – cachinno.

avoids a second parenthesis, but in 'the construction ... "ignoscite sed
sum petulanti splene" ... *sed* does not receive its proper force' (Housman,
p. 14). Although I do not agree that 'These three words, "forgive me, but
I laugh", are the thread on which everything else is strung' (the view
probably contributed to his departure from Hermann) *ignoscite sed
cachinno* is still the more forceful construction.

look ugly on the printed page, but the ugliness, which begins at line 8 with a series of repetitions – *fas, sed fas, tum, cum, cum, tunc tunc, sed* – has expressive value as a mirror of the self-consciously staccato progression towards the harshness of *cachinno*. We find a similar technique at line 119, in preparation for the sham burial of his secret. But here there is an element of evasion: the final answer to his question, *nam Romae quis non?*, has to be delayed in order to accommodate the central onslaught. At line 8, it looks as though an answer will soon be given. But at lines 11–12 Persius sidetracks expectations by telling us that his reaction to Roman gravity is derisive laughter. The final word of line 12, *cachinno*, leads into the rest of the satire, but, no matter how well integrated, it is a delaying tactic. Even though an apposite summary of Persius' treatment of his victims – with *cachinno* compare *rides*, 40 – it follows that Housman's emphasis on the words 'forgive me, but I laugh' is too narrow. If there is any single 'thread on which everything else is strung', it is line 8.

The façade which occasions his laughter will be removed from line 13 onwards, exposing until the completion of his question the various vices which previously lay hidden. Already there are clues. On seeing *canitiem, nostrum istud vivere triste*, and *patruos*, the reader is perhaps at first puzzled. What lies behind the pose? Lines 13 ff. give the full explanation: sexual perversion. But *nostrum istud vivere triste* foreshadows the answer, hypocritical severity being the recognised pose of the homosexual. Now *canitiem* and *patruos* fall into place; our old age is not that of a wise uncle, but of a worn-out reprobate.[1] Persius' derision turns out to be entirely justified. Already armed with private insight, he proceeds to unveil further murky truths.

At line 13, without obvious warning, he begins to talk about the consuming vogue for composition. He may have expected his reader to have the topic of literature in mind from the context of Hor. *Ep.* II. 2.141–2, *nimirum sapere est abiectis utile nugis/et tempestivum pueris concedere ludum,* where wisdom is recommended instead of poetry, a passage which has influenced the previous section. For a moment it seems as if Rome has reached the philosophic state which Horace thinks *utile – sapimus patruos,*

---

[1] *V.* Excursus 1, p. 142.

nucibus . . . relictis – in fact, to our surprise, she combines this with a rage for composition. *nucibus . . . relictis* turns out to be different from *abiectis . . . nugis*; *sapimus patruos*, unlike *sapere*, a mere sham. Horace's precept has not been fully observed, for poetry is still written. Another transitional device might reside in *tristitia*, perhaps a prelude to *grande aliquid*, in that writers of the high style assumed a grave *persona*: the pose prepares for its parallel quality in style.[1] This is perhaps an ancillary factor in the larger connexion between his new subject and prior insinuations: literature suffers from contact with that homosexuality which Persius has detected behind white-haired severity. The recitation[2] which he depicts is a scene of total debauchery, decisive proof that our avuncular wisdom is nothing more than a hypocritical mask. With regard to delivery, pretensions are great, yet the process of composition smacks of the unreal and diseased, lines 13–14:

> scribimus inclusi, numeros ille, hic pede liber,
> grande aliquid quod pulmo animae praelargus anhelet.

Ironically, in view of what follows, the magnitude of *grande* is answered by *praelargus*, a rare word which calls surprised attention to the grotesque nature of the project.[3] Further, the sugges-

---

[1] *V.* Mart IV.14 for Silius' 'scowling brow'.

[2] The recalcitrant satirist traditionally rejects popular recitation: cf. Hor. *Sat.* I. 4.23, *volgo recitare timentis*, and 73, *nec recito cuiquam nisi amicis idque coactus*, *Ep.* I. 19.41–2, *spissis indigna theatris/scripta pudet recitare et nugis addere pondus*; also Juv. I. 1 ff., and perhaps Lucil. 1009 M, *producunt me ad te, tibi me haec ostendere cogunt.* But an attitude is not the same as a reality: Persius himself recited – at least, if we accept the evidence of the *Vita*, where the vulgate *recitantem* of line 23 is hardly likely. Can we really accept that Lucan interrupted his own recitation of another poet's verse with exclamations about its superiority? With Jahn's *recitante eo* (and suitable doctoring of the subsequent readings) sense is restored: when Persius recited, Lucan could hardly restrain himself from remarking on the satirist's superior quality. In general *v.* Mayor on Juv. III. 9.

[3] L & S cite Juvenc. III. 754. *animae* with *praelargus* may help to inflate the image further towards the proportions of *grande*: this is apparently Villeneuve's point, *Essai* p. 377, 'Le mot *anima* appliqué au vent appartient au vocabulaire de la haute poésie (cf. Virg. *Én.* 8.403; 1.153; Hor. *Od.* iv. 12.2) et accentue encore l'emphase voulue de l'expression.' To confine *anima* to its immediate sense of 'breath', is to lose elevation: see *ThLL* sv I, '*spiritus*', listing examples from comedy and prose.

tion of deformity in the image of the bloated lung – *pulmo animae praelargus anhelet*[1] – infects the whole undertaking with an air of perversity. Then *inclusi* at line 13, substituted for *indocti* at Hor. *Ep.* II. 1.117, *scribimus indocti doctique poemata passim*, while contrasting with *populo* at line 15, reprimands those who shut themselves away from the real world, to indulge their sickly inclinations.[2] Now comes the portrayal of the performer, contrasting with the recent depiction of grandiose intentions, the first object of scorn being his meticulous care for appearance, lines 15–17:

> scilicet haec populo pexusque togaque recenti
> et natalicia tandem cum sardonyche albus
> sede leges celsa.

Combed hair and neat toga, if interpreted as correlatives for style, would imply fastidious preciosity; sardonyx ring ornamentation, and high chair grandiosity. The over-all impression is one of affectation and effeminacy.[3]

First of all the combed hair, *pexus*.[4] As an object of satire, such

---

[1] An image from the bellows: cf. Pers. v. 10 f., *tu neque anhelanti, coquitur dum massa camino,/folle premis ventos*, Hor. *Sat.* I. 4.19–21, *at tu conclusas hircinis follibus auras/usque laborantis dum ferrum molliat ignis,/ut mavis, imitare*. Jahn cites Quint. XI. 3.55, Némethy, Cic. *de Or.* III. 41, *nolo verba exiliter exanimata exire, nolo inflata et quasi anhelata gravius*. Cf. also Ar. *Ran.* 829, πλευμόνων πολὺν πόνον. D. Korzeniewski's suggestion, 'Die erste Satire des Persius', *Die Römische Satire*, Wege der Forschung, Band CCXXXVIII (Darmstadt 1970), p. 390 and n. 21 (citing Tib. I. 8.37, Ov. *A.A.* III. 803, Juv. VI. 37, Petron. 100.1, Apul. *Met.* II. 27.3; add Gow-Page, 894 (Asclepiades) with note, 1103–4, and Hor. *Epod.* XI. 10), that the panting is 'ein Keuchen vor Lust' is attractive. But given *grande aliquid* and *pulmo animae praelargus* the sexual overtone can at most be vestigial. P. builds up to his climax only gradually.

[2] *V*. Sen. *Contr.* IX *pr.* 3 on Latro, who needed to declaim indoors, rather than the commonplace Ov. *Tr.* I. 1.41, *carmina secessum scribentis et otia quaerunt*, and Juv. VII. 28, *qui facis in parva sublimia carmina cella*.

[3] *V*. G. A. Gerhard, *Phoinix von Kolophon* (Leipzig 1909), p. 149, for the connexion with concern for personal appearance. At Lucian, *Rhet. Praec.* 16, the orator is advised of its importance: σχήματος μὲν τὸ πρῶτον ἐπιμεληθῆναι χρή; cf. Quint. XI. 3.137, *et toga et calceus et capillus tam nimia cura quam neglegentia sunt reprehendenda*.

[4] Conington suggests (i) that the meaning is perhaps *pexis vestibus*, citing Hor. *Ep.* I. 1.95, *pexae tunicae*, or (ii) that the allusion is to combed hair, Quint. I. 5.14, *ille pexus pinguisque doctor*. Combed hair is the obvious interpretation, since dress figures in the next phase, *togaque recenti*.

fussiness would be a sign of the fop.[1] But hairdressing also provided literary criticism with one of its metaphors: for example, at Dion. Hal. *de Comp.* 25, p. 133, 5, we hear of Plato 'combing and curling' his dialogues, τοὺς ἑαυτοῦ διαλόγους κτενίζων καὶ βοστρυχίζων.[2] The Romans used similar conceits, turning *calamistri*, 'curling-irons', or *cincinni*, 'curls' to the criticism of precious and unmanly style: at *Or.* 78 Cicero advises the writer to dispense with pearls and curling-irons: *tum removebitur omnis insignis ornatus quasi margaritarum; ne calamistri quidem adhibebuntur*; or again, at *de Or.* III. 100 he writes, *eo citius in oratoris aut in poetae cincinnis ac fuco offenditur, quod sensus in nimia voluptate natura non mente satiantur.* On the other hand, a crop of shaggy hair is a symbol of the uncultivated old-fashioned style – the *impexam antiquitatem* of Tac. *Dial.* 20.3. Quintilian concedes that for the Rome of his day this type of unshaven eloquence is outmoded, but at the same time he will not allow an excessively ornamental hair-style, XII. 10.47: *do tempori . . . ne intonsum caput, non ⟨ut⟩ in gradus atque anulos comptum.* However, as he says at VIII *pr.* 22, if the whole body of a composition is well constructed, there is no need for decoration in the shape of either manicure or hair-dressing; *maiore animo aggredienda eloquentia est, quae si toto corpore valet, ungues polire et capillum reponere non existimabit ad curam suam pertinere.* If personal comportment is any criterion for inference, like Seneca's *comptuli*[3] the reciter will be disqualified from attaining to literary excellence, his style, like his hair, being refined to the point of daintiness. The other details of his outward manner may be connected with the stylistic dimension, his immaculate toga – *togaque recenti . . .*

---

[1] Juv.'s servants only comb their hair for a special occasion, XI. 150. Cf. Hor. *Carm.* I. 15.14 f., *pectes caesariem grataque feminis/imbelli cithara carmina divides*, a sign of effeminacy, Cic. *in Cat.* II. 10.22 (Jahn); Ov. *A.A.* III. 433–4, *sed vitate viros cultum formamque professos,/quique suas ponunt in statione comas*, and Sen. *Brev. Vit.* XII. 3. *V.* further Smith on Tib. I. 8.9, Nisbet and Hubbard on Hor. *Carm.* I. 12.41.

[2] J. F. Lockwood, *CQ* XXXI (1937), 196, compares Proclus *in Remp.* p. 199 K, τὸ γὰρ ἐλευθεριώτατον εἶναι τῶν ποιητῶν τὴν ἐκ τούτοις ἄδειαν δηλοῖ, μήτε ὀνομάτων ὥρας φροντίζοντες, οἵαν οἱ πολλοὶ περὶ πλείονος ἄγοντες βοστρυχίζουσι τοὺς στίχους, ...

[3] *Ep.* CXV. 2, *nosti comptulos iuvenes, barba et coma nitidos, de capsula totos: nihil ab illis speraveris forte, nihil solidum.*

albus[1], and ostentatious ring – *natalicia . . . cum sardonyche*, originating in the metaphor from dress and ornament, to image empty pomposity. In addition his high seat, *sede . . . celsa*, suitably matching his *grande aliquid*, backs up the atmosphere of lofty, yet mannered inanity, by what is probably a parody of epic formula, of the kind seen at Virg. *Aen.* VIII. 541 and XI. 301, *solio ab alto*; Albinovanus Pedo p. 115 M, line 12, *sublimis ab alta*; Luc. V. 16, *Lentulus e celsa sublimis sede profatur*; or Stat. *Theb.* II. 385, *sublimem solio*. Ironic replacement of an otiose *altus* by *albus*, to create an air of fragility, would be in the manner of Persius.[2] Alternatively, we might explain the allusion with reference to prostitution: the performer displays his goods in public, like the whore at Juv. III. 135 f., where Ruperti comments 'meretrices in *alta sella* sedebant, ut accedentes scortatores venalem mercem adtentius considerarent, ac membra omnia curiosius perlustrarent, sicut servi etiam venales in catasta prostabant; nam licet togatae essent, pellucebant nihilominus, Cois indutae'.[3]

Now the recitation begins, in the course of which the homo-sexuality disguised by sham *tristitia* is completely uncovered. Persius dramatises contemporary stylistic depravity in a scathing denunciation of the effect of modern literature upon its audience, and of the blatant sexual intent of the performer. The first hint of effeminacy is the preliminary vocal modulation of the reciter, lines 17–18:

> liquido cum plasmate guttur
> mobile conlueris.

Quintilian warns us of the connotations of the pejorative

---

[1] Possibly ambiguous: the white birthday toga (cf. Hor. *Sat.* II. 2.61, Ov. *Tr.* III. 13.14, V. 5.8), and on a secondary level, the diseased *pallor* of the *litterati* (cf. *pallor*, 26), or even the complexion of the reciter as indicative of effeminacy or wantonness (cf. Gerhard p. 155 for derivatives of λευκός used of the κίναιδος or λάγνος).

[2] But cf. the insignificant ἐφ' ὑψηλοῦ θρόνου καθήμενος at Cercidas fr. 2 Knox, where a sophist addresses an insensible audience.

[3] I am indebted to Mr R. A. Harvey for the suggestion. With the whole description cf. Lucian *Rhet. Praec.* 11, aptly cited by Koenig: εὑρήσεις πάνσοφόν τινα καὶ πάγκαλον ἄνδρα, διασεσαλευμένον τὸ βάδισμα, ἐπικεκλασμένον τὸν αὐχένα, γυναικεῖον τὸ βλέμμα, μελιχρὸν τὸ φώνημα, μύρων ἀποπνέοντα, τῷ δακτύλῳ ἄκρῳ τὴν κεφαλὴν κνώμενον, ὀλίγας μὲν ἔτι, οὔλας δὲ καὶ ὑακινθίνας τὰς τρίχας εὐθετίζοντα.

Graecism[1] *plasma*, I. 8.2, *sit autem imprimis lectio virilis* ... *non in canticum dissoluta, nec plasmate, ut nunc a plerisque fit, effeminata,* and our suspicions are amply confirmed by the subsequent portrayal of the lecherous but unmanly glint in his eye as he contemplates the act of literary sexual intercourse, line 18:

patranti fractus ocello.

Literary-critical metaphorics, where a dissolute effeminate style was commonly described by *fractus* or *infractus*, no doubt generated the image: note Sen. *Contr.* VII. 4.8, *non tantum emollitae compositionis sunt, sed infractae,* Sen. *Ep.* CXIV. I, *explicatio* ... *infracta et in morem cantici ducta,* and in a plainly homosexual context, Juv. II. 111–12, *fracta voce loquendi/libertas.*[2] But in order to activate the moral capacity of a conventional word, Persius does not draw on its expected sense by referring it directly to literature, but instead applies it to the reciter himself. In so doing he translates metaphor – *elocutio effeminata* – into the concrete image of a lascivious expression, conflating its literary meaning with its further connotations of emasculation, as at Petron. 119.25, of a mincing gait, *fractique enervi corpore gressus,* where *enervi* reinforces the sexual significance of *fracti.* As Casaubon notes, '*frangere* Latinis est idem ac effeminare, robur virile in muliebrem mollitiem corrumpere.' Placed between *patranti* and *ocello,* the word is paradoxical. For amongst its various senses, the verb *patrare* can denote the act of intercourse: as the scholiast on the passage explains, *patratio est rei Venereae consummatio.* Yet closer is the specification of the Delphin edition, '*patrare proprie est* παιδοποιεῖν',[3] a meaning sufficiently well

---

[1] The others (besides those in parodies of 'neoteric' poetry) are *Romulidae* 31, *elegidia* 51, *heroas* 69, *antithetis* 86, and *heminas* 130. *Romulidae* and *heroas* are elevated, *antithetis* and *heminas* colourless. The evidence is not typical, Graecisms usually being contemptuous like diminutives: *elegidia* thus gains force on both scores. Possibly P. wanted to concentrate his scorn in the parodies.

[2] Cf. Tac. *Ann.* XIV. 20, Plin. *Ep.* II. 14.2, Phaedr. IX. 2, Quint. I. 11.1, and Gell. III. 5, relating a *vox infracta* to homosexuality (Jahn *ad loc.*); add Longin. 41.1, ῥυθμὸς κεκλασμένος καὶ σεσοβημένος, and Sen. *Ep.* CXV. 2, *illum* [*sc. animum*] *non esse sincerum et habere aliquid fracti,* of debauchery exposed by a corrupt style.

[3] London 1820.

known to give rise to the discovery of a *double entendre* in Sallust's *patrare bellum*.[1] It would seem that the reciter can only imagine the pleasures of sex. Because he is *fractus*, worn-out and no longer virile, he is banned from their actual enjoyment. The tension between the active intent evidenced by *patranti*, along with the erotic diminutive[2] *ocello*, and the suggestion of impotence in *fractus*, will supply the basis for Persius' question to the performer at lines 22–3; he is initiating the youth into pleasures the force of which he himself cannot sustain. Near to the weird image *patranti . . . ocello*, but less ambitious, is Quint. XI. 3.76, prescribing that the orator's eyes should not be *lascivi et mobiles, et quadam voluptate suffusi, aut limi et, ut sic dicam, Venerei, aut poscentes aliquid pollicentesve*.[3]

[1] Quint. VIII. 3.44; cf. *expatrare*, Cat. XXIX. 16.

[2] On Pers. I. 33, *rancidulum*, Conington cites Van Wageningen's list of diminutives in P.: (*a*) adjectives: I. 22 *vetulus*; I. 54, *horridulus*; III. 103, *beatulus*; V. 147, *rubellus*; (*b*) substantives: I. 18, *ocellus*; I. 22, *auricula*; I. 51, *elegidia*; I. 57, *aqualiculus*; III. 49, *canicula*; IV. 6, *plebecula*; IV. 15, *popellus*; IV. 18, *cuticula*; IV. 29, *seriola*; V. 74, *tesserula*; V. 116, *pellicula*; *v*. D'Agostino, 'I diminutivi in Persio', *Atti dell' Acc. delle scienze di Torino*, LXIII (1927–8), 5–23. Distribution is uneven, *Sat.* I with six out of fifteen, *Sat.* II and VI with none. As in Juvenal (*v*. Friedländer's list on I. 11), P.'s diminutives tend to be scornful. Contrast Horace where they are sometimes recommendatory, below, p. 162 n. 2.

[3] Conington strays to Hesychius to explain *fractus ocello* as κλαδαρόμματος. Esp. violent here, the image arises from the commonplace idea that sexual desire shows itself in the eyes, particularly during intercourse; *v*. Barrett on Eur. *Hippol.* 525–6, Nisbet and Hubbard on Hor. *Carm.* I. 36.17, Russell on Longinus 4.4, West on Hes. *Th.* 910, and Gow–Page on λίχνοισι at Leonidas 2153 (= *A.Pl.* 306), '*lascivious lickerish* (the word seems connected with λείχειν). A λίχνον ὄμμα is ascribed to paederasts also in Call. fr. 571 (where see Pfeiffer), Meleager 4547; cf. Crat. Theb. fr. 4.' *Anth. Lat.* 902.3, *sunt lusci oculi atque patrantes* probably recalls P. Prior exx. include Ov. *A.A.* II. 691, *aspiciam dominae victos amentis ocellos*, 721, *aspicies oculos tremulo fulgore micantes*, and III. 802; later, Adam. II. 52 (I p. 415, 4 f.), ὑγρὸν βλέπει καὶ ἰταμόν (of the ἀνδρόγυνος: Gerhard p. 153), Juv. VII. 241, *oculosque in fine trementes*, Gell. III. 5.2, *oculos ludibundos* (of the *cinaedus*: Jahn), and Apul. *Met.* III.14, *oculos udos ac trementes*. Persius was perhaps influenced here, and in his later substitution of sexual for aural pleasure (below pp. 79 and 95), by Hor. *Ep.* II. 1.87 f., *verum equitis quoque iam migravit ab aure voluptas/omnis ad incertos oculos et gaudia vana*. The immediately preceding *media inter carmina* (cf. Pers. I. 30), and perhaps *his nam plebecula gaudet* confirm the probability of reminiscence.

The passage beginning at line 19 contains many difficulties and much obscurity:

> tunc neque more probo videas nec voce serena
> ingentes trepidare Titos, cum carmina lumbum   20
> intrant et tremulo scalpuntur ubi intima versu.
> tun, vetule, auriculis alienis colligis escas,
> articulis quibus et dicas cute perditus 'ohe'?
> 'quo didicisse, nisi hoc fermentum et quae semel intus
> innata est rupto iecore exierit caprificus?'   25
> en pallor seniumque! o mores, usque adeone
> scire tuum nihil est nisi te scire hoc sciat alter?

Lines 19–21 are conspicuous for their sexual overtones. But what are we to make of the question at 22–3, of the reply at 24–5, and again, of the retort at 26–7? Has the sexual metaphor disappeared? I think not. Firstly, it would be odd if the erotic colour of the description vanished abruptly after line 21. Persius' question at 22–3, arising as it does from a scene of sexual debauchery, most likely perpetuates the previous dominant colour. Since reply and retort arise from the question, again the probability is that the sexual metaphor is continued. Secondly, there are several details which make better sense if interpreted as part of a literal translation of stylistic effeminacy into a concrete representation of sexual activity. With another touch of parodistic nationalism the Trojan women now become the *ingentes Titi*,[1] the adjective signifying mental grossness,[2] and their reaction to the performance likened to that of a passive homosexual. Verse is substituted for the physical agents of titillation: for *carmina* we expect something like *membrum virile*, for *versu*, *digito*, or perhaps *manu*. Two passages of Juvenal illustrate the idea: VI. 196–7, *quod enim non excitet* inguen/vox *blanda et nequam?* digitos *habet*, and *ibid.* 314–15, *nota bonae secreta deae, cum* tibia lumbos/*incitat*, of the sexual excitement produced by a seductive voice or music.[3] In a literal sense we can adduce Juv. VI. 365.1–2, *in quacumque domo vivit* luditque professus/obscenum, tremula *promittit et omnia* dextra, and

---

[1] Cf. Hor. *A.P.* 342, *celsi Ramnes*. Schol.'s improbable suggestion, '*aut certe a membri virilis magnitudine dicti Titi*', is adopted by Korzeniewski p. 397 n. 40, with bibliography.

[2] Below, p. 156, and Juv. VI. 512–13, *ingens semivir*, of a eunuch priest.

[3] Cf. Hor. *Carm.* IV. 13.5–6.

from the same context, 23–4, *suspectus tibi sit quanto* vox *mollior et quo/ saepius in teneris haerebit* dextera lumbis. In view of *intrant, lumbum* here in Persius must mean *culus*, not 'genitals' as L & S, or as at Juv. VI. 314–15 above.[1] He no doubt started from some such concept as that at Greg. ad Hermog. *Rhet. Gr.* 7.1236 W, αἰσχρῶς μὲν κολακεύει τὴν ἀκοὴν ἐκεῖνα ὅσα ἐστὶν ἐρωτικά, on the poetry of Anacreon and Sappho, or Quint. II. 12.6 *pravis voluptatibus aures assistentium permulcere,* on beguiling the ears of the public, and then decided to make the effect of his reciter's ἐρωτικά, or *voluptates,* more directly physical: instead of *aures* or ἀκοήν, *lumbum* and *intima.* For aural excitement, Juvenal can again be invoked: XI. 170, *auribus atque oculis concepta urina movetur.*[2] Later the image of passive sexual response – *ceves,* line 87 – will be applied to the listener who suspends critical judgement to applaud in return for cheap physical pleasure: but even though *trepidare* here describes the same reaction, it is not necessarily part of a bargain between audience and reciter. However, most important, we now fully comprehend Persius' reasons for rejecting the verdict of Polydamas and the Trojan ladies: it is not true literary merit which interests them, but titillation of the senses.

At lines 22–3 we meet a considerable problem of text and interpretation. I have printed the text with Madvig's emendation *articulis,*[3] supported by Housman,[4] and adopted by Clausen. The MSS transmit *auriculis.* To retain the second *auriculis,* one must either punctuate after it with a comma, explaining *et* as *etiam* or altering *et dicas* to *edicas,* which in itself may not be as inept as Clausen believes (cf. Ter. *Eun.* 962, *dico, edico vobis,* in mitigation of the technical sense of the word; moreover, given the epic cliché *sede* ... *celsa,* 17, and the solemn *patranti,* 18, a 'magisterial' injunction might not be out of place here); or,

---

[1] *arcanaque lumbi,* IV. 35, given *vulvas* at 36 also means *culus.*

[2] For vocal sexual response (*nec voce serena,* 19) cf. Juv. VI. 318, *quae vox saltante libidine.* Generally, on the effect of erotic literature, Cat. XVI. 9–11; for confusion of literary and sexual vocabulary, Ar. *Thesm.* 49–62, *Anth. Pal.* XI. 218 (Korzeniewski p. 395 n. 37). Add Auson. *Epigr.* CVIII. 4 ff., *Anth. Pal.* XI. 139 (Curtius p. 414).

[3] *Adv. Crit.* II p. 128.

[4] *Manilius,* I p. xlv; *CQ* VII (1913), 14.

without punctuation, derive sense from the combination *auriculis
... et cute perditus*. A marginal case could be made for the retention of a second *auriculis* followed by a comma, by appealing to
the prominence of allusions to ears. Since this is the first time that
they are mentioned, and since the joke, *auriculas asini quis non
habet?*, is the point towards which the body of satire gravitates, it
is not entirely inconceivable that Persius wrote *auriculis* in line 23.
But we are then forced to invoke emphasis, and emphasis alone, in
apology for the presence of a repetition which is undeniably
clumsy.[1] Furthermore, *et cute perditus* remains to be interpreted
as a cogent reason for the reciter's exclamation of satiety, directed
at the ears of his audience. Help has often been sought from Hor.
Sat. II. 5.96 ff., a passage about flattery:

> importunus amat laudari: donec 'ohe iam!'
> ad caelum manibus sublatis dixerit, urge,
> crescentem tumidis infla sermonibus utrem.

We might say that the performer is forced to exclaim 'Enough, no
more!' to the acclamations of his audience, because even – *et* – he,
inured to flattery, has reached the limit of endurance, the peculiar
nature of which could be defined by taking *cute perditus* as an
extension of *crescentem ... utrem*. Horace's swollen bladder is
now a bladder about to burst.[2] The physical state of the reciter
now embodies the effect of excessive flattery.

An image of a punctured bladder is far preferable to the allusion
detected by Reckford:[3] 'Persius may have in mind Horace's
tumidis ... dropsy being a more suitable image of a brainswollen
attitude than gout.'[4] Following his line of enquiry, we presumably interpret *tumidis* as an accessory factor in the formation of
cute perditus, adjective leading to image. But the obvious initial
point of departure is not *tumidis* but *crescentem ... utrem*, the
words used of the physical state of flattery's victim.[5] There are

---

[1] E.g. Koenig, 'iteratum hoc auget rei indignitatem'; Dessen p. 35. If
auriculis contains a pun, retention in 23 has more point.
[2] Rudd distinguishes between this and a burst bladder, *CR* ns XXV (1970),
284, it is 'too late to say *ohe* when the balloon has already burst', comparing
Phaedr. I. 24, *intendit cutem/maiore nisu*, of the frog emulating the cow.
[3] *Hermes* XC (1962), 480 n. 2.
[4] Casaubon adduces Lucil. 764 M, *aquam te in animo habere intercutem*.
[5] For *crescere* thus, cf. Hor. *Ep.* II. 2.101, *fit Mimnermus et optivo cognomine
crescit*.

insufficient grounds for positing allusion to dropsy – Reckford is not very clear on this, nor on the reasons for the reciter being *cute perditus* – especially when we remember that the disease was the metaphor for avarice, a vice clearly out of place here.[1]

If Persius *was* thinking of Hor. *Sat.* II. 5.96 ff., interpretation of *cute perditus* as an image of a bladder on the point of being punctured is obviously more in place. Further support for the Horatian explanation might be derived from *A.P.* 27, *professus grandia turget*. After describing the reciter's composition as *grande aliquid*, 14, Persius may have recalled the passage, and, with *turget* in mind, may then have sought a way to develop the image of swelling. An opportunity for conflating the idea of swollen literature with the idea of a reciter swollen with praise may have offered itself in the form of a combination between *A.P.* 27 and the *crescens uter* of *Sat.* II. 5. The process of association would have been from swollen literature (*grande aliquid*), to swollen reciter (via *professus grandia turget*, on the principle that style is the man), to reciter swollen with praise (through reminiscence of *crescentem . . . utrem*).[2] *fermentum* in 24 is again an allusion to swelling.

Such an interpretation is attractive; but the sequence from 22–3 to 24–5 is difficult if Persius has merely said that the writer is bursting from applause, when acclamation is not actually mentioned in context. If we complain with Madvig, '*ohe* de homine laudantium plausibus et clamoribus obruto accipiunt, qui ubi significetur, frustra quaero', line 87 could be invoked, '*bellum hoc.' hoc bellum? an, Romule, ceves?*, where applause is awarded in return for sexual satisfaction, or 28 f., where the interlocutor expresses a liking for public recognition. We have just witnessed the excitement of his audience: it might therefore be argued that they, like Romulus at 87, have graced him with shouts of *bellum* or *euge* as the price for their pleasures. This would carry more weight if 87 or 28 f. came first. As it is, the question of uncritical flattery and applause has not yet been raised. There is therefore nothing in the preceding or immediate context to supplement the ellipse of a reference to acclamation: *nec voce serena* describes the

---

[1] *V.* Russell on Longin. 3.4; Korzeniewski, pp. 391–2 and n. 25.

[2] Cf. *laudis amore tumes*, Hor. *Ep.* I. 1.36, and *inflat* of the effect of an appreciative audience on a writer who is *laudis avarum* at *Ep.* II. 1.178–9.

audience's sexual reaction, not their ovation, and a second *auriculis*, even if 'emphatic', cannot naturally suggest 'ears so corrupted by voluptuous literature that their possessor awards monstrously flattering applause'.[1] Moreover on this interpretation there is a sudden evanescence of the sexual colour of 19–21, the continuation of which the reader has been led to expect through the blatant transposition of *lumbum* and *intima* for *aures* as the area for aural response. Given this preparation, we naturally assume the entry of the word *auricula* to be accompanied by prior erotic associations. Also, the connexion with the reciter's reply is obscure. After being told that the applause with which he is greeted is so great that *even he* would be forced to make a gesture of satiety, he then proceeds to say that the whole point of his training is the communication of an inner urge to expression. This statement is surely a protest against some doubt recently cast on his relationship with his audience. If in fact his audience has been reacting along lines which are quite acceptable to him, by showering him with flattery, then there is no need to reply in a vein which suggests that some aspect of his recital has recently been called into question. To be on the verge of bursting with flattery, in a position where nice deprecating gestures – *et*, line 23 – can be made, does not add up to being in a situation where defensive comments like those of lines 24–5 are naturally made.[2]

The combination *auriculis . . . et cute perditus* removes the problem over *et*, but faces the critic with an intolerably clumsy repetition of *auriculis*, the allusion in line 22 being to the ears of the audience, in 23 to those of the reciter. If we refer *quibus* to *auriculis* in 22, and interpret *auriculis . . . et cute perditus* as meaning 'deaf through flattery, i.e. with ears overwhelmed by

---

[1] Rudd *CR* ns XXV (1970), 284 compares 'those ears which, hearing them, would call their brothers fools', *Merchant of Venice*, Act I scene 1, in support of ears speaking words of flattery. A Roman parallel providing the active force required from a second *auriculis* would be more pertinent.

[2] For the other way of retaining a second *auriculis*, viz. taking *cute perditus* as a reference to impotence, which causes the recognition of an incapacity to continue the process of sexual gratification, *v.* my discussion of *articulis . . . et cute perditus* (an extension of this approach), referring '*ohe*' to *auriculis*, 22. But a second *auriculis*, even with a sexual interpretation of *cute perditus*, still raises problems over *et*.

undiscriminating praise[1] and bursting with excessive acclamation', we again meet the difficulties encountered on the reading
auriculis, quibus et dicas cute perditus 'ohe!' Firstly, where do
we find that excessive praise which accounts for the reciter's
physical state, and occasions his cry of satiety? Secondly, why
should his defensive reply at 24–5 suggest that Persius has cast
destructive aspersions on his profession, if he has merely said
that some halt must be called to the audience's flattering response?
Once more I stress that to the reciter, though not to Persius,
such a response would be quite acceptable: the whole aim of his
performance, in fact. There is therefore no need for him to reply
as if its point has been questioned.

If we refer *quibus* to *escas* in 22, the meaning is 'Are you, old
man, collecting food for the ears of others, food which, if it
were offered to you, you would have to decline, because you are
auriculis et cute perditus?' In this case the problem of sequence is
not so difficult. Since the *escae* are the voluptuous erotica pur-
veyed to the audience, the reciter, told by Persius for whatever
reason that he could not enjoy them himself, now expostulates
at 24–5 after a feature of his profession has been undermined:
there is something about his kind of literature which he himself
is in no state to enjoy. He therefore objects that his training is
wasted if he has to forfeit enjoyment. But what is it that prevents
him from experiencing the pleasures of his own kind of literature?
– that is, what force should we give to *auriculis et cute perditus?*
Literally speaking deafness would disqualify him, and so perhaps
would dropsy, one possible interpretation of *cute perditus*. (If we
refer *quibus* to *escas*, we can no longer take *cute perditus* as suggesting a bladder about to burst through flattery; excessive acclamation cannot be the reason for the reciter's constraint to turn down
his own kind of literature.) But deafness and dropsy have no
special connexion with the type of pleasure so far conveyed by
the performance – a pleasure which has been consistently represented as sexual in origin. Even though a new type of imagery,

---

[1] P. *may* have remembered *gaudent praenomine molles/auriculae* from Hor.
Sat. II. 5.32–3, whence originated the *crescens uter*, in which case we plead
that the reciter is *auriculis . . . perditus* because his ears have taken too
much pleasure in flattery.

namely that of food, appears in 22, the reciter's *escae* are still those same erotic *carmina* whose sexual efficacy has so recently been depicted; also his designation as *vetule*, after a passage of lurid eroticism, probably continues the sexual dimension with the implied question, 'What do you think you are up to, indulging in pursuits from which your age should disqualify you?'[1] Deafness certainly provides no immunity from sexual enjoyment.[2] Nor does dropsy seem to have been regarded as inimical to sexual activity. If we wish to make sense of line 23, while referring *quibus* to *escas*, we must find there a convincing reason for the reciter's inability to experience the particular response produced by his poetry. The most obvious reason would be some kind of sexual debilitation: as I hope to show, *cute perditus* can supply the necessary sexual innuendo. But *auriculis . . . perditus* can yield nothing but an allusion to deafness. Since this has no place side by side with an observation on the reciter's capacity for sexual enjoyment, I turn to the possible meanings of the passage if one accepts the emendation *articulis*.

With the emendation there are still two ways of construing the lines, depending on whether we refer *quibus* to *escas*, or to *auriculis* in 22. Following Madvig in referring *quibus* to *escas*, Housman translates, 'What! catering at your age for others' ears with cates which you, disabled by gout and dropsy, must yourself forgo?'[3] This meets the requirement that 24–5 be a reply to a

---

[1] Though *vetulus* does not always have sexual overtones, it does so sufficiently often, in sufficiently similar contexts (Ov. *Am.* I. 9.4, *turpe senex miles, turpe senilis amor*; Sen. *Contr.* II. 6.4, *senex amans . . . nonne portentum est*) for an erotic interpretation to be natural here, given the reciter's description, 15–18, and audience's response, 19–21. *V.* Saara Lilja, *Terms of Abuse in Roman Comedy* (Helsinki 1965), p. 68, '*decrepitus, ignavus and putidus*, and the contemptuous diminutive *vetulus*, are pejorative adjectives for an old lover'; Korzeniewski, pp. 397–8 n. 42, citing Hor. *Carm.* III. 15; *Epod.* VIII (add *Carm.* I. 25; IV. 13; *Epod.* XII); Mart. III. 93; *Priap.* LVII; p. 402 n. 55, citing *Anth. Pal.* XI. 71 and Mart. X. 67, for the theme of the aged lover.

[2] Cf. Housman, *CQ* VII (1913), 14–15, 'deafness neither prevents a man from perceiving the vibration of his own voice nor from enjoying any excitement which that vibration may happen to set up in his nervous system'. One might object that since the place of sexual enjoyment is aural, deafness is an impediment. But this unravels the metaphor too far: at 19–21 audience-response is straightforwardly sexual.

[3] *Op. cit.* p. 14.

statement of Persius which could be construed as denying the reciter pleasure from his performance. But it glosses over the meaning of *ohe*, and more reprehensibly, specifies gout and dropsy as the reasons for the reciter's exclusion,[1] without attributing sexual significance to either disease: it should be stressed again that the cause for prohibition is inherent in the peculiar nature of the contemplated pleasure. If we take into consideration the type of pleasure from which the reciter is debarred, gout and dropsy must be shown to have affiliations with sexual incapacity. That we should consider the type of pleasure is also borne out by the proper force of *dicas ... 'ohe'*: the reciter would say 'Enough', 'Stop'.[2] In order to say this he has to be in a position where he is hypothetically offered his own *escae*.[3] Such a position would most naturally be that of his audience, those to whom at the moment he dispenses his *escae*. Persius is asking the reciter what he thinks he is up to, offering goods for consumption, which, if he exchanged rôles with his audience, he would himself turn down. To exchange rôles with his audience is to become subject to the same erotic pressure as they; and to be unable to withstand the physical pleasure resulting from such an exchange is to have a smaller capacity for sexual enjoyment. So the words which describe this ineffectuality – *articulis ... et cute perditus* – require an interpretation which will align them with the description of the audience's reaction at 19–21, and make them signify a relative incapability in the reciter's strivings to achieve a similar reaction.

The other method of construing the lines, defining the reference of *quibus* to *auriculis* in 22, has not to my knowledge been canvassed. In this case one would translate along the following lines: 'Are you, old man, collecting food for the ears of others, ⟨ears⟩ to which you, because you are "destroyed in your fingers and in

---

[1] Pers. v. 58 f., *cum lapidosa cheragra/fregerit articulos veteris ramalia fagi*, supposedly explains *articulis ... perditus*; *cum iam cutis aegra tumebit* III. 63, *cute perditus*. But *cute perditus* without a verb like *tumebit* need not suggest the swelling necessary for interpretation in terms of dropsy.

[2] Fraenkel p. 243 variously translates *iam satis, satis iam*, and *ohe iam satis* as 'basta!', 'assez!', 'enough of it!', 'no more of it!', 'stop it'.

[3] Rudd, *CR* ns xxv (1970), 283 (though he refers *ohe* to a repeated *auriculis*), citing Calphurnius on *ohe*, Ter. *Heaut.* 879, 'interiectio est satietatem usque ad fastidium designans', rightly remarks 'The word implies that a process has been going on – a process which must now be stopped.'

your skin", should say "Enough"?' I omit mention of gout and dropsy, since on this interpretation as on the last a sexual allusion is required in 23. For when the reciter is told to say 'Enough', the reference must be to the thing which the ears of his audience have so far been receiving, and which they presumably desire to continue receiving: recitation, and through recitation, sexual stimulus. Martial, who exclaims at the end of a book *ohe, iam satis est, ohe libelle!*, IV. 89.7, because it wants to go on in its previous course, *tu procedere adhuc et ire quaeris*, makes explicit what is implicit in Persius. The exclamation is directed at one who persists in a course of action which must be interrupted: in this context, one of sexually imaged listening. Hence '*ohe*' *auriculis dicere* is to intervene with a refusal to continue a sexually exciting recitation. Persius' audience, like Martial's book, is making demands. The performer, through the medium of poetry, has been the agent of titillation. So when Persius tells him that he should cease from arousing his audience, that he should call a halt to the process he has set in motion, by denying hypothetical requests for continuation, and adds as the reason for this that he is *articulis . . . et cute perditus*, it would seem most likely that here we have an observation on the sexual capacity of the reciter – on some feature of his physical condition which makes it advisable or necessary for him to discontinue the orgy initiated at 18–21. Questioning the abilities of the reciter as a literary and sexual *entrepreneur*, and castigating him for beginning something he cannot finish, Persius makes full use of the opportunity for stating that it would have been better to leave other people alone, if all he can do is induce in them a reaction with which he cannot deal. The objection at 24–5 now has its full weight: told by Persius that he should stop the recitation, the adversary complains that his training is wasted unless he can continue.

So we have two possible interpretations of the passage. Accepting the emendation *articulis*, we can refer *quibus* to either *escas* or *auriculis*, and retain a tolerable sequence of thought between 22–3 and 24–5. Whichever way we construe *quibus*, simple allusion to gout and dropsy in 23 is unsatisfactory: a sexual meaning is required. I now discuss the passage in more detail, dealing first with the consequences of referring *quibus* to *auriculis*.

I hope to have established that on this interpretation the gist is: 'Are you, old man, collecting food for the ears of others, ⟨ears⟩ to which you, because you are unable to meet their requirements, should say "Enough ⟨no more recitation⟩"?' Given the nature of what the audience has been receiving up to this point, recitation, and hence strong sexual stimulus, also given the suggestion of '*ohe*' *dicere* that the audience is making demands, I hope it will be agreed that *articulis . . . et cute perditus*, as a reason for discontinuing the performance, and as a description of the reciter's inability to meet his audience's requirements, must allude to some kind of sexual inadequacy or incapacity. At line 18 the reciter was *patranti fractus ocello*, endowed with an active sexual intent in his eye, but also debilitated. At 19–21 the active sexual intent was realised, transferred from performer to poetry, which was represented as stirring up a violently sexual audience-response. Now, at 22–3, Persius reverts to his earlier portrayal of debilitation, with an innuendo to the effect that the look in his adversary's eye is to be belied by practice. Of the three stages in this progression, from reciter to poetry then back to reciter, the first represents sexual intentions, but intimates that these might not be satisfactorily consummated; the second, with its easy transference from man to style, dwells on the connotations of *patranti* rather than those of *fractus*, showing an audience aroused to the heights of sexual frenzy through the medium of poetry; the third returns to the damaged ruins of *fractus*. Since metaphoric depiction of poetic impotence would be a difficult proposition, its development calling for complicated physical details – to describe active erotic potential would be easier, since less physical specification would be needed to portray the poetry than the reaction of the passive audience – Persius embodies the wreckage of style in the figure of the degenerate performer, who now stands as an outward symbol of literary depravity, a concrete image translated from metaphor. After calling him *vetule* – a ridiculous and culpable *senilis amator*, dedicated to sexual pursuits – Persius first of all demonstrates that he suffers from a disease caused by *paedicatio*, which debars him from further sexual activities, and then that he is impotent. Several passages which link gout with sexual indulgence elucidate the meaning of *articulis . . . perditus*.

Némethy[1] took a step in the right direction when he explained *articulis . . . perditus* with 'arthritide laborans, morbo libidinosorum; cf. v. 57–9: "ille in Venerem putris: sed cum lapidosa cheragra/fregerit articulos, veteris ramalia fagi."' In fact in view of the plural, *ingemuere*, at line 61, it is doubtful whether *cheragra* at v. 58 is the special punishment of the lecherous, or equally applicable to all the types of men enumerated.

But elsewhere gout results directly from lust and similar vices, as, for example, at *Anth. Pal.* XI. 414, Hedylus,

λυσιμελοῦς Βάκχου καὶ λυσιμελοῦς Ἀφροδίτης
γεννᾶται θυγάτηρ λυσιμελὴς Ποδάγρα

an epigram adduced by Smith on Tib. I. 9.73–4,

nec facit hoc vitio, sed corpora foeda podagra
et senis amplexus culta puella fugit

a couplet implying disability; or again, at Sen. *Ep.* XXIV. 16, *libidines ⟨adferunt⟩ pedum, manuum, articulorum omnium depravationes*, and Caelius Aurelianus, *Chronic Diseases* v. ii. 29.[2] At Cat. LXXI, *tarda podagra secat . . . ipse perit podagra*, gout seems to be transmitted from woman to rival. Most important, it is caused by *paedicatio* at *Anth. Pal.* XII. 243, Strato:

εἴ με τὸ πυγίζειν ἀπολώλεκε, καὶ διὰ τοῦτο
†ἐκτρέφομαι ποδαγρῶν, Ζεῦ, κρεάγραν με πόει.

So when Persius inflicts this particular disease on his reciter, he insinuates that sexual antics of the kind witnessed at 19–21, there transferred to his poetry, have so ruined his health that success is impossible and abstinence necessary. Such disqualification is in part paralleled by Apul. *Met.* v. 10, *ego vero maritum articulari etiam morbo complicatum curvatumque ac per hoc rarissimo venerem meam recolentem sustineo*, and as Celsus remarks, sexual activity is bad for the victims of the malady, I. 9.2, *si cui vero dolere nervi solent, quod in podagra cheragrave esse consuevit, . . . Venus semper inimica est.* There may be correspondence between *articulis . . . perditus* and *tremulo scalpuntur ubi*

---

[1] Possibly following Madvig, *Adv. Crit.* II p. 128, 'corpore fracto et debili libidinosae voluptati ineptus'.

[2] I owe the reference to Mr P. G. Maxwell-Stuart.

intima versu, 21 (where, as we have noted, the reader expects *manu* or *digito* for *versu*), so emphasising the physical aspect of the reciter's inability to prolong the response initiated by his poetry. To make his point even more firmly, the satirist then observes that the aged would-be *amator* is impotent: the meaning of *cute perditus*, 'with ruined prepuce', is to be inferred from such passages as Mart. VII. 35.4, *Iudaeum nulla sub cute pondus habes.*[1] A superannuated *paedicator*, the performer is prevented by his debauched condition from continuing his act. He should leave others alone if he is not equipped to gratify them.[2]

Physical impotence may well have been chosen as a parallel to intellectual and moral sterility: in telling the reciter that he cannot meet the requirements of his audience, Persius suggests that his type of literature is so jejune as to be incapable of imparting anything of value. From Dion *Or.* IV. 35 ff., where a sophist is compared to a eunuch,[3] we see what may have been the conceptual origin of the imagery chosen here. Diogenes explains to Alexander καὶ γνώσῃ ὅτι οὐδὲν διαφέρει σοφιστὴς ἄνθρωπος εὐνούχου ἀκολάστου. Alexander asks why he makes the comparison, and receives the answer, 36, ὅτι . . . τῶν εὐνούχων φασὶν οἱ ἀσελγέστατοι ἄνδρες εἶναι καὶ ἐρᾶν τῶν γυναικῶν, καὶ συγκαθεύδουσιν αὐταῖς καὶ ἐνοχλοῦσι, γίγνεται δ' οὐδὲν πλέον, οὐδ' ἂν τάς τε νύκτας καὶ τὰς ἡμέρας συνῶσιν αὐταῖς. This lecherous but ineffectual behaviour is akin to that of the *vetulus*, looking forward to his future pleasures at line 18, but finally proving incapable of consummation. Diogenes continues by demonstrating that to spend one's time with a sophist in an attempt to discover virtue, is as futile and fruitless as to spend time with a eunuch, trying to achieve satisfaction, 37: καὶ παρὰ τοῖς σοφισταῖς οὖν πολλοὺς εὑρήσεις γηράσκοντας ἀμαθεῖς, πλανωμένους ἐν τοῖς λόγοις πολὺ κάκιον ἢ τὸν Ὀδυσσέα φησὶν Ὅμηρος ἐν τῇ θαλάττῃ,

---

[1] *V.* Excursus 3, p. 146.

[2] The impotence theme is common in Hellenistic and Roman literature: e.g., with death-imagery, Ov. *Am.* III. 7; Petron. 20.2; *Anth. Pal.* XI. 30; 29; XII. 232 (Korzeniewski pp. 297–8 and n. 42); add *Anth. Pal.* XII. 11 and 216; Cat. LXVII. 21; Mart. XII. 86.

[3] *V.* Gerhard p. 148 n. 1 for another such comparison, in the Arabic version of Polemo *de physiogn.* 1 p. 162, 10 F; also *Com. adesp.* fr. 15 K, κεκολλόπευκας· τοιγαροῦν ῥήτωρ ἔσει, an equation between homosexuality and rhetoric.

καὶ πρότερον εἰς ᾅδου ἄν τις ἀφίκοιτο, ὥσπερ ἐκεῖνος, ἢ γένοιτο ἀνὴρ ἀγαθὸς λέγων τε καὶ ἀκούων. The reciter, like the eunuch–sophist, cannot adequately satisfy his listeners. Taking account of his own sterility, he should cease to assault the ears of those who have nothing to gain.[1]

Lines 24–5 constitute a whining objection to these last observations on his shortcomings: 'But my training is wasted unless continued performance achieves my desired aim.' Metaphorically, his aim is the gratification of his paederastic urges, a goal which, by allusion to his inability to meet his listeners' demands, Persius has implied to be unattainable. If the audience has nothing to gain, then neither has the reciter: his impotence works both ways. What he dwells on now is his personal predicament – how the charge of impotence affects the contemplation of his pleasures. But his mode of expression is unfortunate, an ironic corroboration of previous innuendo about his sterility, 24–5:

> 'quo didicisse, nisi hoc fermentum et quae semel intus
> innata est rupto iecore exierit caprificus?'

The imagery has not been satisfactorily explained. Macleane provides a clue, in his remark on *iecore*, 'lust ... was supposed to have its seat in the liver' (referring to his citation of Schol. on I.12: *et hoc secundum physicos dicit, qui dicunt homines splene ridere, felle irasci, iecore amare*): given context, lust is surely the point of the allusion.[2] But what exactly do we make of the combination *rupto iecore*, and the other bizarre images? As for *iecore*, we can back up Macleane from the entry in *ThLL*. With the comment

---

[1] Cf. Plut. *Rect. Rat. Aud.* 38 a–b, where virtue's only way of access to the body is via the ears, which must be kept uncontaminated: vice enters through many other parts of the body. To protect the ears of the young, Xenocrates advised ear-guards for children, rather than athletes, since their characters can be ruined by what they hear. In P., vice's entry to young ears is represented by the body-image, offering not satisfaction, but a cheap titillation from which they should be protected.

[2] At *Aen.* VI. 596, '*amorem* ..., hoc est libidinem, quae secundum physicos et medicos in iecore est, sicut risus in splene* (cf. Pers. I. 12), *iracundia in felle*', Servius mentions Tityos at Lucr. III. 992, a symbol of lust because of his liver; cf. Koenig on 24–5, '*iecur, ut sanguinis officina, sedes omnium adfectuum, praecipue libidinis, quae hujusmodi carmina, de quibus h.l. sermo est, dictat*', citing Hor. *Carm.* I. 25.15, Theocr. XIII. 72; also Mayor on Juv. I. 45 and VII. 117.

'habet vim ad movendum amorem vel tollendam pubertatem', e.g. Ov. *Am.* III. 7.30 is cited, where damage to the liver is a possible reason for impotence:

> sagave poenicea defixit nomina cera
> et medium tenuis in iecur egit acus?

Liver is an ingredient of a love-potion at Hor. *Epod.* v. 37:

> exsecta uti medulla et aridum iecur
> amoris esset poculum.

At *Carm.* I. 25.15, *iecur ulcerosum*, Lydia's liver is ulcerated with unsatisfied lust;[1] at IV. 1.12, *si torrere iecur quaeris idoneum*, Venus makes for the liver when she wants to set someone alight with love; and at [Sen.] *H.O.* 574, *sed iecur fors horridum/flectam merendo*, Deianira hopes to move the liver of her husband. So when Persius' adversary observes that the vindication of his 'training' – which is grounded as much in sex as literature – involves a bursting of the liver, the most natural way to construe the action is in terms of lust: *rupto iecore* refers to the production of orgasm, of sexual satiety. But there is a slight irony. In conjunction with *iecur*, *rumpere* has a sense similar to that found at Cat. XI. 20, *ilia rumpens*, LXXX. 7, *Victoris rupta miselli ilia*, or Prop. II. 16.14, *rumpat ut assiduis membra libidinibus*. In these cases the verb refers to the achievement of orgasm, but more especially to the deterioration produced by excessive sexual activity. For the reciter, 'bursting his liver' means the release of pent-up sexual impulses. But there is a shade of meaning in *rumpere* which implies that the process is very exacting in physical terms – a shade of meaning which in part accounts for the next comment, *en pallor seniumque*.

If *rupto iecore* has this erotic significance, what of *fermentum* and *caprificus*? So far on this interpretation, the reciter has been represented as an aged and ineffectual *paedicator*, who claims achievement of satiety as the point of his training. In itself, *fermentum* appears to be devoid of precise erotic connotations: Fulgentius, *Aet. Mund.* p. 164, 16 Helm, *Olympias draconis squami-fero fermentante complexu . . . ediderit gravidata puerulum* does not

---

[1] Cf. *Ep.* I. 18.72, *non ancilla tuum iecur ulceret ulla puerve*; Nisbet and Hubbard on *Carm.* I. 13.4.

warrant their attribution.[1] The verb *fermentare* can mean 'to make swollen', as at Cels. II. 8.33, *si venter est quasi fermentatus, pinguis atque rugosus*, and *fermentum* can be used of an internal swelling of the emotions, as at Plaut. *Merc.* 959, of anxiety, *uxor tota in fermento iacet*, or *Cas.* 325, of rage, *in fermento tota est mulier, ita turget mihi*, where *turget* assists the metaphor. When the reciter employs the word, he depicts the urge to communicate his inspiration as something which swells and distends him.[2] Though final proof is impossible, the image of tumidity may have been intended as an ingredient of the dominant sexual *double entendre*.[3]

The majority of commentators appear to believe that bare citation of Juv. x. 144–5, *ad quae/discutienda valent sterilis mala robora fici*, or similar passages, is sufficient explanation of *caprificus*. Perhaps the commonplace association of the wild fig with fissures in tombs is relevant. If so, the commentators should take the step of noting that Persius here represents the reciter as a tomb, split open by the force of his supposed inspiration.[4] His old age can then be related to the fig-tree: there are several comic depictions of old men as tombs,[5] which invite enquiry like that developed by Korzeniewski pp. 397 ff., who links this passage to the funerary allusions at 36 ff. – note *tumulo* 39 – arguing that the poet is a 'nobody', ἔμψυχός τις τάφος (Lucian *dial. mort.* 6.2), dead before his proper time.[6] If on the other hand the connexion

---

[1] *Pace* Korzeniewski p. 394, who also appears, n. 33, to take the Plautine *loci* above of sexual excitement.

[2] Despite the lack of logical connexion (leaven activates reciter, not poetry), *fermentum* may in the first instance have been suggested by the food metaphor, *escae*.

[3] If Virgil's *incipiunt agitata tumescere* (*Georg.* I. 357) could be interpreted in sexual terms by Celsus (Quint. VIII. 3.47), given context a sexual overtone, besides the possibly alimentary, might have been detected by the Roman reader.

[4] Macleane, Némethy and Conington, with little or no comment, compare only Juv. x. 144–5. Jahn, '*caprificus* in commissuris saxorum ortus, postea dum crescit, ipsa saxa dirumpit', refers to Sen. *N.Q.* II. 6, Mart. x. 2.9, Isid. *Orig.* XVII. 6, and Schol. Hor. *Epod.* v. 17. Add Prop. IV. 5.76. But he is still peremptory on the less relevant point.

[5] E.g. *sepulchrum vetus*, Plaut. *Pseud.* 412; *capuli decus, Asin.* 892; *capularis, Mil.* 628; *quam odiosum est mortem amplexari, Bacch.* 1152 (Lilja p. 68); Enk on *Merc.* 290 f.

[6] Add Juv. IV. 109, *quantum vix redolent duo funera* to his exx.

with tombs is not thought so important as that with sterility (although the two reinforce one another to some extent), the critics should conclude that the image suggests the barrenness of the commodity which the reciter feels he must communicate: *sterilis* at Juv. x. 145 is backed up by Plin. *N.H.* xv. 79 f., of caprification: *caprificus vocatur e silvestri genere ficus* numquam maturescens, *sed quod ipsa non habet alii tribuens . . . ergo culices parit, hi fraudati alimento in matre e* putri *eius* tabe *ad cognatam evolant.*[1] Too often the image is passed over as though it were devoid of meaning. My own opinion is that *caprificus* was intended to suggest sterility, both literary and sexual. Adducing the comparison of a eunuch with a sophist who has nothing genuine to teach at Dion *Or.* IV. 35 ff., we have seen that the charge of impotence in lines 22–3 possibly mirrors the moral worthlessness of the reciter's poetry. Another editorial suggestion of sterility in his objection to Persius' charge would be final proof that he does indeed have nothing to impart to his listeners. Soph. ῾Ελέν. Γαμ. *Satyr.* fr. 182 p. 172 N², πέπων ἐρινὸς [ἀχρεῖος ὢν/ἐς βρῶσιν] ἄλλους ἐξερινάζεις λόγῳ, parallels the image of barren literary *caprificatio,* used of communication at 24–5. The reciter deceives himself into thinking he has something to give his audience, only to be foiled by the insinuations of worthlessness contained in his unhappy metaphor from the process of caprification. His urge to communicate, to let others know, is as jejune as implied in the recent accusation of debility.

Sexually, it is possible to align *caprificus* with immediate metaphoric context, which represents the reciter as an impotent *paedicator,* who nonetheless desires satisfaction. If 'the exit of the fig-tree' is to be integrated with the pattern of imagery so far established, the connotations of *caprificus* must be derived from *membrum virile,* a sense attested by the simple fig at Ar. *Pax* 1349–50, τοῦ μὲν μέγα καὶ παχύ./τῆς δ᾽ ἡδὺ τὸ σῦκον, where σῦκον applies to both male and female, and *Eccl.* 707–8, θρῖα . . . /διφόρου συκῆς. Also relevant is Buchheit's interpretation of the

---

[1] Theophr. *Hist. Pl.* II. 8; *Caus. Pl.* II. 9; Gow on Theocr. x. 45 (σύκινοι ἄνδρες) for proverbs based on the worthlessness of the cultivated fig.

word-play on *ficus* and *caprificus* at Mart. IV. 52: '*capris gestari nisi desinis*, wirst du von einem passiven Liebhaber (*ficus*) jetzt zu einem aktiven, sei es als *paedicator*, sei es als *amator cunni*, eben ein *caprificus*.'[1] But Persius does not write *caprificus* instead of the simple *ficus* in order to differentiate between active and passive, as in Martial's epigram: his point is that the wild fig is sterile.[2] In his wish to communicate – on the metaphoric level, in his desire to extract[3] his member after finding satisfaction – the reciter unfortunately uses a word which the reader recognises as justifying the earlier charge of sterility.

The reader's experience at *CIL* 4, 2360, *amat qui scribit*, pedicatur qui legit, *qui obscultat*[4] *prurit, pathicus est qui praeterit*, is probably parallel to that of the audience here, despite logical difficulties over *innata est*: his member is not actually 'born' within his audience. But (i) all details are not always equally apposite in a sexual *double entendre*;[5] (ii) *innāta est* might be a pun on *in năte est*. Elision obscures the cases, and the harsh metre after the caesura perhaps allows a metrical anomaly in the first part of the line.[6] Persius may recall Hor. *Sat.* I. 8.47, *diffisa nate ficus*, *nate* changed to the ambiguous *innata est*, *diffisa* to *rupto*, and *ficus* to *caprificus*. With *intus*, the pun would suit the situation

---

[1] 'Feigensymbolik im antiken Epigramm', *RhMus* CIII (1960), 221. He argues from caprification (*v.* above, and p. 221 n. 71 of his article); cf. Korzeniewski p. 393 n. 29 following B., who takes *caprificus* as 'Metapher für Phallos', noting Hor. *Epod.* XII. 20, where *arbor* is compared with *membrum virile.* Besides the male and female genitals, figs also symbolise *culus* (cf. ἰσχάς at Argentarius, *A.Pl.* 241 = Gow–Page *Philip* 1507; σῦκον at Philip *A.Pl.* 240 = *ibid.* 3133), and piles (cf. *ficus* at Mart. I. 65; VI. 49, not *membrum virile*, as Korzeniewski p. 393 n. 29; VII. 71; XIV. 86; *marisca* at Juv. II. 13 (Schol. '*stupri vestigia medici rident*'). At Cels. VI. 3.1 *ficus* is used of swollen excrescences in the hair and beard.

[2] The prefix *capri-* may augment sterility associations: *v.* ThLL sv caper, 'de castrato capro', Mart. III. 24.14, *dum iugulas hircum, factus es ipse caper*, Gell. IX. 9.9, *auctore enim M. Varrone is demum Latine caper dicitur, qui excastratus est*; cf. Lilja p. 68 on the connotations of impotence in *cantherius* and *vervex*. But *caper* and cognates can have the opposite force: *Physiogn.* 112.7, *oculos caprinos libidini esse deditos*; *ibid.* 117.3.

[3] Given *rupto iecore*, we might feel there is some violence in *exierit*, e.g. 'burst out', which would not quite suit the metaphor. But in itself *exire* is not particularly violent.

[4] *auscultat*, Marx.

[5] Cf. e.g. *Anth. Pal.* V. 204, Meleager, comparing an old prostitute to a ship.

[6] Cf. Mart. I. 92.11–12 for a pun on *cūlus* and *ocŭlus*.

better than the face-value meaning of *innata est*.[1] Another punning division, of *auriculis* 22, into *auri-culis*, is possible.[2] As we have noticed, Persius conflates the vocabularies of sex and hearing at 19–21. For *lumbum* and *intima* we expect *aures*: compare *scalpere aures*, Sen. *Ep.* LXXV. 5,[3] with Persius' *scalpere intima*. Noting the substitution of *lumbum* and *intima* for *aures*, the reader is on the alert for signs of a continued conflation between sex and hearing: *auriculis* fulfils anticipations.

At 26–7 Persius replies that his haggard look is only to be expected if he insists on straining to succeed in something which is beyond his powers:

> en pallor seniumque! o mores, usque adeone
> scire tuum nihil est nisi te scire hoc sciat alter?

At 22–3, because of his physical state, the satirist advised him to discontinue his performance. At 24–5 he objected, asserting the urgency of full sexual satisfaction as the end of literary training. But he described his pursuit of that satisfaction in an unfortunate manner. The image *rupto iecore* was too strong, leaving room for wry comment on his appearance: 'If you use language which implies that you have to be *effututus* before you come within

---

[1] Quintilian's examples of κακέμφατον at VIII. 3.44–7 prove a Roman ear for less apposite obscenities: *ductare exercitus, patrare bellum, cum notis hominibus loqui, incipiunt agitata tumescere* (Virg. *Georg.* I. 357; cf. Gell. IX. 10.5–6 for Cornutus' objections to *membra* at *Aen.* VIII. 406). The example of *divisio* at 46, *intercapedo (interca-pedo)* parallels this suggested resolution of *innata est*. Persius was a Stoic, and some Stoic doctrine on ambiguity was extreme: cf. Gell. XI. 12.1, *Chrysippus ait omne verbum ambiguum natura esse, quoniam ex eodem duo vel plura accipi possent*; *v.* P. de Lacey, 'Stoic Views of Poetry', *AmJPh* LXIX (1948), 258 and n. 98, 259 and notes 100, 101, 'to clarify the relations of words to the things they signify the Stoics found it necessary to differentiate eight kinds of ambiguity, and they recognised that the use of words in altered meanings is especially common in poems'. On ambiguity, *v.* Ar. *Rhet.* 3.5, 1407a; legally, *ad Her.* I. 12.20, II. 11.16, and Cic. *de Or.* II. 26.111; along with fables, caricatures, ironical inversions, puns, paradoxes etc., *ad Her.* I. 6.10; in a context of wit, Cic. *de Or.* II. 61.250; full discussion at Quint. VII. 9.7 ff.; Brink on Hor. *A.P.* 449; Petron. 118, *ambages*; for allegory, Demetrius 99–102.

[2] Cf. Mart. I. 92.11–12 again, also Lilja p. 34, for a link between the Plautine *cuculus* and *culus*.

[3] Cf. Clem. Al. 328, κνήθειν τὰς ἀκοάς; Casaubon, 'scalpere obscoena notione, ut apud Graecos ξύειν et κνήθειν.'

reach of your objectives, then it's not surprising that the strain leaves you looking white and decrepit.' Also the connotations of barrenness and infertility inherent in *caprificus* look back to the warning at 22–3, where the *vetulus* was told that it would be better to leave other people alone, being unequipped to gratify them:

> If you insist that the communication of your literary talents is akin to sexual intercourse, that there is a pressing need for personal satisfaction, what can I do but think back to your impotence, when you yourself remind me of it through your unhappy image of the *caprificus*. I'm not at all surprised you look as you do, when you are physically prohibited from success in the sexual feats you so vehemently, yet so vainly, attempt to accomplish. It really would be better to keep your sexual and literary 'know-how' to yourself, since other people stand to benefit nothing from your futile attempts to consummate the act of communication.[1]

I now consider the consequences of referring *quibus* to *escas*, and the meaning then required from *articulis . . . et cute perditus*. I have argued that exclamation of 'Enough' or 'Stop it' depends on the hypothesis of a situation in which the reciter is offered his own *escae*. Since such a situation is most naturally that of his audience, by notional identification with them he becomes subject to the same erotic pressures as they, pressures which have been represented as an active force producing a passive reaction. So to be *articulis . . . et cute perditus*, and therefore under the necessity of exclaiming 'Enough', is to be physically incapable of experiencing the passive delights induced by listening to his own kind of literature. A paraphrase of 22–3 would run as follows: 'Are you, an old man, providing for others a type of pleasure which you personally are no longer capable of enjoying, and would therefore turn down if offered it yourself?' *articulis . . . et cute perditus* must imply some diminution in his capacity for passive enjoyment. No longer a *paedicator* as on the last interpretation, he is asked to merge his identity with that of his audience for a moment, in order to realise the relative extent of his physical shortcomings: he emerges as a decrepit *pathicus*, unable to withstand

[1] For my argument that *pallor seniumque* describes a condition resulting from 24–5, not a condition prior to that act, *v.* Excursus 4, p. 148.

the active stimulus of his own type of poetry. Presumably there is a moral purpose behind the request: as a result of contemplating his physical state, caused by listening to erotic literature, he should desist from exposing others to the danger of similar physical deterioration. Emphasis on his disabilities is now a cautionary illustration of the consequences of sexual immoderation, intended to awaken the performer to his responsibilities as regards the young: 'Are you, an old man, corrupting the young with pleasures which have wrecked you – pleasures of whose disastrous effects you are fully aware?'

Do the words *articulis . . . et cute perditus* support the necessary hypothesis of portrayal of the reciter as a failed *pathicus?* Beginning with *cute perditus*, there are several parallels for allusion to passive homosexuality: Paul. Fest. p. 110, 23, *inter cutem flagitatos dicebant antiqui mares qui stuprum passi erant*; Gell. XIII. 8.5, *nihil enim fieri posse indignius neque intolerantius dicebat quam quod homines ignavi ac desides, operti barba et pallio, mores et emolumenta philosophiae in linguae verborumque artes converterent et vitia facundissime accusarent, intercutibus ipsi vitiis madentes* (the situation resembles that in Persius, false gravity and pretended moral concern cloaking homosexuality); Prisc. *G.L.K.* II p. 271, 5, *Cato autem quasi adiectivo eo est usus, dicens intercutibus stupris obstinatus pro 'intestinis'* or again, Paul. Fest. p. 113, 13, *intercutitus, vehementer cutitus, hoc est valde stupratus.*[1] Simple references to passive homosexuality, none of these passages mention failure or disability within that sphere. Since on this interpretation *perditus* would mean much the same as *flagitatus* at Paul. Fest. p. 110, 23,[2] it is difficult to derive the required sense from the words: *cute perditus* might be referred to passive homosexuality, but not to a particular failing or shortcoming on the

---

[1] Cf. also Tertull. *de Pallio* 4, *inter cutem caesum*; not Mart. VII. 10.1 f. (quoted p. 147 n. 4), where Housman, *Hermes* LXVI (1931), 410 suggests two possibilities: wrongly, that Prisc. *G.L.K.* II p. 271, 5 and Paul. Fest. p. 110, 23 may illustrate Eros' activities; rightly, use of the proverb *de suo* or *alieno corio ludere* (e.g. Mart. III. 16.15 f.). One might object against this interpretation of *cute perditus* that the *loci* cited contain the adjective *intercus*, or the prepositions *inter* and *intra*. But Paul. Fest. p. 113, 13 attests the simple form *cutitus*, which looks as though it could stand independently of *intercutitus*; and *intus* does in fact follow *cute perditus* at 24.

[2] For *flagito, v. ThLL* sv A.2, 'speciatim de stupro'.

part of that kind of deviant. Another difficulty presents itself with regard to *articulis ... perditus*. As we have seen, gout can be caused by *paedicatio*, as well as prohibiting its victim from further sexual activity. Although the latter point would still hold good if the reciter were a *pathicus*, there is an unfortunate dearth of parallels for the malady being caused by, or particularly associated with, passive as opposed to active homosexuality.

The evidence is against the reference of *quibus* to *escas*, with the retention of a sexual allusion in *articulis ... et cute perditus*. Additional problems arise if we pursue this line of enquiry. For in order to have become an ineffectual *pathicus* the reciter must have experienced his audience's passive response on several occasions, so reaching a stage where he can no longer enjoy their reaction. Such an exchange of rôles, even if only notional, or momentary, is rather difficult, especially in view of the fact that '*ohe*' should mean 'No more, I've had enough', not, as required here, 'No thank you, none for me'. Is it likely that the reciter, in the imagined position of his audience, should sample his own *escae* before turning them down? If it is impossible to say 'Enough, no more', without tasting the *escae*, the reciter cannot, as expected, refuse them at once, being in no state to stomach them, but must begin by tasting them, only exclaiming 'Enough' after proceeding some way towards satiety. Since the nature of his exclamation involves participation in his own goods, the required idea – of offering something for consumption which he would not eat himself – becomes difficult.[1] Another problem arises out of 24–5. If the reciter has been told that his kind of literature has been his ruin, with the tacit exhortation to refrain from leading his audience astray, there is a marked change of direction in the depiction of the factor responsible for his physical state. At 19–21 Persius described the pleasures of others; at 22–3, he remarked that these pleasures cannot be enjoyed by their purveyor, implying that his knowledge of their noxious effects should dissuade him from infecting others; at 24–5, the reciter objects that pleasure is the whole point of the exercise. Disregarding the injunction to consider his own jaded condition, and therefore not tamper with his listeners, he thinks only of the personal consequences of his

---

[1] Housman's interpretation is vulnerable on this point.

98

condition, his attention fixed on his capacity for pleasure, instead of moral deduction from the diminishment of that capacity. He regards erotic literature from his stance as performer, not from identification with the position of his audience: hence a switch of focus to inspiration, the agent of pleasure during delivery, away from the finished *carmina*, at present pleasurable to his audience, whose ruinous force has just been illustrated through description of his ravaged physical state. This interpretation is generally consistent with the rejoinder at 26–7:

> Because you insist that pleasure is the whole point, and because you describe its sexual aspect in such grotesque terms, I'm not surprised you look so debauched. What I said about your physical condition at 23 was quite justified. Since you refuse to see the ulterior significance of my remarks about your state, and dwell instead on the purely selfish business of finding passive satisfaction with the *caprificus* of your inspiration, I feel it necessary to revert to my earlier point about 'others', and the desirability of leaving them alone. You really should keep your *didicisse* – what I now call your *scire* – to yourself.

But the fact remains that at one moment it is poetry like his own, hypothetically experienced as listener, which accounts for the wreckage, at another, the *caprificus/membrum virile* of inspiration, a stimulus experienced as performer. Given his selfishness about deprivations possibly to be undergone because of his feeble condition, the change of emphasis, as regards achieving pleasure, from listener to performer, is necessary, but awkward. In view of these problems, and the absence of parallels for a passive sense in *articulis . . . et cute perditus*, it is preferable to adopt the previous interpretation, where the reciter, represented throughout as an ineffectual *paedicator*, exclaims '*ohe*' to the ears of his audience.

Taking up *alter*, the interlocutor extends the topic of communication into a sketch of the rewards of publicity, 28–30:

> 'at pulchrum est digito monstrari et dicier 'hic est'.
> ten cirratorum centum dictata fuisse
> pro nihilo pendes?'

He cannot keep his literary training to himself: above all, and in this unlike Persius the self-sufficient Stoic, he requires public renown. But his concept of popularity is depicted in incongruous or ambivalent terms: *digito monstrari* is an obscene gesture as well as an indication of fame;[1] the curly hair of line 29, *cirratorum*, points again to effeminacy;[2] while *dictata* refers to the fate which the true poet conventionally abhorred, that of becoming a popular text in the schools.[3] At first it seems as if line 30, bringing a dinner-party to our notice, institutes a new theme. But on closer inspection a unitary sequence can be detected in lines 28–43. At 28–30, the interlocutor asks if Persius is utterly careless of public fame. With *ecce* a situation is singled out in which the verse of a dead, or metaphorically dead poet – note the funerary clichés at 36 ff. – is recited at a banquet, in exemplification of the public recognition despised as worthless by the satirist. Then at 41–3 the interlocutor insists a second time on the importance of public fame. So the dinner-party is framed on both sides – *os populi*, 42, looking back to *dictata*, 29 – with the adversary's emphasis on publicity.

Recitation at banquets was common practice,[4] and the *cena* itself a traditional satiric theme. Associating bad literature with food and drink, Persius condemns the audience's judgement as dependent not on literary criteria, but on the dictates of the stomach, perhaps guided in his general scheme by Hor. Ep. II. 1.109–10:

> pueri patresque severi
> fronde comas vincti cenant et carmina dictant,

[1] *V.* the commentators for the more flattering aspect, e.g. Hor. *Carm.* IV. 3.22, *monstror digito praetereuntium*; C. Sittl, *Die Gebärden der Griechen und Römer* (Leipzig 1890), p. 52 n. 2; Gerhard p. 148 for '*hic est*', citing Juv. I. 161, Mart. V. 13.3, D.L. VI. 34, Epict. III. 2.11. Sittl p. 101 for the insulting aspect. Apposite here is the homosexual connotation of the sign: *v.* Ruperti on Juv. X. 52, 'extentus ille digitus reliquis contractis pudendam speciem exhibet eoque cinaedi vel molles designabantur' (hence the Greek name καταπύγων for the middle finger; cf. καταδακτυλικός = *pathicus* at Ar. *Eq.* 1381); Mayor on Juv. X. 52; Jahn on Pers. II. 33. Korzeniewski pp. 402–3 links this passage with 58–62 (without mentioning the obscene aspects), where the bad poet is pointed out by disrespectful animal signs.

[2] Jahn cites Mart. IX. 30.7, *matutini cirrata caterva magistri*; cf. X. 62.2, of a schoolmaster, *sic te frequentes audiant capillati*.

[3] Cf. Hor. *Sat.* I. 10.73 f. *neque te ut miretur turba labores,/contentus paucis lectoribus. an tua demens/vilibus in ludis dictari carmina malis?*; *Ep.* I. 20.17–18, Juv. VII. 226–7, and Mart. I. 35.2.

[4] Cf. Plin. *Ep.* I. 15.2, III. 5.12, VIII. 1.2, IX. 17.3, 36.4; Suet. *Aug.* 78; Juv. VI. 433 ff., XI. 180 ff. with Mayor's note; Petron. 55, 59 and 68. For symposia in early Greek times, *v.* Fraenkel pp. 36–7 n. 1, criticising Reitzenstein.

where the absurd juxtaposition of *severi* with *fronde*, and the combination of *cenant* with *dictant*, ridicule the two activities by treating them as if of equal moment. Like Horace, who implies that Rome does not know the difference between a good dinner and a good poem, Persius suggests that his contemporaries are similarly confused about precise demarcations. As often his language is taut and economical, setting up, in an intuitive but unassuming manner, a neat tension between mundanities and smart cultural professions. Disapproval is not directly conveyed through a designing sermon: instead it is quietly implied in a seemingly detached but carefully arranged collocation, lines 30–1:

> ecce inter pocula quaerunt
> Romulidae saturi quid dia poemata narrent.

The specious solemnity of the occasion is presented through *ecce*, the grandiose *Romulidae*, the exaggerated poeticism *dia*,[1] and *poemata*. But pretence to high interests is completely undercut by the materialistic *inter pocula* and *saturi*, along with the trite colloquialism *quid...narrent*.[2] The sons of Romulus are a disgrace to their origins, their concern for poetry analogous to their cultivation of the palate.[3]

The recital then begins, once again with preliminary observation on the performer's appearance. Emphasis is on the edible and liquid qualities of his maudlin verses, creating the impression that such poetry is a rather nasty course at a banquet, lines 32–5:

> hic aliquis, cui circum umeros hyacinthina laena est,
> rancidulum quiddam balba de nare locutus
> Phyllidas, Hypsipylas, vatum et plorabile siquid,
> eliquat ac tenero subplantat verba palato.

---

[1] At Hor. *Sat.* I. 2.32, *sententia dia Catonis* (cf. Lucil. 1316 M, *Valeri sententia dia*; Marx suggests Ennian influence), *dia* illustrates the old man's quaintness in approving brothel-frequenting (a Cynic theme: Rudd p. 25). Henss (above, p. 3 n. 1) p. 288 cites *ego mira poemata pango*, *A.P.* 416; but cf. *Sat.* I. 10.6, *pulchra poemata mirer*. Juvenal's method of deflation, *et divina opici rodebant carmina mures*, III. 207, is like that of Persius.

[2] Villeneuve *Essai* p. 382, of *narrent = dicant*, 'locution familière'; cf. Lejay's exx. on Hor. *Sat.* I. 9.52.

[3] In a muddled note Conington relates Hor. *Sat.* II. 2.4, *inter lances mensasque nitentes* to Pers. I. 30, *inter pocula*. In both the delights of the table hinder moral and critical sensibility. Against the parallel, cf. Cic. *Fam.* VII. 22, *inter scyphos*, and Juv. VIII. 217, *media inter pocula* (Buscaroli p. 52 n. 16).

As on my argument about the details of presentation at 15 ff., the purple cloak, *hyacinthina laena*, derided by moralists and satirists,[1] may also continue the literary dimension, a concrete analogue of excessive *ornatus* in style. Given the correspondence principle, it is possible for a literary man to wear on his person a sign of the mannerism we might expect to find in his style; we remember that purple is the symbol for the obtrusive stylistic device.[2] Once inaugurated, the recitation is in part presented through metaphors from food and drink. Replete with associations from rotten food, the contemptuous *rancidulum*[3] prepares for the unpleasant image of salivation applied to a watery delivery at lines 104–5. The entertainment demanded by the bloated *Romulidae* consists of a questionable poetic morsel, more in place at a *cena* than in the world of letters. After the service of literary

---

[1] Cf. Mayor on *coccina laena*, a sign of importance, at Juv. III. 283; Juv. x. 212; [Cercidas] fr. 5 Knox p. 220, τῷ περι⟨σσὰν⟩/θηροπέπλου μανίας/ ὕβρέος τε περιστάσιμον/στοὰν ἔχοντι/Πυθαγόρου πελάτᾳ; Lucian *Rhet. Praec.* 15, on the clothing of the shameless orator, καὶ ἡ ἐσθὴς δὲ ἔστω εὐανθὴς ἢ λευκή, ἔργον τῆς Ταραντίνης ἐργασίας, ὡς διαφαίνεσθαι τὸ σῶμα; Epict. III. 23.35, of a reciter, ἐν κομψῷ στολίῳ. P. may have remembered Hor. *Ep.* II. 1.207, *lana Tarentino violas imitata veneno*, where the actor's cloak wins more applause than his speech.

[2] *A.P.* 15–16 where see Brink, *purpureus pannus* (another instance of the clothing analogy, enlivened by *adsuitur*), cf. Quint. VIII. 5.28, of a style streaked with disjointed *sententiae*: *porro, ut adferunt lumen clavus et purpurae in loco insertae, ita certe neminem deceat intertexta pluribus notis vestis.* In moderation, purple enhances a composition; in excess, it ruins cohesion. Cf. Quint. XI. 1.31; a style which is *plenum et erectum et audax et praecultum* is denied to old men on grounds of impropriety, the following simile implying that this style is too rich, *sicut vestis quoque non purpura coccoque fulgentibus illa aetas satis apta sit.* Cf. Lucian *Quom. Hist. Conscr.* 15, καί μοι ἐννόησον ἡλίκον τὸ ἀξίωμα τῆς ἱστορίας καὶ ὡς Θουκυδίδῃ πρέπον, μεταξὺ τῶν Ἀττικῶν ὀνομάτων τὰ Ἰταλιωτικὰ ταῦτα ἐγκεῖσθαι, ὥσπερ τὴν πορφύραν ἐπικοσμοῦντα καὶ ἐμπρέποντα καὶ πάντως συνᾴδοντα.

[3] '*Rancidus* si dice propriamente dei cibi stantii e che hanno preso cattivo gusto; traslatamente di ogni cosa che muove nausea' (Ramorino). Of food, Hor. *Sat.* II. 2.89, *rancidum aprum*, Juv. XI. 134–5, *obsonia . . . /rancidula*, Plin. *N.H.* XXII. 92, *rancido aspectu*, of poisonous mushrooms. In literary contexts, e.g. Mart. VII. 34.7, *qui sic rancidulo loquatur ore*, Gell. XVIII. 11.2, *rancide ficta verba*, and XVIII. 8.1, of Lucilius' complaints against Isocratean rhetoric, *in conlocandis verbis immodice faciunt et rancide. putidus* too is used of both food and literature. By localising the recitation at a *cena*, P. brings out the literal meaning of *rancidulum*: without the preparatory *saturi* and *inter pocula* it might not have had its full force; with them, food associations are inescapable.

food, the metaphoric equation of poetry and wine, lines 34–5. Answering the original request made in the middle of a drinking bout – *inter pocula* – Persius substantiates the idea that luxury and literature are now interchangeable by applying *eliquat*, a metaphor from wine straining,[1] to the reciter, who decants another bottle – of poetry. And this activity originates in his mouth: *palato*, the final word of the description, abandons the reader to a corrupt indulgence of the senses, literary quality no longer an object of concern.[2] An adherent of the plain style, Persius has dramatised a simile like that of Cicero at *Or.* 83, where the modest orator shuns grandiosity 'as in the trappings of a feast'.[3] He transforms metaphor into reality, spurning a *cena* whose menu includes poetic food and wine.

But the imagery is not only that of the table: the sexual imputations of the earlier recitation scene are transmitted to the later part of the satire through the epithet *tenero*, and the image of a weak nose in line 33, *balba de nare*.[4] The interlocutor's later accusation, *nimis uncis/naribus indulges*, 40–1, is intended as criticism of Persius' unnecessarily fastidious attitude.[5] But his curled nostrils are

---

[1] Colum. XII. 27, *vinum a faecibus*, XII. 19.4; of water, Sen. *N.Q.* III. 26.6; metaphorically as here, Apul. *Flor.* II. 15.54, *canticum ... ore tereti semihiantibus in conatu labellis eliquare*.

[2] The metaphor changes briefly before *palato* (cf. Hor. *Ep.* II. 2.62, *vario ... palato*, of readers' tastes), from wine to wrestling; but the mouth is emphasised at the end of a passage which alludes to both food and drink. The new metaphor, *subplantat* (= ὑποσκελίζειν: *v.* Marx on Lucil. 915, perhaps the first incidence of the word), contrasts the manliness of wrestling with the effeminate *tenero*: the poetry retailed is far from virile. *subplantat* has literary-critical affiliations: the orator was often compared to an athlete, to enhance, like military imagery, his profession's pretence of active bravura (*v.* Austin on Quint. XII. 2.12 and XII. 10.41; Peterson on X. 1.4, 33; Assfahl, pp. 38 f.); in Persius the reciter is anything but an athlete.

[3] Above, p. 51 n. 2.

[4] Hor. *Sat.* II. 3.274, *cum balba feris annoso verba palato*, contributes to 33 and 35, the nose, then the palate; cf. also *Ep.* II. 1.126, *os tenerum pueri balbumque poeta figurat*, and κόρυζα (literally, a running at the nose) at Plat. *Rep.* 343 a. Affected pronunciation, *os blaesum ... debilisque lingua* at Mart. X. 65.10, is a sign of effeminacy.

[5] Cf. Horace's complaints about the keen noses of those able to see others' faults, but not their own, *Sat.* I. 3.29–30, *acutis/naribus*; I. 6.5, *naso suspendis adunco* (Maecenas is praised for not despising the low-born H.), and *Ep.* I. 5.23, *corruget nares*. *nasus* corresponds to the Greek μυκτήρ.

ironically a manly contrast to the reciter's wet nose, marking a mental attitude consistent with the sarcastic, critical attitude of his genre. Lucilius, according to Plin. *N.H. praef.* 7, *primus condidit stili nasum;* Horace, Pers. I. 118 below, was *callidus excusso populum suspendere naso.*[1] The interlocutor intends disparagement: in fact he compliments the satirist on adherence to the precepts of genre. Then there is the nature of the subject matter chosen for the recital: for *Phyllidas* and *Hypsipylas,* with their dulcet and effeminate '*Y*' sounds[2] bring to mind the mincing, professionally inconsolable heroines of the Ovidian type,[3] admirably suited to the posturings of the performer. The lofty connotations of inspiration in *vatum,*[4] and the parodistic depiction of the heroes' applause, line 36:

adsensere viri

aimed at epic formulae like *adsensere omnes,*[5] or *adsensere dei,*[6] and perhaps evoking the epic banquet itself, including its recitatations – *Phyllides* and *Hypsipyles* being unheroic counterparts of Homer's Demodocus, Virgil's Iopas, or Lucan's Acoreus[7] – besides their provision of ironic contrast to the situation before us, these mock grandiose touches also serve a serious function as

---

[1] Cf. Quint. VIII. 6.59, μυκτηρισμός, *id est dissimulatus quidam sed non latens derisus;* XI. 3.80, *naribus labrisque non fere quidquam decenter ostendimus, tametsi derisus iis, contemptus, fastidium significari solet;* Russell on Longin. 34.2.

[2] Grammarians call *Y* the 'peregrina littera': the choice of alien-sounding Greek titles illustrates the decline of the Roman tradition. Cf. H. J. Rose *CR* XXXVIII (1924), 63, citing Quint. XII. 10.27 for the sweetness of υ and φ: cf. *Berecyntius,* 93, and *lyncem,* 101.

[3] Ov. *Her.* II and VI; Villeneuve, *Essai* p. 196, for Ovidian themes, and Lucian, *quom. Hist. Conscr.* 57, for exaggerated emotionalism in Parthenius, Euphorion, and Callimachus, forerunners of the Roman Alexandrianism culminating in Ovid.

[4] Cf. Pers. V. 1, *vatibus hic mos est;* Juv. I. 18. In general cf. Claud. *in Eutrop.* I. 261 f., *verbisque sonat plorabile quiddam/ultra nequitiam fractis,* and for the opposite vice in pronunciation, Sidon. Apoll. *Ep.* IX. 7, *orationem salebrosas passam iuncturas per cameram palati volutatam balbutire* (Casaubon).

[5] Virg. *Aen.* II. 130; Lucan VIII. 536.

[6] Ov. *Met.* IX. 259; XIV. 592. Juvenal parodies a similar formula at VII. 115, *consedere duces.*

[7] *Od.* VIII. 62 ff.; *Aen.* I. 740 ff., with Austin's note; *B.C.* X. 172 ff.; cf. Sil. XI. 288 ff.

media for the recollection of betrayed values. After the great men, the lesser guests, probably with mock elevated tones,[1] and with slightly more enthusiasm:

> laudant convivae.

Through a cynical use of funerary clichés – perhaps implying that the poet is only metaphorically dead: *cinis ille poetae* may be ambivalent, and *tumulo* may continue the imagery initiated by *caprificus*, where we have seen the reciter possibly represented as a tomb – also through sardonic reference to the conventionally attractive violet, Persius shows his utter scorn for the interlocutor's concept of fame.[2]

Now he imagines an objection to his position. He is being too critical. Nobody would turn down poetic fame, lines 40–3:

> 'rides', ait, 'et nimis uncis
> naribus indulges. an erit qui velle recuset
> os populi meruisse et cedro digna locutus
> linquere nec scombros metuentia carmina nec tus?'

Traditional formula and ridicule are interwoven: as the commentators note, *os populi meruisse* and *nec scombros metuentia carmina nec tus* are founded on two conceits, the first concerning the durability of good poetry, the second the fate of bad poetry. Mackerel and spice are easily paralleled, e.g. by Cat. xcv. 7 f., *Volusi annales ... laxas scombris saepe dabunt tunicas*, or the similar imagery at Hor. *Ep.* II. 1.269, *deferar in vicum vendentem tus et odores/et piper et quidquid chartis amicitur ineptis*: bad poetry is used as wrapping paper.[3] Manipulated by Persius, the interlocutor does himself a disservice by reminding the reader of this fact: interposition of a mere *nec* is insufficient to separate this

---

[1] Given *adsensere viri*, the corresponding *laudant convivae* most likely has a similar mock elevated tone, though Jahn's note '*convivarum* nomen ita accipiendum est, ut παράσιτον notet, cf. Hor. *Sat.* I. 10.80; Juv. v. 74; IX. 10', is probably correct: but class distinction can be treated without any loss in grandeur.

[2] *V.* Korzeniewski pp. 397 ff., esp. p. 400 n. 49, for the poet as a nobody; p. 401 n. 51, with bibliography, for funeral epigrams on the living; p. 405 n. 60 for *viva cadavera*, Sen. *Contr.* VII. 4.9, and analogous expressions.

[3] Cf. Mart. III. 2.3–5, 50.9; IV. 86.8; VI. 61.8; Juv. XIII.116.

type of poetry from the fate due to it.[1] Then, based on schemata of the type *volito vivus per ora virum* (Enn. *Epigr.* 2 V[3]), *victorque virum volitare per ora* (Virg. *Georg.* III. 9), *venies tu quoque in ora virum* (Prop. III. 9.32) or *Romana brevi venturus in ora* (Hor. *Ep.* I. 3.9), Persius' *os populi* replaces the mouths of men with the mouth of the people: the heroic *virum* found in conventional formulations has become the vulgar *populi*. When taste in poetry is arbitrated by the common people the corollary is a devaluation of the eternal fame it bestows. Perhaps the idea of scandal is present.[2] But there is more to *os populi* than this: from the beginning of the fifth satire we have seen the double function of the mouth as the medium for poetic delivery and eating; given alimentary metaphorics, it was no difficult task to convert the mouth from a proper to an improper use. In view of this, and the satire's other representations of literature as something to eat or drink, it seems fair to say that it has here again assumed its relationship with food, Persius expecting his reader to imagine the mouth of the people as not only intoning lines from its favourite authors, but also savouring them as though they were poetic *escae* served up to whet a jaded palate.[3]

A new section now begins, lines 44–62, the theme of which arises from the recent topic of public fame, namely the nature of true praise, as opposed to the recognition on sale for any poetaster of sufficient means. Persius protests against the facile approval awarded with suspect regularity to worthless compositions by venal and undiscerning tastes. Meaningless adulation can be purchased by the wealthy dilettante from his needy clients: the truth can only be told by the incorruptible satirist – a truth which

---

[1] *cedro digna locutus*, before *scombros* and *tus*, a conflation of Virg. *Aen.* VI. 662, *quique pii vates et Phoebo digna locuti*, and Hor. *A.P.* 331 f., *speramus carmina fingi/posse linenda cedro* (cf. Brink *ad loc.* and Vitruv. II. 9 for this use of cedar oil), may, with its echo of epic, condemn the petty self-seeking of its new context.

[2] Cf. Cat. XL. 5, *an ut pervenias in ora vulgi?* (the threat of the scurrilous iambist); Livy II. 36.3, *ne in ora hominum pro ludibrio abiret*; Cic. *Lael.* I. 2; Sen. *de Ira* III. 23.4; perhaps Hor. *Ep.* I. 3.9 above. Cf. the ambivalence of *digito monstrari*, 28, notoriety replacing fame.

[3] The mouth can have a sexual, as well as an alimentary function in literary contexts: at Lucian *Rhet. Praec.* 23, the declaimer is advised to keep his mouth open for everything, including sexual exercise.

involves judgement on the moral imperfections responsible for
literary deterioration. Persius here adapts and recasts a passage of
the *Ars Poetica*, lines 419 ff.:

> ut praeco, ad merces turbam qui cogit emendas,
> adsentatores iubet ad lucrum ire poeta
> dives agris, dives positis in faenore nummis.
> si vero est, unctum qui recte ponere possit
> et spondere levi pro paupere et eripere atris
> litibus implicitum, mirabor, si sciet inter-
> noscere mendacem verumque beatus amicum.
> tu seu donaris seu quid donare voles cui,
> nolito ad versus tibi factos ducere plenum
> laetitiae: clamabit enim 'pulchre! bene! recte!'

This has been conflated with another passage of Horace, *Ep.* I.
19.37–8:

> non ego ventosae plebis suffragia venor
> impensis cenarum et tritae munere vestis.

While satirising the wealthy poet-patron, Persius employs
Horatian echo to convey the notion that honest critical judgement
is impossible in a society eroded by considerations of worldly
well-being.[1]

Adopting his routine *persona* of ironic self-depreciation, he says
that he is not averse to real praise where praise is due, 44–7, and
proceeds to impugn the modish vocabulary of approval which is
mindlessly extended to undeserving trifles, lines 48–53:

> sed recti finemque extremumque esse recuso
> 'euge' tuum et 'belle'. nam 'belle' hoc excute totum:
> quid non intus habet, non hic est Ilias Atti
> ebria veratro? non siqua elegidia crudi
> dictarunt proceres? non quidquid denique lectis
> scribitur in citreis?

---

[1] For enticements for praise during recitations or law-court cases, *v.* Mart.
II. 27, *laudantem Selium cenae cum retia tendit/accipe, sive legas sive patronus
agas:/'effecte! graviter! cito! nequiter! euge! beate!'/hoc volui: facta est iam
tibi cena, tace*; III. 50, *haec tibi, non alia, est ad cenam causa vocandi,/versi-
culos recites ut, Ligurine, tuos*; VI. 48; Petron. 10.2, *multo me turpior es tu
hercule, qui ut foris cenares poetam laudasti*; 137.9, *quisquis habet nummos* . . .

Exclamations of *euge* and *belle* are too promiscuous, including as they do inferior epic, and after-dinner epigrams. Significantly, the impeachment moves from style to morals, the tone already established by the philosophic language of 48: *finis* and *extremum* in the sense of τὸ τέλος are paralleled by Cic. *Fin.* II. 2.5 and III. 7.26, as Jahn and Villeneuve note. Relevant also is Némethy's note on Pers. v. 65, 'certum finem, quem sine philosophia non possumus invenire', and his citation at III. 60 of Aristotle, *Eth. Nic.* I. 2, 1094 a 22, ἆρ' οὖν καὶ πρὸς τὸν βίον ἡ γνῶσις ⟨τοῦ τέλους⟩ μεγάλην ἔχει ῥοπὴν καὶ καθάπερ τοξόται σκοπὸν ἔχοντες μᾶλλον ἂν τυγχάνοιμεν τοῦ δέοντος;, and Sen. *Brev. Vit.* 2.2, *quibusdam nihil, quo cursum derigant, placet, sed marcentes oscitantesque fata deprendunt.* Contrasts to the trivial *euge* and *belle*, Persius sets ethical absolutes against temporal fashions, as in the similarly sarcastic IV. 17–18:

> quae tibi summa boni est? uncta vixisse patella
> semper et adsiduo curata cuticula sole?[1]

Here in the first satire *intus* evokes the commonplace motif of corruption concealed by seductive façade.

The *Ilias Atti/ebria veratro* is faulted mainly on literary grounds, as a product of artificial *furor poeticus*, uncontrolled, but falsely induced inspiration. For to be 'drunk with hellebore' is to have taken deliberate steps to join the company of crazy poets from Helicon:[2] the small genre 'satire' levels its usual criticism at grandiose epic. Nothing much so far to indicate that Persius has

/carmina componat, declamet, concrepet omnes/et peragat causas sitque Catone prior./ iuris consultus 'parret, non parret' habeto/ atque esto quicquid Servius et Labeo; Juv. XIII. 31 ff., nos hominum divumque fidem clamore ciemus/quanto Faesidium laudat vocalis agentem/sportula; Plin. *Ep.* II. 14.4 f., where *claqueurs* are called *laudicenae*; *Anth. Pal.* XI. 394 (Koenig on I. 53).

[1] Cf., without irony, on the theme of moral objectives, Pers. III. 48, *est aliquid quo tendis et in quod dirigis arcum?*, and IV. 64 f., *petite hinc iuvenesque senesque/finem animo certum.*

[2] Note P.'s scorn for the *Heliconides* at prol. 4. Ramorino *ad loc.*, 'l'elleboro nero, più forte dell'altro, si credeva nascesse sul monte Elicona, il monte della poesia'; cf. Jahn's reference to Plin. *N.H.* XXV. 49, for black hellebore on mount Helicon, 'a quo sanos poetas exclusit Democritus (Hor. *A.P.* 296 f.)'. The drug produces artificial inspiration: cf. Plin. *N.H.* XXV. 51, *plerique studiorum gratia ad pervidenda acrius quae commentabantur saepius sumptitaverint*, of its use by scholars.

moral, besides literary-critical, objections in mind, except possibly the slight innuendo of real drunkenness in *ebria*, and real madness in *veratro*. But this moral colour, if present at all, is submerged well below the surface. However, the next charge is unequivocally moral, divided into two parts, each of which contains in a single word a wealth of satiric associations. First of all, its literary-critical burden confined to the sneer in *elegidia*, we find, lines 51–2:

> non siqua elegidia *crudi*
> dictarunt proceres?

where *crudi* shows that the modish *euge* and *belle*, as well as perpetuating low standards in literature, connive at dubious gourmandise. Once more Persius has recreated Horace: as the commentators rightly note, *crudi/dictarunt* is indebted to *Ep.* II. 1.110, *cenant et carmina dictant*, conflated with *Ep.* I. 6.61–2, *crudi tumidique lavemur/quid deceat, quid non, obliti*, the first linking food and poetry as though of parallel importance, and the second succinctly suggesting that gluttony results in moral suicide. From this Horatian basis Persius intimates that the composition of poetry is as crass as the process of eating, and that Rome's unquestioning sanction extends to pandering to the sensual appetites. *crudi* recalls 30–1, *inter pocula . . . saturi*, and 22, *escas*, continuing the connexion between literature and food, and points to 92, where the interlocutor misuses the term. Clashing with *elegidia*, its grossness augments the scorn of the diminutive. These supposedly fine elegies are written by careless hacks. Persius may have been influenced by Hor. *Sat.* II. 5.40–1, *pingui tentus omaso . . . conspuet*, where the over-fed Furius physically retches up his poetry: compare with line 51 Quint. XI. 3.27, *nam crudum quidem aut* saturum (cf. 31) *aut* ebrium (cf. 30) *aut eiecto modo vomitu, quae cavenda quidam monent, declamare neminem, qui sit mentis compos, puto*. Amidst this compact image of decadence, the insertion of the elevated mockery of *proceres*[1] acts as another

---

[1] Cf. Juv. II. 121, *o proceres, censore opus est an haruspice nobis?* (for the epic background, e.g. Virg. *Aen.* I. 740, *post alii proceres*); also P.'s transmutation of Horace's colourless *at bona pars hominum, Sat.* I. 1.61, into *at bona pars procerum*, II. 5, another attack on a nobility failed in its duties; Mart. VI. 64.9, *non aspernantur proceres urbisque forique*, of his own poetry (Korzeniewski p. 409 n. 68).

reminder of values lost. The second recrimination is found at lines 52–3:

> non quidquid denique lectis
> scribitur in *citreis*?

Here the final word conjures up an image of imported splendour. Reference to citrus-wood[1] symbolises the air of ostentation investing the occasion, which is still one of composition at the dinner table.[2] More than bad literature has been found within the *euge* and *belle* of line 49: once they have been 'shaken out' – *excute* – they have been found to conceal and approve gluttony and luxury.

The stage is now set for what at first seems a pronounced movement from the criticism of literature to an exclusive denunciation of morality. Persius singles out one of the *proceres*, but instead of delivering a verdict on his poetry, dwells on the failings of his character as symbolised in his body. However, as we shall see, the literary dimension, though relegated to a secondary position, has not disappeared completely: the tone of the five lines from 53 to 57 looks suspiciously like an extension of literary-critical moral colour:

> calidum scis ponere sumen,
> scis comitem horridulum trita donare lacerna,
> et 'verum', inquis 'amo, verum mihi dicite de me.'   55
> qui pote? vis dicam? nugaris, cum tibi, calve,
> pinguis aqualiculus propenso sesquipede extet.

In the primary moral situation, taking up *crudi* and *lectis* . . . *citreis*, Persius turns to the wealthy poet-patron, to tax him with the material rewards he uses for seducing his client-audience. With *calidum scis ponere sumen*, we are still at a banquet, not concretely localised, but a symbolic banquet of falsehood, like that at the opening of Hor. *Sat.* II. 2. At line 55 we are again in the world of this same Horatian satire: for when the patron asks for a

---

[1] Prominent in the moralists' repertoire for reproof of imported foreign imports: in general, Plin. *N.H.* XIII. 29.91 ff., Mela III. 104; in particular, Varro *Men.* 182 B, *R.R.* III. 2.4, Luc. IX. 426 ff., X. 144 f., Petron. *B.C.* 27 f., Sen. *Ben.* VII. 9.2, *Tranq.An.* I. 7, Plin. *N.H.* V. 1.12, Mart. IX. 22.5, Sil. XIII. 354; also Mayor on Juv. I. 137 ff.

[2] The *lectus tricliniaris* suits context better than the *lectus lucubratorius*: a reference to food – *calidum scis ponere sumen* – follows immediately in 53.

true verdict on his poetry – Persius no doubt means 55 as a cliché, the patron making a conventionally stupid request: with *vis dicam?*, 56, compare *vis dicam quid sis?* at Mart. II. 7.8, to another *littérateur*, Atticus, likewise followed by abuse: *magnus es ardalio*[1] – he solicits the opinion of a *corruptus iudex*,[2] a judge who has already been bribed with gifts of food and clothing. Persius therefore steps in personally to offer his services, evading the intention behind the rich man's request, by giving a truthful opinion, not of his literary abilities (as requested at e.g. Epictet. III. 23.11, below) but on his character: *verum mihi dicite* de me, 55, allows movement from poetry to morals. Persius' caricature is not merely a scurrilous gibe. The patron's baldness – *calve* – is the baldness of debauchery and lustfulness, a reminiscence of the earlier recitation scene.[3] The image of a fat stomach – *pinguis aqualiculus* – has many moral connotations. First, after the preparation of *crudi* and *calidum scis ponere sumen*, the words describe the effects of gluttony. Second, they insinuate that the patron is no higher than an animal: since, according to Isidore, *aqualiculus* is properly a pig's belly,[4] the connexion with *sumen*[5] suggests that the patron's identity has become conflated with his vulgar

---

[1] *V.* also Jahn on 55, citing Plaut. *Most.* 181, *ego verum amo, verum volo dici mihi, mendacem odi*, and Mart. VIII. 76, '*dic verum mihi, inquit, Marce, dic amabo;/nil est, quod magis audiam libenter*' / ... *vero verius ergo quid sit audi:/verum, Gallice, non libenter audis*, where the poet similarly cheats the expectations of the petitioner, who is a reciter and an advocate. Cf. Epict. III. 23.11, πρῴην ἐπαινεθεὶς περιήρχου καὶ πᾶσιν ἔλεγες 'τί σοι ἔδοξα;' 'θαυμαστῶς, κύριε, τὴν ἐμήν σοι σωτηρίαν.' 'πῶς δ' εἶπον ἐκεῖνο;' 'τὸ ποῖον;' 'ὅπου διέγραψα τὸν Πᾶνα καὶ τὰς Νύμφας.' 'ὑπερφυῶς' (Korzeniewski p. 403).

[2] Cf. Hor. *Sat.* II. 2.8–9, *male verum examinat omnis/corruptus iudex*, of a judge corrupted by *mensae nitentes*. At Pers. *prol.* 8 ff., not the critic, but the poet, is seduced by mercenary incentives. Poetry other than that of the satirist is either written, or applauded, with material rewards in mind.

[3] For its sexual significance, *v.* Gerhard p. 154; for the premature baldness of debauchery, e.g. Apul. *Apol.* 59, *caput iuvenis barba et capillo populatum*.

[4] *Etym.* XI. 1.136. The word is transmitted at Sen. *Ep.* XC. 22, but usually emended to *aequali fervore*; at Vegetius, *Mulomedicina* 40, it is used of a horse's stomach (Jahn).

[5] Cf. Mart. VII. 78.3; XIII. 44; Juv. XI. 138 (Jahn); *abdomina* at Plin. *N.H.* VIII. 209, *hinc censoriarum legum paginae interdictaque cenis abdomina, glandia, testiculi, vulvae, sincipita verrina*; Hor. *Ep.* I. 15.41, *nil vulva pulchrius ampla*, spoken by a glutton.

skills.[1] Thirdly the words imply that through debauchery,[2] the patron has forfeited all finesse of intellect: as the scholiast notes, 'tractus sensus ex Graeco versu, quo significatur ex ventre crasso tenuem sensum non nasci'.[3] Moreover, several *loci* adduced by Jahn show that fatness is variously symbolic of stupidity, viciousness, drunkenness, and social insufficiency.[4] The upshot then, is that on account of his material and carnal preoccupations, the patron has declined into a physical grotesque, his mind as crass and dull as that of an animal, and therefore deserving censure.

The development of lines 50–7 has been away from the criticism of literature, towards the criticism of morals: from the predominantly literary-critical 50–1, with only faint moral overtones in *ebria* and *veratro*, to the intermediate stage of combined literary and moral denunciation in lines 51–3, with their emphatic *crudi* and *citreis*, and finally to the mainly moralistic 53–7. But the literary level in this last passage is not completely submerged. There are signs of connexion with critical vocabulary. A literal translation of line 53:

calidum scis ponere sumen

is 'you know how to serve up a hot sow's paunch'. But *ponere* is ambiguous: in addition to its culinary sense, of serving up a dish,[5]

---

[1] Cf. the identification at Pers. III. 27 ff., where the idea of *eques* suggests *equus*, in the trappings of line 30, *ad populum phaleras!* The knight is conflated with his horse, his *insignia* now those of an animal. Here in the first satire we may have a Stoic's objection to Epicureanism: *v.* Nisbet *in Pisonem* p. 195 and his note on 37.24, for comparisons of Epicureans to pigs, as well as the observation that 'Epicureans pointed to animals to show that the aim of creatures was ἡδονή', and that 'their enemies accused them of putting men on a level with the beasts', citing Cic. *Fin.* II. 32 and 109, and Epicurus fr. 398 Us.

[2] For the connexion between lust and fatness, *v.* Gerhard pp. 151 ff., Korzeniewski p. 402 n. 54, citing, *inter alia*, *Trag. adesp.* fr. 186 N², πλήρει γὰρ ὄγκῳ γαστρὸς αὔξεται Κύπρις.

[3] παχεῖα γαστὴρ λεπτὸν οὐ τίκτει νόον (Galen v p. 878 K; *Com. adesp.* 1234 K).

[4] Below, p. 157.

[5] Cf. Pers. III. 111, *positum est algente catino/durum holus,* VI. 23, *rhombos libertis ponere lautus*; Hor. *Sat.* II. 2.23, *posito pavone,* II. 4.14, and esp. *A.P.* 422, *unctum qui recte ponere possit.*

it can also refer to pictorial, and hence, verbal, description.[1]
When taken in conjunction with lines 70-1:

> nec ponere lucum
>   artifices,

where we are told that the modernists cannot even handle an
elementary poetic commonplace, the proposed ambiguity in 53
is to the effect that poetic skill has sunk so low that cookery
demands more skill than writing. Instead of simply translating
'you know how to serve up a hot sow's paunch', we now have
an element of surprise: 'you know how to compose – a hot
sow's paunch'. There may also be a pun on *calidum/callidum*.
Admittedly, *callidum* would be unmetrical, but Persius may
have chosen to be clever rather than correct. A pun would suit
the suggested ambiguity: 'you have the wit to compose a clever –
sow's paunch'. Perhaps *scis* in 53, repeated in 54, belongs to the
literary undercurrent: at 27 *scire* was used three times, of literary
(and possibly sexual) 'know-how', the lessons learnt in school.[2]
An ambiguity of this kind would look back to the *elegidia* of the
nobility, and the works written on citrus-wood couches. In a
society dedicated to corporeal appetites, the summit of 'poetic'
expertise is no longer literary: it is nothing more than a dish of
food. As Martial says to a wealthy patron who buys approval, it is
your dinner that is eloquent, not you, VI. 48:

> quod tam grande sophos clamat tibi turba togata,
>   non tu, Pomponi, cena diserta tua est.

Likewise in Persius, the patron is fully capable of composing an
eloquent dinner – with the ulterior motive of capturing praise
from an audience insensible to the virtues of true poetry. Food,
the object to which literary critics compared literature, now
replaces it, causing us to lose all sight of literature itself. Or

---

[1] *A.A.* III. 401, Hor. *Carm.* IV. 8.8, *A.P.* 34.
[2] Cf. 65, *scit tendere versum*. P. elsewhere uses words of knowledge ironically, implying false or superficial understanding: *scit*, 132, *scis*, IV. 10;
calles, IV. 5, *callidior*, III. 51; *sollers*, VI. 24 and 75; cf. Hor. *Sat.* II. 2.52,
pravi docilis Romana iuventus, and Juv. IV. 142, *callebat*, of pointless knowledge about oysters. Contrast the real cleverness of Horace at Pers. I. 118,
callidus excusso populum suspendere naso.

perhaps I should say we almost lose sight of literature. For the postulated ambiguity is based on a term from literary vocabulary, so leaving us with a negative awareness of the higher pursuit never attained by the patron, and never required by his audience.

Similarly, the words describing the fat stomach at line 57, *pinguis aqualiculus*, assume a new appearance when taken in the line of imagery running from *crudi*, through *lectis . . . citreis*, and into *calidum scis ponere sumen*; also, when regarded in the light of Callimachus *Iamb.* II. 192, 5 ff. Pf. On the theory advanced so far, the topic of literature has been fast disappearing, but disappearing in a particular way – down a channel charted by the food metaphors of literary criticism. Primarily it seems that the fat stomach embodies intellectual and moral crassness. But it could also be regarded as the logical outcome of an argument which has conflated literature with food, so that literature has finally become food; alternatively, as a variant on the animals listed in the passage of Callimachus recently mentioned. But in the absence of a direct Callimachean parallel, it is probably better to argue that Persius' verdict of moral incapacity answers a question about literature: 'tell me the truth about my poetry'. When that truth is told, although a personal moral comment on the bizarre physique of the patron, it is still a truth firmly grounded in a literary context: how could a man in such a state claim the name of poet? It is as though the literary-critical metaphors of *turgidus* and *pinguis* have been realised in an actual representation of physical corpulence; Persius appears to have progressed through the notion of a 'fat' style, into the notion of a 'fat' mind, and from there, into the concrete image, perhaps intending his literal *sesquipede* to be interpreted as a pompous externalisation, at two steps remove, of Horace's literary image for bombast, *sesquipedalia verba*, *A.P.* 97. When we reach the final image, style is not to the forefront. But we could argue that it was there in its origins, part of its presence still felt, however slightly. If we retrace the hypothetical stages in the formation of the image – working from physique back to the bluntness of the patron's *pingue ingenium*, and thence to his dull turgid style, *pinguis oratio*,[1] the image of the fat stomach then

---

[1] The phraseology of παχεῖα γαστὴρ λεπτὸν οὐ τίκτει νόον, the immediate source of *pinguis aqualiculus*, is not far from the terms of Callimachus'

appears as an independent, but not self-contained, development of a moral aspect of literary-critical vocabulary: its genesis may have been assisted by the alimentary metaphor and the bodily analogy, hovering behind it in the form of the rhetorical conception of turgid style as a bloated, or over-fed body.[1] But this concept can only stand at some distance behind it, and the image, primarily moral in function, can at most be an indirect reflection on style, in the absence of Callimachean analogues. First and foremost, given the state of our evidence, the image requires interpretation as an external symbol of an interior moral state, its origins in style only tenuous. Some support is available from *nugaris*, the *mot juste* for inconsequential versification:[2] the patron is devoted to writing frivolous nonsense, when he would be better occupied in curing his moral faults. As it is, he has not grown up, but squanders his life amidst trivialities: we remember the implications of *nucibus . . . relictis*, line 10, that avuncular airs have not really replaced childish pursuits.

Persius now enters territory where the critic can rely on the guidance of Callimachus, whose second *Iambus* proves the literary significance of the animal imagery in lines 58–62:

> o Iane, a tergo quem nulla ciconia pinsit
> nec manus auriculas imitari mobilis albas
> nec linguae quantum sitiat canis Apula tantae.
> vos, o patricius sanguis, quos vivere fas est
> occipiti caeco, posticae occurrite sannae.

The asses' ears – *auriculas . . . albas*, line 59 – are especially

objection to Antimachus' Lyde as παχὺ γράμμα καὶ οὐ τορόν (fr. 398 Pf.). A 'fat' and inflated style, *pinguis oratio*, is the logical product of a 'fat' mind, *pingue ingenium*.

[1] Longin. 3.4, κακοὶ δὲ ὄγκοι καὶ ἐπὶ σωμάτων καὶ λόγων οἱ χαῦνοι illustrates the way in which P.'s *pinguis aqualiculus* may have come into being. The only requirement was a divorce between human and literary components: for omitting the literary part of the comparison, ὄγκοι . . . ἐπὶ σωμάτων would be close to *pinguis aqualiculus*. In Persius the ellipsed, literary part of the statement may give the image vestigial literary-critical force.

[2] Cf. I. 70, dismissing those who are *nugari solitos Graece*, v. 19–20, *non equidem hoc studeo, pullatis ut mihi nugis/pagina turgescat*; Fordyce on Cat. I. 4, citing *loci* from Martial; Hor. *A.P.* 322, *versus inopes rerum nugaeque canorae* with Brink's note; *Sat.* I. 9.2 and *Ep.* I. 19.42, depreciating his own works, after the precedent of Lucil. 1039 M, *ludo ac sermonibus nostris*.

noticeable, lack of taste again the object of the reference. The blue blood of Rome – *o patricius sanguis*, another allusion to deserted standards[1] – is asked to awaken to the animal gestures made behind its back. As Callimachus shows, these signs are vehicles for the criticism of poor quality in literature. Apart from *ciconia*, perhaps symbolising cacophony,[2] the animals in Persius – dog[3] and ass, and including the prologue, parrot – have equivalents in the second *Iambus*, 192, 5 ff. Pf.:

> δίκαιος ὁ Ζεύς, οὐ δίκαια δ' αἰσυμνέων
> τῶν ἑρπετῶν μὲν ἐξέκοψε τὸ φθέ[γμα,
> γένος δὲ τ[.]υτ[. . .]ρον – – ὥσπερ οὐ κάρτος
> ἡμέων ἐχόντων χἠτέροις ἀπάρξασθαι – –
> . . .]ψ ἐς ἀνδρῶν. καὶ κυνὸς μὲν Εὔδημος,   10
> ὄνου δὲ Φίλτων, ψιττακοῦ δὲ [ῥητῆρες
> οἱ δὲ τραγῳδοὶ τῶν θάλασσαν οἰ[κεύντων
> ἔχουσι φωνήν.

Unlike Janus, the nobility unfortunately is not endowed with eyes in the back of its head to preserve itself from gestures suggesting literary incompetence. A nobleman can buy praise at the price of a dinner or threadbare cloak. But true admiration is not for sale. After making a show of appreciation, the client will not restrain his inner feelings of contempt for his patron once his back is turned. This passage was probably suggested by Hor. *A.P.* 433, *derisor vero plus laudatore movetur*, a line which occurs in the important passage beginning at 419, on the dangers inherent in being a wealthy poet (quoted above p. 107). The client is Horace's *derisor*, quite willing to snigger behind his patron's back, 58–62, but all agog with enthusiasm, 49, and never a word of criticism to his face, 55–6: *dicam* means that Persius has to do this. The Horatian tag, *vero plus laudatore movetur*, suits the client

---

[1] Cf. Hor. *A.P.* 291–2, *vos o| Pompilius sanguis*, with Brink's comments on its solemnity.

[2] E.g. Conington, 'The fingers seem, according to the Schol., to have been tapped against the lower part of the hand, so as to imitate the appearance and the sound of a stork's bill.'

[3] For the sign of the thirsty dog, 60, cf. also the less relevant Callim. *ia.* I. fr. 191, 82 f, Pf., ὁ δ' ἐξόπισθε Κωρυκαῖος ἐγχάσκει/τὴν γλῶσσαν †ἕλων ὡς κύων ὅταν πίνῃ (Korzeniewski p. 403 n. 57).

down to the ground. A *verus laudator* is not at hand for the patron, but, ironically, a true critic, in the guise of Persius.[1]

Ignoring the unwelcome truths expounded by the satirist, the interlocutor briefly reverts to the very thing which provoked Persius to inspect the meaning of *euge* and *belle* – the opinion of the uncritical and undiscriminating crowd, lines 63–8:

> 'quis populi sermo est?' quis enim nisi carmina molli
> nunc demum numero fluere, ut per leve severos
> effundat iunctura ungues? scit tendere versum
> non secus ac si oculo rubricam derigat uno.
> sive opus in mores, in luxum, in prandia regum
> dicere, res grandes nostro dat Musa poetae.

Persius did not conceal the moral tone when offering his verdict. Popular opinion, on the other hand, is represented as confined to obsequious and amoral trivialities.[2] Forestalling its answer to the question '*quis populi sermo est?*' Persius ironically announces that now, at last, perfection has been achieved in the techniques of versification: with *nunc demum* he indicates the arrogant progressivism of the moderns. The smooth *molli| . . . numero* of lines 63–4, a good description of the metrical technique of the modern verse pilloried later, especially with regard to its lack of elision, smacks of effeminacy, and the technological simile of 65–6:

> scit tendere versum
> non secus ac si oculo rubricam derigat uno,

applied to glib metrical proficiency, is obviously condemnatory. Again, *oculo . . uno*, perhaps an instance of eyesight symbolising mental state, may imply that the poet is not fully aware of what

---

[1] *V.* further Buscaroli p. 60.

[2] Korzeniewski pp. 406 and 432 ff. argues that 63 marks the division of the main part of the satire: 13–62, *artifex*, 63–106, *ars* (Bo unnecessarily abbreviates with a lower limit of line 91, but correctly observes of 63–91 '*poetas novos irridet* P., *qui* formam, *non* rem *curent, sublimia tangant, cum ne minima quidem apte tractare sciant, qui veteres poetas contemnant et poeticam elocutionem corrumpant itemque oratores quibus cordi sunt* figurae, *non* causae'); an attractive theory, but there is still dramatic continuity between 63 ff. and what precedes: Persius the satirist is most naturally concerned with moral truths about the *artifex*; the superficially-minded crowd, with unimportant details of *ars*.

he is doing,[1] while contempt again accompanies the use of the verb *scire*.[2] There is further irony at 67–8:

> sive opus in mores, in luxum, in prandia regum
> dicere, *res grandes* nostro dat Musa poetae.

Corresponding formally to *grande aliquid* at line 13, the point of *res grandes* is that elevation is inapposite to the proposed themes. For satiric invective[3] against morals, luxury, and gluttony requires a plain style, not inflation. The patron's[4] corpulence – his *pinguis aqualiculus* – finds its literary counterpart in his bombastic compositions: he is shown as seizing every opportunity for display, even where tradition dictated simplicity.[5] The chosen topics prove total hypocrisy. Already we have seen the

---

[1] Cf. *pede in uno*, Hor. *Sat.* I. 4.10. For the technological *rubrica*, *v.* Jahn *ad loc.*; perhaps the building simile at Lucr. IV. 513 ff., employing *regula* and *norma*; also Pers. IV. 12, *pede regula varo*, the crooked ruler (so Jahn, '*prave distorto*', not as Conington, '*varo* possibly may denote that the ruler branches into two parts'). For the image of the crooked and the straight, originating in Plato, *v.* Summers on Sen. *Ep.* XI. 10: Pers. III. 52, *haud tibi inexpertum* curvos *deprendere mores*; IV. 11–12, rectum *discernis ubi inter/* curva *subit*; V. 38, *apposita* intortos *extendit regula mores* (the skilful ruler); VI. 18–19, varo ... *genio*; Hor. *Ep.* II. 2.44, curvo *dignoscere* rectum, 56, *alterum et huic* varum *et nihilo sapientius*.

[2] Cf. 27, 53, 54, also (not of literature) 132.

[3] If not to *satura*, 67 refers to moral diatribe, where simplicity was again in order. Villeneuve, *Essai* p. 201, decides on satire in the widest sense – not only the genre *satura*, but also moral commonplace. P. agrees with Hor. *A.P.* 86 f., *descriptas servare vices operumque colores/cur ego si nequeo ignoroque poeta salutor?* implying that the choice of *res grandes* ignores the *lex operis*; cf. Juv. VI. 635–6, quoted below, p. 165, a sign that the satirist is deserting his genre. *prandia regum* are more likely to be the feasts of wealthy gluttons (cf. Hor. *Sat.* II. 2.45, *necdum omnis abacta/pauperies epulis regum*; also the feasts of the rich at *Ep.* I. 7.33; I. 17.43, and perhaps *A.P.* 434), than Thyestean banquets: *mores* and *luxum* would be awkward in conjunction with a reference to tragedy.

[4] Structure is neater if *nostro ... poetae* is the patron. Persius gave a truthful answer to his request, 55, but that was on his morality: now he attributes to the people a flattering, not a truthful, verdict on his poetry.

[5] *Musa* is also contemptuous, an ironic echo of Horace. From the prologue, and the beginning of the fifth satire, we see that P. has no time for the hackneyed apparatus of inspiration and Helicon: with *dat Musa*, cf. the somewhat high-flown *Musa dedit*, *A.P.* 83, rather than the other Horatian *loci* adduced there by Brink, in that the phrase is close to the exposition of the doctrine of propriety (above, n. 3), the whole context therefore probably being to the front of Persius' mind.

warped morality, the luxury, the gluttony of Rome; and the
decline of literature has so far been associated with the material
excess which deadens the sensibility. Yet, according to the
sarcastic innuendo, the effete presume to pontificate on the very
things which have caused their ruin.[1]

Persius continues the *propria persona* argument instigated by
res grandes to remark that the modernists are taught to attempt
heroics when their only experience is of epigrammatising in
Greek, lines 69 f.:

> ecce modo heroas sensus adferre docemus[2]
> nugari solitos Graece.

The clash between *heroas sensus* and *nugari . . . Graece*, with its
hint of satiric xenophobia,[3] and scornful verb,[4] implies that
these poets lack the stamina demanded by their propositions.
What is more, they cannot even manage elementary poetic
exercises in a satisfactory manner, lines 70 ff.:

> nec ponere lucum
> artifices nec rus saturum laudare, ubi corbes
> et focus et porci et fumosa Palilia faeno,
> unde Remus sulcoque terens dentalia, Quinti,
> cum trepida ante boves dictatorem induit uxor
> et tua aratra domum lictor tulit – euge poeta!

---

[1] Cf. the hypocrisy of 9 ff., where Rome's sham respectability provoked
Persius' laughter. Juvenal is more explicit, IV. 106, *tamen improbior
saturam scribente cinaedo*; cf. Trimalchio's inapposite recitation of a
moralistic piece by 'Publilius' (probably a Petronian pastiche) at Petron.
55.6.

[2] *videmus*, αΧΦS(LU)Σ; *docemus* PGL Bob.Sang.S (M). The latter is preferable, since immediate context concerns education: *v.* 76–9, where the
study of archaic texts is criticised; also *didicisse* 24, *didicit* 93. At Tac. *Dial.*
28.2, decay in the arts arises from *desidia iuventutis et neglegentia parentum
et inscientia praecipientium et oblivione moris antiqui*; cf. Petron. 1–2,
blaming the teachers, and 4, the parents, for educational decline.

[3] Cf. the alien *Phyllidas* and *Hypsipylas*, 34. Horace opposed unintegrated
Hellenisms: *v. Sat.* I. 10.31 f., for his own rejection of composition in
Greek, the more forceful because of the warnings of the Roman *Quirinus*,
and I. 10.20–30, for his strictures on Lucilius for mixing Latin with Greek
(*v.* Rudd, pp. 111 ff., noting that Horatian Hellenisms tend to the
satirical).

[4] Cf. *nugaris*, 56.

Description of a grove is a rudimentary *locus communis* of the schools,[1] in which one might expect some degree of proficiency, as also in descriptions of rural life. To expose the incompetence of the *Graecissantes* when faced with a typically Roman theme, Persius writes an incongruous précis of a panegyric on the *rus saturum*, a parody on their deficient sense of propriety. The chosen details attest their lack of stylistic *constantia*: the normal prescription, *in oratione constanti ... omnia sint apta inter se et convenientia ... tanta vis est loci et temporis*, is ignored.[2] As Conington notes, the 'homely' details would not offend in a Wordsworth – I would add, or in a Hesiod, according to Pound, the Roman Wordsworth – but in Roman poetry they are breaches of decorum. As we have seen, country life easily lent itself to parody: Juvenal's sarcastic exercises on the theme are not far from more serious treatments such as Prop. IV. 2.39–46. Out of their inability to treat quintessentially Roman topics – particularly their mismanagement of the Palilia, Remus, and Cincinnatus, expected ingredients in praises of the agricultural virtues of earlier days, which for all their hackneyed nature cause us to glimpse lost values[3] – out of their incongruous treatment arises a tacit indictment of their moral sense, which, granted literary form, has distorted the relationship of present to past. The final ironic *euge* applauds not only literary incompetence, but also the perversion of once simple traditions.

At line 76, there is a switch to the topic of archaism:

> est nunc Brisaei quem venosus liber Acci,
> sunt quos Pacuviusque et verrucosa moretur
> Antiopa aerumnis cor luctificabile fulta.

---

[1] Virg. *Aen.* VI. 179 ff., with Norden's note, VIII. 597 ff.; Prop. IV. 4.3 ff.; Hor. *A.P.* 16; Luc. III. 399 ff.; Sen. *Oed.* 530 ff.; Sil. VI. 146 ff.; Juv. I. 7.

[2] Cic. *de Off.* I. 144; on decorum, cf. *Or.* 71–4, Gell. IX. 9.

[3] The juxtaposition *boves/dictatorem*, with which cf. Martial's parodistic *dum prandia portat aranti*, of Curio's wife, VI. 64.2, strikingly links potentially related subjects in a violent and unrelated manner. *Palilia faeno* is imitated from Prop. IV. 1.19 (for the ceremony, *v.* Smith on Tib. II. 5.87–90); *sulcoque terens dentalia* is reminiscent of Virg. *Georg.* I. 46, *sulcoque attritus splendescere vomer*, and *Aen.* VI. 844, *vel te sulco, Serrane, serentem*. For the plough, *v.* Korzeniewski, p. 412 n. 79; for Remus, Prop. II. 1.23, IV. 1.9; Juv. X. 73 and Mart. XIII. 3.6; for Cincinnatus, Livy III. 26 and Cic. *Cat. Mai.* 16.56 (Jahn). Possibly *sulcoque terens dentalia* has sexual overtones, a reminder of virility amidst effeminacy: for *sulcus* = *pudenda muliebria*, *v.*

It is hard to decide whether Persius speaks the lines, or the interlocutor: but whatever our ascription, *fulta* should not be followed
by a question-mark, since this would imply recommendation of
archaic tragedy by a Persius who thinks the moderns would
benefit from reading Accius and Pacuvius. Such a situation is
intolerable in satire. The fashion for archaising is a symptom of
decadence, and Persius, like other classicising critics, here assails
that affectation. Our conclusion must be that the topic is either
brought up by the interlocutor in proud opposition to Persius'
criticisms of contemporary education: 'Ah, but we read Accius
and Pacuvius: you are wrong in attacking our educational
system, which according to you debars us from proper treatment
of old-fashioned themes.' Or else Persius himself raises the
subject, as another sign of the malady infecting literary education:
'and then on top of our incompetence, there is that unhealthy
tendency to pore over diseased archaic texts'.[1] Whatever the
case, Accius and Pacuvius come in for criticism. Their works
suffer from the same maladies that infect their revivalist advo-
cates; the text of Accius is *venosus*, varicose-veined, and the
Antiopa of Pacuvius is *verrucosa*, covered in warts.[2] A transition
from literary to hitherto latent moral criticism is effected by the
continued imagery of old age and disease at 79 f.:[3]

> hos pueris monitus patres infundere lippos
> cum videas,

Lucr. IV. 1272, Virg. *Georg.* III. 136; for *arare* of intercourse, Plaut. *As.*
V. 2.24, *Truc.* I. 2.48; Theogn. 582, ἄρουραν ἀροῦν, and Juv. IX. 45–6,
fodere. Cf. the sexual slant of the agricultural imagery at Pers. IV. 35 ff., and
the comparison between the flower untouched by the plough with unspoilt
virginity at Cat. LXII. 39 f.

[1] *V.* Appendix 1.
[2] Cf. Tac. *Dial.* 21.8, quoted p. 37 n. 2.
[3] *Brisaei*, one of the names of Bacchus (Macrob. *Sat.* I. 18), here an extension
of Callimachean criticism of a frenzied, ungainly manner (not an allusion
to the Dionysiac beginnings of tragedy, as, with some reservations,
Conington: *bacchari* used of the tragic style, e.g. Juv. VI. 636, is a literary-
critical, not a literary-historical term), refers primarily to style, dubbing
Accius as a wine-drinker, but has perhaps some active moral force, looking back to 36, *inter pocula*. The liquid image, *infundere*, 79, perhaps
reinforces this aspect: cf. Hor. *Ep.* I. 2.67, *nunc adbibe puro/pectore verba
puer*; Cic. *de Or.* II. 355, *infundere in aures tuas orationem*; Lucil. 610 M,
haec tu si voles per aures pectus inrigarier; Hor. *Ep.* I. 8.16, *praeceptum
auriculis hoc instillare memento*.

where the allusion to defective vision – *lippos* – recalls the idea
of inner deficiency and lack of judgement,[1] while the reintro-
duction of the age motif – *patres* – furthers the theme of dis-
reputable and hypocritical old age.[2] The proximity of *patres*
... *lippos* gives a moral twist to the predominantly literary
venosus and *verrucosa*: a pair of past writers are now convicted of
failings similar to those which afflict their modern devotees.

Given the state of education, it is not surprising that poetic
diction[3] is in decline, or that sexual excitement accompanies
public literary display, lines 80–2:

> quaerisne unde haec sartago loquendi
> venerit in linguas, unde istud dedecus in quo
> trossulus exultat tibi per subsellia levis?

Two basic motifs recur, concrete form now embodying metaphoric analogy: the association of literature with food and
effeminacy. Poetic diction is a hash cooked up in a frying-pan:
sartago is a cheap kitchen utensil,[4] here probably an image for
the exotic variety in diction produced by study of Accius and
Pacuvius, as seen in the 'quotation', *aerumnis cor luctificabile
fulta*, 78,[5] rather than an allusion to an irksome amount of noise,
as suggested by Isidore and Augustine,[6] while *in linguas*, like
os populi at 42, and *saliva* at 104, places the poetic 'food' in the

---

[1] '*lippus* ad animi vitia translatum ut II. 72' (Jahn). Juvenal perhaps imitates
at X. 130–2, *quem pater ... lippus ... ad rhetora misit*. Cf. also XIV. 210,
talibus instantem monitis quemcumque parentem, and 228, *laevo* monitu
pueros *producit avaros*.

[2] *luctificabile* (cf. Lucil. 608 M, *monstrificabile*) is perhaps not only tragic
parody, but also, if taken with *nostrum istud vivere triste*, 9, an evocation
of the solemn *tristitia* which hides debauchery – a debauchery which here
consists of the agitation of the *trossulus*, 81–2.

[3] Cf. Cic. *Brut.* 258, *Caecilium et Pacuvium male locutos videmus*, finding
fault with P.'s Latinity, and Némethy on 76–82, 'sunt qui antiquissimos
poetas, Accium Pacuviumque, sectantur eorumque obsoletum dicendi
genus inepte imitantur. quare non est mirandum elocutionem poeticam in
dies magis magisque corrumpi.'

[4] *V.* Juv. X. 64; Plin. *N.H.* XVI. 22; Isid. *Etym.* XX. 8; Eubulus fr. 109, 2 K,
λοπὰς παφλάζει βαρβάρῳ λαλήματι (Jahn).

[5] Cf. Martial's choice of *Lucili columella hic situ' Metrophanes*, and *terrai
frugiferai* in his attack on archaism, XI. 90.4–5.

[6] *Etym.* 20.8, *a strepitu soni vocata, quando in ea ardet oleum, Conf.* III. 1, *veni
Carthaginem et circumstrepebat me sartago flagitiosorum amorum.*

mouth, to the surprise of the reader, who has been led to expect *in mentem*.[1] Then with the loaded terms *trossulus, exultat,* and *levis* we return to the metaphorics of the recitation scene: *levis* means that the listener is a depilated effeminate, the antithesis of the values symbolised by the Stoic's beard at 133;[2] *trossulus* implies that the higher classes are now degenerate;[3] and *exultat*, like *trepidare* at 20, describes the physical titillation produced by depraved compositions.[4]

Having dealt with the shortcomings of education, Persius directs his attention to the law-courts, moving from verse to prose: in view of the preceding attack on archaic tragedy, *sartago loquendi* must refer to poetry. But 81–2, *unde istud dedecus . . . subsellia levis*, prepare for the law-court scene, which 'properly' starts at 83. In these one and a half lines, the transition begins.[5] Interpretation of *dedecus* as a foreshadowing of the disgrace about to be witnessed in the court-room, translation of *in quo* as 'during which', construction of *exultat* as a preparation for *ceves*, 87, and explanation of *subsellia* as the seats in the court-room[6] serve the function of catalysts. The *monitus* of the old lead to the corruption of poetic diction; also, but less logically, to the experience of physical pleasure during a disgraceful law-court scene (*istud dedecus . . . subsellia levis*). If there is a further connexion, between *capiti . . . cano*, 83, and *patres . . . lippos*, 79, then the bad educational advice of 79 has made way for the bad

---

[1] Cf. Villeneuve, *Essai* p. 391, comparing IV. 48, *in penem . . . venit*, where again the reader might have expected *in mentem*.

[2] *V.* Buscaroli, pp. 79–80, and Korzeniewski, p. 415 n. 83.

[3] The word (a title for a Roman *eques*) acquired pejorative connotations: Varro *Men.* 480 B, *nunc emunt trossuli nardo nitidi vulgo Attico talente equum*; Sen. *Ep.* LXXXVII. 9, *o quam cuperem illi* [*sc. Catoni*] *nunc occurrere aliquem ex his trossulis in via divitibus*; LXXVI. 2, *quid ergo? idem faciam, quod trossuli et iuvenes?*

[4] *V.* Quint. II. 2.9, above, p. 44 n. 1; Gell. IX. 15.9, *clamore magno exultantibus*, of an audience at a recitation; generally, Juv. VII. 86, of the sexual excitement produced by Statius' *Thebaid, fregit subsellia versu.*

[5] *sartago loquendi*, though a reference to poetic diction, possibly contributes to the transition, if P. has Hor. *Sat.* I. 10.20 ff. in mind, where the Lucilian '*sartago*' of Latin mixed with Greek leads to observations on the impracticability of such a style in the law-courts when faced with the Roman advocate Pedius.

[6] So Jahn, against Conington with 'benches occupied during a recitation'.

example set by old men who prefer to hear applause (*decenter*, 84), rather than ward off the serious charges which face them. In this case, *istud dedecus . . . subsellia levis* would have more of a prospective connexion with the bad example set by the old to the young during the court-room scene of 83 ff., than a retrospective connexion with the *monitus* inculcated by the old at 79. Though advice will have given way to example, the conjunction of *capiti . . . cano* with *patres . . . lippos* has the advantage of strengthening the transitional force of *istud dedecus . . . subsellia levis*. It is *the old men* who lead the youth astray, by poor education in the first place, and now through their performance in court, which has already begun to make their audience quiver on the benches, a reaction like that produced by the reciter at 19 ff., another corrupt old man.

From 83–7, we see that stylistic affectation has smothered realities; *verba* no longer bear any relationship to *res*:[1]

> nilne pudet capiti non posse pericula cano
> pellere quin tepidum hoc optes audire 'decenter'?
> 'fur es', ait Pedio. Pedius quid? crimina rasis
> librat in antithetis, doctas posuisse figuras
> laudatur: 'bellum hoc.' hoc bellum? an, Romule, ceves?

Literature now connives at the concealment of crime. When corrupt old age – *cano*, perpetuating the imagery instituted by *canitiem*[2] – is threatened with real dangers, its primary concern is with applause, with hearing the exclamation *decenter*, which like *euge* and *belle* at 49, is squandered alike on morals and literature. Abruptly accused of criminality, Pedius sidesteps the moral issue, weighs the charges in shaved antitheses – *rasis/ . . . antithetis*, 85–6, continues the idea begun by *levis*, 82, depilation acting as a prelude to *ceves*, 87[3] – and finally, with an emphatic *laudatur*, is

---

[1] *V*. Tac. *Dial*. 20, on the 'new' style in the law-courts; the listeners want detachable conceits and exciting figures.

[2] Cf. Plaut. *Merc*. 305, *tun' capite cano amas, senex nequissime?*

[3] Korzeniewski, pp. 416–17, suggests, probably correctly, a sexual *double entendre* in *doctas posuisse figuras*. For *figura = schema concubitus*, he cites, n. 85, Ov. *A.A*. II. 679, *Venerem iungunt per mille figuras*; III. 772, *non omnis una figura decet*; *Trist*. II. 523 f., *sic quae concubitus varios Venerisque figuras/exprimat*; also Suet. *Tib*. 43; *Priap*. LXIII. 17; Mart. XII. 43.5; Ov. *R.A*. 407. With *posuisse* he compares *disponere* at Tib. I. 9.64 and Ov.

praised for his style.[1] Values are reversed, his crime forgotten, hidden beneath the apparatus of his false rhetoric. Yet further reversal is present if Conington's theory about the advocate Pedius at Hor. *Sat.* I. 10.28 is correct. Noting that the gist of the Horatian passage is 'Would you do so [*sc.* mix Latin with Greek] if you had to plead in a criminal trial for a great criminal, with the famous Pedius against you, pulling out all the powers of his mother tongue?', he thinks that Persius may mean 'Even the eloquence of the bar, to which Horace would point as a genuine unaffected thing, has caught the taint – even our Pediuses talk like schoolboys or pedants.' It is not a case of Pedius talking like a schoolboy or a pedant; Persius is more concerned with the evasion of the moral issue by means of a corrupting rhetoric which deceives and titillates the audience. But there is something in Conington's suggestion about 'the bar catching the taint'. Horace's Pedius judges the new Pedius,[2] who contravenes the standards of his predecessor: once respectable, he has fallen short of his duties, like the solemn *Polydamas* and *Troiades* at the opening of the satire. With the violent obscenity *ceves*,[3] Persius explodes the irresponsible *bellum*,[4] demonstrating its real nature as an acclamation of empty praise, extended to an amoral and

Am. III. 7.64 (*disposuitque modos*; *modos* in the same sense as *figura*); and as a parallel for the device of sexual content couched in rhetorical or grammatical imagery he quotes Lucillius, *Anth. Pal.* XI. 139.

[1] Cf. Plin. *Ep.* II. 14.12, on delivery and audience-reaction in the law-courts, *pudet referre quae quam fracta pronuntiatione dicantur, quibus quam teneris clamoribus excipiantur*; Sen. *Ep.* LII. 12, for praise as a clue to character, *qualis quisque sit scies, si quemadmodum laudet, quemadmodum laudetur aspexeris*.

[2] We can dismiss the Pedius Blaesus of Tac. *Ann.* XIV. 18, who was tried only two years before P.'s death.

[3] Conington compares *trepidare* and *exultare*; Jahn, '*cevere* verbum est de pathicis, qui in libidinis actu clunes agitant', citing Juv. II. 21, IX. 40, and Mart. III. 95.13, gives the full explanation. *V.* also J. Mussehl, *Hermes* LIV (1919), 387 ff.

[4] The repeated *bellum* of 86 is perhaps imitated from Lucilius' close investigation of the word at 805 M, *aetatem istuc tibi laturam et bellum, si hoc bellum putas.* P. employs simple repetition: on seeing the word a second time, we immediately realise that there is something faulty about it. Cf. Hor. *Ep.* I. 6.65–6, *si Mimnermus uti censet, sine amore iocisque/ nil est iucundum, vivas in amore iocisque*, where, meeting *in amore iocisque* for the second time, we literally think twice about it, to realise the shortcomings of a formula expressive of the boredom ensuing from satiety.

seductive rhetoric, which glosses over the hard fact of criminality. Romulus, a symbol of prior greatness,[1] has sunk so low as to buy homosexual gratification in return for convenient blindness in the presence of crime. As listener he awards exclamations of *belle* and *decenter*, thrilled by his passive experience of Pedius' rhetoric. This is a parallel state of affairs to the passive excitement of the *trossulus* at 81–2, where he began to experience fits of sexual excitement, instigated by the disgraceful performance of the old. Once more the rhetorical metaphor of *elocutio effeminata* is presented in quasi-dramatic terms.

After a few more comments from Persius, on the need for sincerity, the interlocutor praises the superior techniques of modern poetry, to the detriment of the 'archaic' Virgil, lines 92–7:

> 'sed numeris decor est et iunctura addita crudis.
> cludere sic versum didicit "Berecyntius Attis"
> et "qui caeruleum dirimebat Nerea delphin",
> sic "costam longo subduximus Appennino".
> "Arma virum", nonne hoc spumosum et cortice pingui
> ut ramale vetus vegrandi subere coctum?'

For the moderns, who claim to have achieved technical perfection, the *Aeneid* is outmoded and archaic. The tag is obviously relative: a little while ago, at lines 76–8, we saw the modernist penchant for 'archaic' tragedy; now we see their distaste for the 'archaic' Virgil. There is no inconsistency in their position: indulging a fashionable preference for the exotic flowers to be culled from early tragedy, they daringly disparage the now classical Virgil, so unmasking themselves, from the satiric viewpoint, as empty-headed *obtrectatores*, who refuse to award due credit to the classics, on account of their boastful and eclectic 'neoterism'. Persius, on the other hand, dismisses their modernism, with its unhealthy courtship of the archaic, and aligns himself with the sanity of the *Aeneid*.[2]

---

[1] I doubt direct influence from Cat. XXIX. 5, *cinaede Romule* (Jahn), where see Kroll, 'Romulus nannte man Leute von grossen Verdiensten um den Staat und von grossem Einfluss, wie Ps. Sall. inv. 7 den Cicero *Romule Arpinas* nennt oder Sulla Sall. or. Lep. 5 *scaevus Romulus* heisst', implying a proverbial quality in the word.

[2] *V.* further Appendix 2.

The first instance of modernist *decor* and *iunctura* is unfortunate: the rhythm of *Berecyntius Attis* can be faulted on stylistic grounds, but inherent in the word *Attis* is another gibe at effeminacy, preparatory to the searing tirade of lines 103–6.[1] Their chosen subject matter, a story of frenzied self-emasculation, incriminates the sexually ambiguous *litterati*. Two more examples of modernist *decor* intervene[2] before the interlocutor's wrongheadedness leads him to an ill-advised attack on Virgil. The formal criticisms levelled apply more properly to his own type of poetry, as also the moral features of his charges. For accusations of inflation, *spumosum*, fatness, *pingui*, old age, *vetus*, and rottenness, *coctum*,[3] intended by him to denigrate the *Aeneid*, have been

[1] 'The point of ridicule appears to be the rhythm, which the poet doubtless thought excellent, a long sweeping word like "Berecyntius" being a great point gained' (Conington). P. was probably offended by Ovid's *Cybeleius Attis*, *Met.* X. 104, and *Berecyntius heros*, *Met.* XI. 106; perhaps by Cat. LXIII, or some more recent composition, as implied by Mart. II. 86.4–5, *nec dictat mihi luculentus Attis/mollem debilitate galliambon*, which would accord with the charge of effeminacy, and of mere verbalism amongst the *Graecissantes*. On the quoted verses (parody, or direct citation from elsewhere), *v.* Marmorale pp. 190 ff., Korzeniewski pp. 417 ff., with bibliography n. 90; J.-P. Boucher, *Études sur Properce* (Paris 1965), pp. 273–97, esp. 280 ff. on the *Eclogues*, for deliberate inaccuracy in résumés.

[2] The Graecisms, *Nerea delphin*, the spondeiazon, *Appennino* (*v.* Cornelius Severus, *pinea frondosi coma murmurat Appennini*, Schol.; Hor. *Epod.* XVI. 29, *in mare seu celsus procurrerit Appenninus*; Ov. *Met.* II. 266, *aeriaeque Alpes et nubifer Appenninus*, and Luc. II. 396, *umbrosis mediam qua collibus Appenninus/erigit Italiam*; cf. Quint. IX. 4.65, *est permolle . . . cum versus clauditur 'Appennino' et 'armamentis'*) and the bold metaphor *costam* (*v.* Seneca's strictures on *audax translatio ac frequens*, *Ep.* CXIV. 10) seem to be the main offenders. If the *locus communis* of Nature ravaged is behind 95 (Némethy), the question of hypocrisy arises, as at 67 above. Nature is defaced at Sall. *Cat.* 13, Hor. *Carm.* II. 18.17–22, Tib. II. 3.44–5, Ov. *A.A.* III. 125 f., Plin. *N.H.* XXXVI. 1.2; add Fabianus *ap.* Sen. *Contr.* II. 1, and for the bodily metaphor, Cat. LXVIII. 111, *caesis montis . . . medullis*, Virg. *Aen.* III. 575, *viscera montis*.

[3] For the image of rotten branch and diseased bark, cf. Varro *Men.* 424 B, *tum ut si subernus cortex aut cacumina/morientum in querqueto arborum aritudine* (object of comparison unknown); Pers. V. 58–9, in a metaphor for gout (where *fregerit* is the right reading, not *fecerit*: cf. the violent *contudit*, Hor. *Sat.* II. 7.15 f.). Possibly Persius remembered *cortice sicco* and *ramaliaque arida* from Ov. *Met.* VIII. 642 ff., in which case, given antipathy to Ovid, we might have a sample of the tasteless vacuity of the interlocutor's critical terminology. *vegrandis* seems to have an archaic colour (*v.* the *loci* in *The Classical Papers of A. E. Housman*, ed. J. Diggle and

directed not only at the literature for which he acts as spokesman, but also at the morality of which that literature is symptomatic: his reproaches rebound on himself. Moreover, citation of the *Aeneid* as *Arma virum*, though standard procedure,[1] is an ironic reminder of the virile standards which he lacks, contrasting with the castrated *Attis* of 93, and with the effeminate *tenerum* and *laxa*[2] – opposites of the recent implication that Virgil's style is *durum* – of Persius' next question, line 98:

> quidnam igitur tenerum et laxa cervice legendum?

In answer, we are given a sample of modernist perfection, lines 99–102:

> 'torva Mimalloneis inplerunt cornua bombis,
> et raptum vitulo caput ablatura superbo
> Bassaris et lyncem Maenas flexura corymbis
> euhion ingeminat, reparabilis adsonat echo.'

This supposedly exemplifies the thesis that the moderns have attained a degree of facility unknown to the writers of *numeri crudi*, Virgil himself included. But *tenerum* means two things: to the interlocutor, rhythmical fluency; to Persius, enervated softness; hence the double edge of the quoted verses, not only

---

F. R. D. Goodyear, Cambridge 1972, vol. II, pp. 876–7) and hence is peculiarly apt for the castigation of Virgil as 'archaic' by modernists with yet more pronounced archaising tendencies. For *coctum* cf. the usual Prop. IV. 5.62, Pers. III. 5–6, and add the pun at Hor. *Sat.* II. 2.40–1, *at vos/praesentes Austri, coquite horum obsonia. decoctius,* 125, on the other hand is not pejorative.

[1] The opening words stand for the *Aeneid* as a whole: cf. Ov. *Tr.* II. 533, Mart. VIII. 56.19, XIV. 185.2, Auson. *Epigr.* 137.1; Sen. *Ep.* CXIII. 25 for a joke on *Arma virum,* as also *Anth. Lat.* 1936, *fullones ululam[que] cano, non arma virumq[ue].* Lucretius' poem is cited as *Aeneadum genetrix* at Ov. *Tr.* II. 261, Cicero's *de Senectute* as *O Tite si quid* at *ad Att.* XVI. 3.1; 11.3. *V.* further H. D. Jocelyn, *The Tragedies of Ennius* (Cambridge 1967), p. 350 n. 4.

[2] For *laxa cervice,* cf. Quint. I. 11.9, warning against bending the neck while speaking; for its effeminacy, Meineke's citations at *Frag. Com. Graec.* IV p. 612 (Jahn). Add Cicero's censure of *mollitia cervicum* at *Or.* 59; Quint. XI. 3.69, *in latus inclinato (capite) languor ... ostenditur;* Pers. III. 58–9, without sexual overtones, *stertis adhuc laxumque caput compage soluta/oscitat,* where the metaphor is one of shipwreck.

ridiculed for their formal properties,[1] but also tacitly denounced because of their uncontrolled Dionysiac subject matter, which yet again sets forth that sexually orientated emotionalism which has pervaded so much of the satire.

The sexual and moral overtones of the sample occasion an explosion on the causes of decay, lines 103–6:

> haec fierent si testiculi vena ulla paterni
> viveret in nobis? summa delumbe saliva
> hoc natat in labris et in udo est Maenas et Attis
> nec pluteum caedit nec demorsos sapit ungues.

All previous innuendo is made explicit: Romans write as they do on account of the loss of every vestige of virility. Some proverb, such as *si nos coleos haberemus*,[2] appears to be the source of line 103: but as Villeneuve points out, 'Perse remplace le mot grossier *coleus* par le mot savant *testiculus*', the more learned word adding technical precision to the appeal to virility.[3] Effeminacy of character is then equated with effeminacy of style through the parallelism of *delumbe*[4] and *testiculi vena ulla paterni*: the style itself is 'weak in the loins', just as the writers themselves are enervated and effete.

---

[1] With 99, cf. Cat. LXIV. 263, *multis raucisonos efflabant cornua bombos* (Lucret. IV. 544; Diomedes I p. 499, 21 K., *teretes sunt (versus dactylici) qui volubilem et cohaerentem continuant dictionem, ut 'torva Mimalloneis inflatur tibia bombis'*); with 100, Eur. *Bacch.* 743 f.; with 102, Ov. *Met.* I. 654, *ingeminat*, and III. 358, *resonabilis Echo*. Echo supplied easy oblique effects in 'Alexandrian' literature: *v.* Callim. *Epigr.* XXX (cf. *Aetia* fr. 75.10–11, for reflection in water); Prop. I. 20.48 ff.; Virg. *Georg.* IV. 526; Nisbet and Hubbard on Hor. *Carm.* I. 20.6. There are twelve Graecisms in 99–102 and 93–5; five nouns – *delphin, bombis, lyncem, corymbis, echo*; five proper names – *Attis, Nerea, Bassaris, Maenas, Euhion*; and two adjectives – *Berecyntius, Mimalloneis*.

[2] Petron. 44.14; Otto sv *coleus* and *vir* (e.g. Apul. *Met.* II. 17, *si vir es*); Petron. 134.9, *lorum in aqua, non inguina habet*; Ar. *Lys.* 661, ὅστις γ' ἐνόρχης ἔστ' ἀνήρ, and Hor. *Epod.* XV. 12, *siquid in Flacco viri est*.

[3] Besides the overt sexual reference of *testiculi* there may be allusion to the equation *vena = membrum virile*; P. himself employs *vena* thus at VI. 72; cf. also Hor. *Sat.* I. 2.33.

[4] Cf. Cic. *Or.* 231, of the enervating effect of Asianism, *concidat delumbetque sententias*; Tac. *Dial.* 18.5, *Ciceronem ... male audisse ... a Bruto, ut ipsius verbis utar, tamquam fractum atque elumbem*.

The other charge against the interlocutor's quotations is that they are 'wet', floating on the saliva at the front of the mouth:

> summa delumbe saliva
> hoc natat in labris et in udo est Maenas et Attis.

The images add up to a rejection of facile insincerity. Except for saliva, the literary-critical implications of natat, in labris and in udo est can be sufficiently explained by parallels from criticism: for example, the tone of in labris is illustrated by Sen. Ep. x. 3, non a summis labris ista venerunt: habent hae voces fundamentum, also Plut. Cat. Mai. 12, where ῥήματα ἀπὸ χειλῶν are contrasted with those which come ἀπὸ καρδίας, 'words from the lips' being trite and insincere. With natat, we can compare Quint. x. 7.28, innatans illa verborum facilitas, while in udo est can be elucidated by the proverbial ἐν ὑγρῷ ἐστιν ἡ γλῶττα, used of a talkative man at Theophr. Char. 8. Wetness and fluidity drench any wholesome quality of style.[1] But saliva cannot be paralleled as the other terms; rather, along with sapit in 106, it looks like an attempt at rejuvenating their original physical qualities. For natat, in labris and in udo est, being conventional, and therefore tired metaphors,[2] would probably have forfeited much, if not all of their efficacy as physical images, even though they suffice as a purely literary-critical judgement on the quoted lines. saliva and sapere on the other hand, sandwiching the other images, are direct and physical, centering the reader's attention on the mouth. The function of the unconventional noun is one of producing immediate surprised realisation that literary-critical metaphor is

---

[1] Cf. also ad Her. IV. 11.16, eius generis, quod appellamus dissolutum, quod est sine nervis et articulis; ut hoc modo appellem fluctuans, eo quod fluctuat huc et illuc nec potest confirmate neque viriliter sese expedire, combining, as here, wetness with effeminacy; Quint. x. 3.2, verba in labris nascentia; Gell. I. 15, qui nullo rerum pondere innixi verbis umidis et lapsantibus diffluunt, eorum orationem bene existimatum est in ore nasci, non in pectore, (Jahn). Add Sen. Ep. cxiv. 23, cum vero cessit ⟨mens⟩ voluptati, artes quoque eius actusque marcent et omnis ex languido fluidoque conatus est; Van Hook p. 13, citing Alcid. περὶ σοφιστῶν 16; Dion. Hal. de Dem. 20, p. 1013; Pl. Theaet. 144 b; Cic. de Or. II. 15, and Longin. 34.3; also Fronto II pp. 102–4, cited below, p. 144.

[2] in udo, with its proverbial nature (v. schol. ad loc., deriving it from ἐν ὑγρῷ; Otto sv udum), had probably lost all metaphoric qualities.

adopting a new shape.[1] Helped by *sapit*, the physical emanations of *saliva* renovate the other terms, reminding us that the mouth is used for eating, as well as poetic recitals: the word has associations with food, sometimes employed as metonymy for *sapor*, as by Propertius, Pliny, Petronius, and Persius himself,[2] a usage particularly relevant here, given the verb in 106. We have witnessed actual banquets, the consequences of gluttony for the gross poet-patron, and the degeneration of poetry to the status of food: a chain of associations now finally wound up by *saliva* and *sapit*.

So ends the main part of Persius' attack on literature and morals. There are two further sections. The first, lines 107–23, has two sub-divisions: from lines 107–14, Persius ironically makes as if to abandon his undertaking in view of the attendant dangers, but then, at lines 114–23, remembering the precedent of his ancestors Lucilius and Horace, he decides that out of duty to the principle of satiric *libertas* he must finish the inchoate joke of line 8. In fact the whole argument is ironic, since in itself, apart from its function within the framework of the satire as a whole, the joke is meagre, hardly deserving elaborate preparation: also his conception of *libertas* is played down, the joke not being broadcast publicly, but remaining a private secret – at least, until the ditch finally promulgates the truth, as in the myth of Midas. Distinctive features in this section are Persius' exaggeration of the dangers attendant on writing satire, his desire for a place in the great

---

[1] Its surprise value is probably increased through its unpoetic nature: *v.* H. Tränkle, *Die Sprachkunst des Properz und die Tradition der lateinischen Dichtersprache* (Wiesbaden 1960), *Hermes* Einzelschrift 15, p. 125. Satire frequently uses unpoetic diction which has a vigour and directness unattainable by the self-contained neatness of the well-turned phrase, making it difficult to gauge the conscious aggression here. Most likely it is strong: cf. Juv. VI. 623, *longa manantia labra saliva*, scornfully, of the idiot Claudius.

[2] Prop. IV. 8.38, Plin. *N.H.* XXIII. 40, Petron. 48.2, Pers. VI. 24; cf. Pers. V. 112, *salivam Mercurialem*, 'hunger for gain', a metaphor from food applied to money, and the similar metaphor for enthusiasm ('tickles your palate') at Sen. *Ep.* LXXIX. 7, *Aetna tibi salivam movet. saliva* is also used in erotic contexts: e.g. Cat. LXXVIII. 8; XCIX. 10; Lucr. IV. 1108, *adfigunt avide corpus iunguntque salivas/oris et inspirant pressantes dentibus ora*, savagely maligning idealistic lovers' kisses by accentuation of physical realities.

tradition, and his retention of the pose of exclusiveness. He emerges as the complete satirist, having made a personal bow to programmatic conventions. As far as 106 the reader has seen him at work on Neronian Rome, his behaviour inviting us to penetrate his irony and deprecatory gestures, to see the true meaning of his final joke, which is only inconsequential when confined to immediate context. Regarded in the light of all previous developments, it becomes a reflection on, and consummation of, the predominant theme, the asses' ears a symbol for the pervasive decay which stems from lack of moral and literary discernment.

The interlocutor begins this section by taxing Persius with the point of his criticism, lines 107–8:

> 'sed quid opus teneras mordaci radere vero
> auriculas?'

Once again, the diminutive implies disease: in other words, Roman tastes are degenerate. An impression of fragility and unmanliness is evoked by the epithet *teneras*, while *radere*,[1] and, on the usual interpretation, *mordaci*,[2] present the truth – *vero*[3] – as a medical cure for the soft ears of corruption. Offered a truthful diagnosis of her disease, Rome finds it harsh and unacceptable. The satirist is a dog, barking at the vices of the

---

[1] For interpretation in terms of a surgical instrument scraping a diseased surface, rather than as simply the opposite of, e.g., *aures mulcere* (Quint. XI. 3.60; cf. III. 1.3, *ne . . . aures . . . tam delicatas raderet*), *v.* above, p. 3 n. 2.

[2] For the image of therapeutic vinegar (here supposedly replacing truth), cf. Pers. v. 86, *aurem mordaci lotus aceto*; H. Lackenbacher (above p. 36 n. 2), p. 139, citing Cels. VI. 7.7, *si durae (sordes aurium) sunt, acetum et cum eo nitri paulum coiciendum est; cumque emollitae sunt eodem modo elui aurem purgarique oportet*. An alternative possibility (but not an inevitable corollary of the reference of *canina littera*, 109–10, to the satirist, rather than the *maiores*: P. may be mixing his metaphors, or preparing for a medical *radere*), is that *mordaci* alludes to the 'snappishness' of the cynical satirist (κύων): cf. Hor. *Ep.* I. 17.18, *mordacem cynicum*, and perhaps *Sat.* I. 4.93, *lividus et mordax videor tibi*.

[3] The reading of PR, *verbo*, is wrongly adopted by Scivoletto. At 55 the patron asked for the truth – *verum mihi dicite de me* – and the truth has since been told. Persius has 'shaken out the *belle*', exposing the decay it concealed – an operation better described by the general *vero*, than the needlessly specific *verbo*. The interlocutor objects to the satiric habit of 'telling the truth', Hor. *Sat.* I. 1.24–5, *ridentem dicere verum/quid vetat?*

great, and running the danger of forfeiting their patronage, lines
108–10:

> 'vide sis ne maiorum tibi forte
> limina frigescant: sonat hic de nare canina
> littera.'

But of course, he is not interested in such patronage: *limina*, not
the station of a guardian animal, but the place where Persius
snarls his insults, is a noticeable addition to Horace's *o puer, ut sis/*
vitalis metuo, et maiorum nequis amicus/frigore te feriat, *Sat.* II.
1.60–2, perhaps with *Epod.* II. 7–8, *superba civium/potentiorum*
limina in mind, representing the satirist as a client. We have
already been given an insight into the decadent relationship
between noble and client, so when we read the word *maiorum*
we know that the values it supposedly enshrines are meaningless;
and when we read *limina* we know that the position of a client
involves servility and hypocrisy. The patronage of the great is
now synonymous with the patronage of the corrupt – to be a
client is to lose the faculty of telling the truth. Better, then, to
stand outside society and snarl.[1]

Pretending to disregard the warning, Persius temporarily
abandons his mission, to award an ironically promiscuous *euge* to
the whole of society, lines 110–11:

> per me equidem sint omnia protinus alba;
> nil moror. euge omnes, omnes bene, mirae eritis res.[2]

Previously, except for 49 ff., the acclamation was reserved for
literature. Now it is extended to embrace Rome's failure in
morals. Resigning all discrimination, Persius indicates the extent
of the interlocutor's amorality: to countenance bad literature with
a fashionable *euge* is to maintain the absence of every kind of
standard. Literary congratulations amount to moral connivance.
However Persius has no real intention of betraying his concern for
the truth to complaisant flattery. Momentarily he makes as if to
abandon his accusation; but he finally decides to give evidence

---

[1] *V.* Excursus 5.
[2] Perhaps imitated from Lucil. 1026 M, *omnes formonsi, fortes tibi, ego*
improbus, esto.

at line 120: *nil moror* and *vidi* are legal metaphors.[1] First though, a highly sarcastic representation of Rome's deification of her own sterility, lines 112–14:

> hoc iuvat? 'hic' inquis 'veto quisquam faxit oletum.'
> pinge duos angues: 'pueri, sacer est locus, extra
> meiite.' discedo.

Such formulae appear in temple inscriptions, invoking the anger of the gods on anyone who defiles the sanctity of the spot by relieving themselves there: besides Persius, Horace, Juvenal, and Petronius make satirical capital out of the opportunities they offer.[2] In the parody the satirist is a wilful boy,[3] attempting to besmear the sacred vices of society. The uncompromising implication that satire is akin to excretion sets the genre on a belligerently realistic level, at a far remove from the counterfeit attractions of modish literature. The unpleasant imagery represents the satirist as an outsider, someone who refuses to abide by the usual laws of decency because those very laws are corrupt. Society has usurped the name of sanctity, but sanctity itself is nowhere to be seen. Obeisant court-poetry supplies Persius with ammunition at this point. Calp. Sic. II. 55, *ite procul – sacer est locus – ite profani* (adduced by Koenig) is more likely to have been Persius' source than vice versa, given the image of sanctity at Hor. *Sat.* I. 1.71–2, *tamquam parcere sacris/cogeris* (of a miser's avarice, represented by his bags of money), a passage which includes the words *hoc iuvat*, and is therefore, by conflation, another influence on 112–14. Calpurnius is not likely to have

[1] For the latter, *v.* below, p. 137 n. 2; for the former, 'the customary formula for abandoning an accusation and dismissing an accused person' (L&S), cf. Livy IV. 42.8, *C. Sempronium nihil moror*, also VIII. 35.8, XLIII. 16.16; Lejay on Hor. *Sat.* I. 4.13; following Villeneuve *Essai* p. 397, Buscaroli p. 100, '*nil moror*, frequente nei comici, era originariamente la formula con la quale dal presidente si scioglieva l'assemblea o dal console si licenziava il senato o dall'accusatore veniva abbandonata la lite'; he also suggests, p. 101, that *alba* may be technical, related to the ψῆφος λευκή (cf. Hor. *Sat.* II. 3.246; Pers. v. 108; Otto sv *calculus*). Another possibly legal image is *excute*, 49: 'The idea is taken from the shaking of a suspected person's clothes to see that he has nothing secreted in them' (Macleane).

[2] *V.* Jahn *ad loc.*, and Hor. *Sat.* I. 8.38, *atque in me veniat mictum atque cacatum*, Juv. I. 131, *cuius ad effigiem non tantum meiere fas est*, Petron. 71.8, *ne in monumentum meum populus cacatum currat.*

[3] *V.* Appendix 3.

drawn on an allusive source, dependent in turn on another author. Persius rejects the deceptive appearance, imaging his repulsion and disgust in an urge to befoul the temple of sanctioned vice. Open obscenity and dirt are valid weapons against concealed obscenity and dirt – that which is hidden from sight by a conspiracy of respectable sinners.[1]

With a transition which is not altogether unprepared, he turns to his predecessors, lines 114–18:

> secuit Lucilius urbem,
> te Lupe, te Muci, et genuinum fregit in illis.
> omne vafer vitium ridenti Flaccus amico
> tangit et admissus circum praecordia ludit,
> callidus excusso populum suspendere naso.

As a result of being banned from defiling the temple, he has been reminded of satire's usually drastic dealings with vice – of those criticisms which occasion society's interdiction on *libertas*: hence, partly, the violent representation of Lucilius. He falters during exit. Why should he refrain from justified sacrilege, why be inhibited, when his predecessors gave vent to their satiric urges? Can he, Persius, add nothing of his own to the tradition which he so recently seemed to join, line 119?

> me muttire nefas? nec clam? nec cum scrobe? nusquam?

The mild colloquialism *muttire* contrasts with the bolder freedom

---

[1] *V.* Marmorale pp. 65–6, for Persius' obscenities; also Fiske pp. 93–6. Besides those in *Sat.* I, M. lists IV. 35–6, 38, 48, and VI. 71–3: perhaps add IV. 15, for *cauda = membrum virile*, supported by Hor. *Sat.* I. 2.45 and II. 7.49. Persius' candour – 'l'ingenuo candore della sua anima di fanciullo' – is neither here nor there. Obscenity is a literary device, not a sign of spiritual candour; it probes beneath the veneer, shocking us into a frame of mind receptive to the castigation of the vices found. If society will not admit to its corruption, the satirist unmasks the truth: e.g. at Varro *Men.* 104 B, *divitum amphoras Chias ad communem/revocat matellam*, the vices symbolised by Chian wine are shorn of their attractions by the reminder that the fate of all liquids is the same. Hence a realistic insight from an unexpected angle. If the truth is unpleasant or obscene, it is painted starkly in its own colours, thereafter to be easily recognisable. Stoic doctrine, dictating an uninhibited naturalism (Cic. *ad Fam.* IX. 22.1, *nil esse obscenum, nihil turpe dictu*: cf. D'Alton, *Roman Literary Theory and Criticism* (London 1931), p. 35, on the principle 'naturalia non sunt obscena' citing Cic. *de Off.* I. 127–8, and the unimportant *de Or.* II. 252, also p. 326 f.; D.L. IV. 52 for obscenity in Cynic diatribe), obviously helped: a spade was to be called a spade. *V.* further Excursus 6.

of Lucilius and Horace, a quiet spirit against more adventurous predecessors.[1] Here we are in familiar territory – the traditional conception of satiric humility. Persius refuses to speak openly in facile language, maintaining instead a reserved and introverted posture. This attitude has been seen in the way he keeps himself to himself at lines 2, *min tu istud ais?*, where he expressed surprise at the interruption of his thoughts; 7, *nec te quaesiveris extra*, where he enjoined self-sufficiency; 8–12, where his diffidence ended in a private outburst of laughter; 88, *men moveat?*, where he refused involvement in the trial; 110, *per me equidem sint omnia protinus alba*, where he dissociated himself from Roman decadence. Now we see him stuttering about his secret, and talking, significantly, to his own book, the staccato repeated questions representing his nervous striving towards self-expression.[2] His reserved attitude contrasts strongly with the easy, and evil, communication indulged in by the rest of Rome. At first sight, *nec cum scrobe* looks like another manifestation of the expected humility, an analogous variation on *clam* – Persius is not able to speak aloud in public – but we are now very close to the joke about the ass's ears: consequently, he has the myth of Midas in mind. In that myth, Midas' barber whispers his secret knowledge about the king's ears into a hole in the ground, only to be foiled by reeds which spring up and broadcast the information.[3] So when Persius entrusts his secret to his book, we can make an important prediction: as in the mythological situation, the truth will out in the end. The burial is a sham, lines 120–1:

> hic tamen infodiam. vidi, vidi ipse, libelle:
> auriculas asini quis non habet?

[1] Lucilius thought he might burst if he did not give vent to his feelings: 957–8 M, *mihi necessest eloqui,/nam scio Amyclas tacendo periisse.* Cf. Varro fr. 59 B, *cum Quintipor Clodius tot comoedias sine ulla fecerit Musa, ego unum libellum non 'edolem' ut ait Ennius?*

[2] *V.* above, p. 70, on 8–12. For *nusquam* followed by a question-mark *v.* J. G. Griffith, 'The ending of Juvenal's first satire and Lucilius xxx', *Hermes* XCVIII (1970), 60 and n. 2.

[3] *V.* Ov. *Met.* XI. 180–93, depicting Midas' tastelessness (he has a *pingue ingenium* at *Met.* XI. 148, and prefers the barbaric song of Pan to that of Apollo), developed by P. and transferred to Rome. Cf. Hygin. *Fab.* 191.2, *tunc Apollo indignatus Midae dixit, 'Quale cor in iudicando tales et auriculas habebis'*, linking Midas' lack of judgement to the ass's ears.

Like the ditch, the book lets out the secret.[1] What seemed the end of censure turns out as its culmination. Through the repeated *vidi*, 'the form of giving evidence',[2] Persius becomes a witness in a court-room; Rome has been on trial for crimes observed by the satirist. A contrast with the corrupt law-court scene may be intended: unlike his compatriots, Persius is incapable of deceit. The passage which intervenes between the institution of the joke at line 8, and its completion at line 121, has illustrated all its ramifications, supplying evidence for our condemnation of literature, and of the society in which that literature thrives. Line 121 turns out to be far more than a frivolous joke: lack of taste is a pointer to total moral abdication. It need hardly be denied that here originally stood an allusion to Nero: in Kenney's words,[3]

> It was long ago remarked by Conington (and no doubt by others before him) that *Mida rex* . . . installed in the text by Casaubon . . . would ruin the point of the verse and of the satire. Hence a simple illation. Persius did not write these words and neither he (so Σ) nor Cornutus (so the *Vita*) expelled them from the text; *ergo*, the story is a fabrication; *ergo*, the whole passage, which in any case has no very firm footing in the *Vita*, is evidence for nothing.

Lines 121–3 keep up the pretence of secrecy:

> hoc ego opertum,
> hoc ridere meum, tam nil, nulla tibi vendo
> Iliade.

Secrecy and autobiography were facets of the satiric pose – note e.g. Hor. *Sat.* II. 1.30, of Lucilius, *ille velut fidis arcana sodalibus olim/credebat libris*. Likewise, Persius talks to his book, or rather pretends to talk to his book – the truth now being known – not to any human being. His joke may seem unimportant, but he would not exchange it for any swollen epic: *tam nil* is contrasted

---

[1] J. G. Griffith, *op. cit.* p. 60, takes *hic*, 120, as referring to *scrobe*. It surely refers to *libelle*, the book being the thing which concerns Persius as a writer (*v.* Hor. *Sat.* II. 1.30 f.); the ditch, to which it is related by *infodiam*, is the thing which announces publication, finally issued at 121.

[2] Conington, citing Juv. VII. 13, *hoc satius quam si dicas sub iudice 'vidi'/ quod non vidisti*, and XVI. 29–30, '*da testem*' *iudex cum dixerit, audeat ille/nescioquis, pugnos qui vidit, dicere 'vidi'*; cf. e.g. Ov. *Am.* I. 2.11.

[3] Reviewing F. Ballotto, *Cronologia ed evoluzione spirituale nelle Satire di Persio* (Florence 1964), in *CR* ns XV (1965), 120–1.

with the strategically placed *Iliade*.[1] The satirist can ironically disparage his chosen form – indeed it is common practice to do so – but when it comes to competition with the other genres, then satire takes precedence.

Mention of popular epic occasions the last section of the piece, where Persius chooses his prospective readers. The large genres can have their big audiences, but satire will only admit the discerning few. At Cic. *de Or.* III. 66, the Stoics are said to write an *orationis ... genus ... inusitatum, abhorrens ab auribus vulgi*. Popularity is not courted. Lucilius is the least exclusive of the satirists, in so far as he fears the trenchant critic and asks for a more ordinary kind of reader.[2] Horace makes an advance in exclusiveness, admitting only his immediate circle at *Sat.* I. 10.81 f.: 'The very satire which has found fault with Lucilius' poetic standards ends by demanding a more discriminating type of reader than Lucilius did.'[3] Elsewhere, he usurps several of the Callimachean images for esotericism. Persius goes beyond this, subscribing to a less conventional rejection of the *profanum vulgus*: his exclusiveness is introverted and moralistic, written in on a personalised, and therefore no longer conventional, interpretation of the traditional images for esoteric composition. Nobody except the reader of Old Comedy is allowed within distance of his works. The question of line 2, *quis leget haec?*, finds its answer, lines 123–5:

> audaci quicumque adflate Cratino
> iratum Eupolidem praegrandi cum sene palles,
> aspice et haec, si forte aliquid decoctius audis.

Derogatory motifs from the earlier part of the poem are here redefined, applied to virtues instead of vices: *adflate* refers to true inspiration, not to the panting of an oversized lung, line 14, or the wild fig-tree, lines 24–5; *praegrandi* describes real greatness, not

---

[1] *vendo* may allude to the venality of the materialistic interlocutor, in which case the *Iliad* would be a saleable commodity, satire a private possession. Cf. Petron. 52.4, *meum intellegere nulla pecunia vendo* (Jahn); Sen. *Ep.* XXVII. 8, *bona mens nec commodatur nec emitur. et puto, si venalis esset, non haberet emptorem. at mala cotidie emitur*, a kind of sentiment perhaps leading to an image of literature as something on sale to the public.

[2] Cf. Cic. *de Or.* II. 25 for his demands, *Persium non curo legere, Laelium Decumum volo*. Similarly, Martial fears the grammarian Probus at III. 2.12.

[3] Brink, *Prolegomena* p. 169.

the false bombast of *grande aliquid*, line 14, or *res grandes*, line 68; *palles* is now applied to the virtuous whiteness of study, not exhausting sexual exertions, line 26. For the first time in the poem old age – *sene* – has dignified and honourable connotations, just as *decoctius* sheds the previous condemnatory tone in culinary metaphors for style. Normally used of boiling down or cooking, *decoquere* describes the refined density of Persius' manner, the opposite of the undigested style – the *crudum* or *turgidum* – of his opponents.[1] Old Comedy will cleanse the ears of Persius' designated reader, line 126:

> inde vaporata lector mihi ferveat aure.

At last the healthy *auris* replaces the diseased *auricula*: *vaporata* describes the process of cleansing with steam. Because of her tastes and morals – symbolised by the infected, uncomprehending ears of an ass – the rest of Rome cannot profit from the satirist. But there are a select few, open to cure, who will constitute his audience.

Exclusion of the common herd, whose sense of humour is childish and unconstructive, concludes the satire, lines 127–34:

> non hic qui in crepidas Graiorum ludere gestit
> sordidus et lusco qui possit dicere 'lusce',
> sese aliquem credens Italo quod honore supinus
> fregerit heminas Arreti aedilis iniquas,
> nec qui abaco numeros et secto in pulvere metas
> scit risisse vafer, multum gaudere paratus
> si cynico barbam petulans nonaria vellat.
> his mane edictum, post prandia Callirhoen do.

Persius subscribes to the traditional distinction between liberal

---

[1] For *decoquere* in literary contexts, *v.* the not esp. analogous Cic. *de Or.* III. 26.104, *suavitatem habeat orator austeram et solidam, non dulcem et decoctam* and Quint. II. 4.7, *multum inde decoquent anni*, of the young orator's imagination; Anderson, above, p. 34 n. 3, 409 ff., 'Persius does not assert that he is cooking ordinary, plebeian fare (as if for ordinary people). He has a special meal to serve, and only trained palates will enjoy it, for his purpose has been to boil down ideas to their minimum, then to combine them in a meal that must prove indigestible to all but the elect.' I agree that he has 'boiled down ideas to their minimum' – an excellent characterisation of the complexity of his style – but cannot see an allusion to indigestibility in *decoctius*. Rather, this meal is cooked through and through, unlike the meal of his opponents.

and illiberal humour, established in the main by Aristotle, and transmitted by him to later rhetorical theory: the *sordidus* here behaves like the βωμολόχος of the *Nicomachean Ethics*.[1] He laughs without reason at peculiarities of national dress – the Greeks naturally wear sandals[2] – his activity perhaps partly modelled on Horace's bow to the theory of humour at *Sat*. I. 3.30–2, *rideri possit eo, quod/rusticius tonso toga defluit et male laxus/in pede calceus haeret*, where a man with hidden qualities is undeservedly mocked for his hair and dress. Worse, the *sordidus* finds amusement at the sight of physical deformity:

> lusco qui possit dicere 'lusce'.

Various factors seem to have influenced the choice of the image of a one-eyed man: Aristotle, who illustrates his proposition τοῖς μὲν γὰρ διὰ φύσιν αἰσχροῖς οὐδεὶς ἐπιτιμᾷ with the similar example of blindness;[3] Ciceronian theory that ridicule should not be directed *in calamitatem*, '*ne inhumanum sit*', *Or*. 88, and more relevant, his statement at *de Or*. II. 246 that a joke at the expense of a *luscus* is *scurrile*; and, if we follow Hendrickson,[4] Horace's praetor of Fundi, Aufidius Luscus, *Sat*. I. 5.34, interpreted as the link between lines 128 and 129, *lusco ... dicere 'lusce'* leading via Horace to the image of a provincial magistrate. Another influence on lines 128–9 may have been Nero's satire 'The One-Eyed Man', 'directed against the former praetor Clodius Pollio, a man of bad character'.[5] An unflattering gesture to Nero at this point need not lead to acceptance of the story of a similar, suppressed gesture at 121. In rejecting those who feel self-important on the basis of some minor achievement, 129–30, Persius shares Horace's superior attitude towards political position, *Sat*. I. 6.15 ff.: *populo, qui stultus honores/saepe dat indignis et famae servit ineptus,/qui stupet in titulis et imaginibus*. He also dismisses those who show disrespect for learning by scoffing at mathematics or philosophy,

---

[1] Below, pp. 190 ff.

[2] But not the Romans: *v*. Nisbet on Cic. *in Pis*. 13.6, 92.3, and p. 194.

[3] *Eth. Nic*. III. 5.15, 114a 24; cf. IV. 8.3 ff., 1128a 4 ff. Though sharing Aristotle's views on βωμολοχία, Persius nonetheless parts company over Old Comedy: *v*. below, p. 192, and Hendrickson, *AJPh* XXI (1900), 140.

[4] *Op. cit*., p. 140 n. 1.

[5] J. Wight Duff, *Roman Satire* (Cambridge 1937), p. 86, referring, n. 27, to Tac. *Ann*. XV. 49; schol. on Juv. IV. 106; Suet. *Dom*. I.

in line 133 imitating Hor. *Sat.* I. 3.133–4, *vellunt tibi barbam/ lascivi pueri*, and following Cicero's interdiction on ridicule which is *petulans*, in case it appears *improbum*, *Or.* 88. From his strictures on those who find private amusement to the detriment of the innocent and the worthwhile, we infer repudiation of malice and alignment with the liberal tradition. When *he* directs ridicule at peculiarities of dress – as at lines 15, 16, and 32 – or at deformity and disease – as at lines 57 and 79 – unlike the *sordidus*, he has ulterior, positive aims. He only reproves such physical and moral deformities as lie within the range of human responsibility: his victims are to blame for their appearance, their disease is self-induced. Here then is a clue to the function of Persius' imagery, constructive in its derision of outward appearances, in that it cuts through the symbolic surface to expose an interior malady, for which, given cooperation on the part of the patient, some remedy is implicitly proposed.

Liberal humour is the legitimate tool of the reforming satirist. Illiberal humour, on the other hand, lacks purpose. To its adherents Persius finally offers the kind of literature which he has so consistently pilloried: *post prandia Callirhoen do*, 134.[1] His model at this point is probably Horace *Satires* I. 10, where we find the comparable pattern of a parting shot delivered at undiscerning readers – 90–1, *Demetri, teque, Tigelli,/discipularum inter iubeo plorare cathedras* – after a treatment of the audience which he will permit. The word *Callirhoe*, referring to some inferior work constructed along the lines of a '*Phyllis*' or '*Hypsipyle*', or some kind of comedy (if a mime, then there is a link back to the recent subject of misdirected humour),[2] seems intended to conjure up all the disrepute with which Persius has stigmatised Rome's jaded tastes: the unthinking crowd is damned forever.[3] The satirist is left

---

[1] For *edictum v.* Némethy *ad loc.* (citing Hor. *Ep.* I. 6.22, and esp. *Ep.* I. 19.8–9, *forum putealque Libonis/mandabo siccis, adimam cantare severis*), 'quod Horatius dixit, "*forum mandabo iis, qui a Musis alieni sunt*", Persius ita expressit "*edictum do alienis a philosophia*"'.

[2] Jahn's explanation, 'notum scortum', is unconvincing. A second-rate work of literature caters for the topic of Rome's lack of taste, and contrasts with the strength of Old Comedy.

[3] *V.* Excursus 7. Like Horace, Persius is *a volgo longe longeque remotus*, *Sat.* I. 6.18; cf. *Ep.* I. 1.70 ff., for idealistic avoidance of the haunts of the money-minded.

standing alone, with the same air of self-sufficiency that he assumed at the beginning of the piece.

EXCURSUS I

Nuts and uncles at Persius I. 10–11

Here I wish to argue for sexual overtones in the contrasting *nucibus . . . relictis* and *patruos*, the first an image from childhood alluding to homosexuality, the second a reference to the suspect gravity of the pervert. That the *patruus* was the type of moral severity is clear from Cat. LXXIV, Cic. *Cael.* XI. 25, *pertristis patruus*, Hor. *Sat.* II. 2.97, 3.88 (cf. Pers. III. 96), *Carm.* III. 12.3, Manil. V. 452. Housman, *CQ* VII (1913), 13, wrongly ignores the connexion between these hints and the recitation scene which follows, writing of *canities*, 'There is no allusion to anything so irrelevant as premature decrepitude brought on by vicious indulgence.' In fact Persius laughs because he has penetrated the masquerade: *sed habet tristis quoque turba cinaedos.*

 nucibus facimus quaecumque relictis is based on Horace: *nucibus . . . relictis* has been exchanged for *abiectis . . . nugis* and *sapimus patruos* for *sapere* at *Ep.* II. 2.141–2, *nimirum sapere est abiectis utile nugis,/et tempestivum pueris concedere ludum.* I would endorse Némethy's interpretation. On the basis of schol. cod. Par. 8272 (Serv. *Ecl.* VIII. 29), *pueri meritorii, id est catamimi* [i.e. *catamiti*], *quibus licenter utebantur antiqui, recedentes a turpi servitio nuces spargebant, ut significarent, se puerilia cuncta spernere et in robur virile venire*, and Cat. LXI. 119 ff., he interprets the words as an allusion to the retention of 'boyish', that is homosexual, habits, even after formal departure from boyhood: 'Nos etiam pueritiam egressi idem facimus, quod pueri delicati ante nuces relictas facere solent: virili aetate muliebria patimur. Cinaedi sumus, non sumus viri. Et hoc facimus eodem tempore, cum iam *patruos sapimus*, cum agimus partes acerbissimi morum censoris.' This would be unwarranted if it were not for the other indications of homosexuality in the passage; but given *canitiem, vivere triste*, and *patruos*, it would be surprising if *nucibus . . . relictis* were merely an elaborate way of saying 'when we have grown up'. Persius need not have expressed himself in this particular way. Admittedly, we have to supply the notion of the *puer delicatus*, and also suppose that Persius implies the opposite of what he says (we have not in fact 'grown up'), but this is not too difficult in view of 13 ff. Cf. also Epict. III. 19.6, 24.53, quoted pp. 188–9.

'Escae' at Persius I. 22

The commentaries are deficient in illustrative material for the sense of *escas*, a metaphor from food, at Pers. I. 22:

> tun, vetule, auriculis alienis colligis escas.

It is not enough to cite Cic. *Cat. Mai.* 13.44, *divine enim Plato escam malorum appellat voluptatem quod ea videlicet homines capiantur ut pisces*, as, for instance Némethy *ad loc.*, referring to his note on II. 154 (in fact, v. 154) and noting Cicero's source as *Timaeus* 69 d, ἡδονὴν . . . κακοῦ δέλεαρ. True, the reciter in Persius is leading his audience astray. However they are not captivated by sheer pleasure, but by pleasurable poetry. A literary parallel is required. Aelian's metaphor from feasting the ears, *V.H.* III. 1, κατᾴδουσι δὲ καὶ ὄρνιθες . . . καὶ ἑστιῶσιν εὖ μάλα τὰς ἀκοάς, adduced by Némethy and Jahn, and partly implied by Conington's comment, 'Causaubon compares the Greek phrases εὐωχίαι and ἑστιάσεις ἀκοῶν', is not very helpful.[1] Better is Petron. 3.4, cited by Villeneuve, *sic eloquentiae magister, nisi tamquam piscator imposuerit hamis escam, quam scierit appetituros esse pisciculos, sine spe praedae morabitur in scopulo*, where teachers lure the young with tasty morsels of rhetoric. But the meaning of *escas* is capable of closer definition. Three further passages – from Petronius, Fronto, and Quintilian – clarify its implications.

After an attack on declamation Petronius states at 1.3 that the youth of his day have lost contact with reality, and spend their time pampering a taste for the dainty turns of the modernist style: *mellitos verborum globulos et omnia dicta factaque quasi papavere et sesamo sparsa.* At 2.1 he continues, *qui inter haec nutriuntur non magis sapere possunt, quam bene olere, qui in culina habitant*, where the imagery instituted by *mellitos verborum globulos* is carried over into *nutriuntur* and *culina*.[2]

---

[1] Ramorino and Bo cite no parallels; Scivoletto refers to Schönbach, *De Persii in saturis sermone et arte* (Diss. Weidae Thuringorum, 1910), pp. 21 f., which was unfortunately unavailable to me.

[2] There is perhaps a pun in *sapere*; they have no sense, and, literally, no taste. If so, 'taste', *sapere*, may have led to 'smell', *olere*, the metaphoric potential of the latter verb (cf. *redolere*, of literature, Tac. *Dial.* 21.4;

Those who feed on rich declamatory titbits have the smell of the kitchen about them. Though more explicit, enlisting disapproval as if against a manifestation of luxury, the image is akin to Persius' *escae*, likewise an example of enticing food served up during a recitation.

Another analogy is at hand in Fronto's colourful warnings on the subject of Seneca and his school. Displaying abhorrence from the 'soft and fevered plums' of their style, he writes, II p. 102, *confusam eam ego eloquentiam, catachannae ritu partim pineis nucibus Catonis partim Senecae mollibus et febriculosis prunulis insitam, subvertendam censeo radicitus, immo vero Plautino ut utar verbo, exradicitus*. During an unfavourable comparison between Seneca and Sergius Flavius, he proceeds to develop the imagery of a meal, II pp. 102–4:

> quid vero, si prandium utrique adponatur, adpositas oleas alter digitis prendat, ad os adferat ut manducandi ius fasque est ita dentibus subiciat, alter autem oleas suas in altum iaciat, ore aperto excipiat, ut calculos praestigiator, primoribus labris ostentet? ea re profecto pueri laudent, convivae delectentur; sed alter pudice pranderit, alter labellis gesticulatus erit.

Seneca is an impresario, a conjurer who can throw his verbal olives in the air, and catch them in his mouth, slowly then on the tip of his lips; *primoribus labris* and *labellis* suggest the presence of the idea that 'words from the lips' are insincere and lacking in substance. Affinity with Persius is clear: in both cases a literary expert displays a suspect skill with scraps of food.

Finally, there is the word *frustum*, another pejorative image from food, indicative of the meretricious attraction of inorganic detail. When decrying the deleterious effects of cultivating the individual *sententia*, Quintilian writes, with what is obviously a classicist's objection, VIII. 5.27, *unde soluta fere oratio et e singulis non membris sed frustis collata structura caret, cum illa rotunda et undique circumcisa insistere in vicem nequeant*. The offending style resembles that of Seneca: we remember the criticism at Quint. X. 1.130, where his liking for *obliqua*, disregard of *recta*,[1] and dissolution of *rerum pondera* into *minutissimae sententiae* is castigated, along with his influence on susceptible youth. If not Seneca himself, Quintilian surely has in mind

Varro *Men.* 63 B, attributing the smell of vegetables to the *sermo* of early Rome, *avi et atavi nostri cum alium ac caepe eorum verba olerent, tamen optume animati erant*: the vegetarian image enhances the worth of such *sermo*, *tamen* a false apology for praiseworthy *rusticitas*) probably assisting the simile's creation: from the 'smell' of literature we revert to that of the kitchen.

[1] For the textual difficulties, *v.* Peterson's edition of Quint. X, pp. 207–8.

the type of pointed declamatory style which appears to have held sway in many quarters for much of the first century.[1] Its features were a preference for dispersion – *soluta* – against concentration; for the part against the whole – *e singulis non membris* . . . *collata*; for incoherence against order – *structura caret*; for the autonomous verbal unit against organic arrangement – *rotunda et undique circumcisa*; for elliptical, tonal juxtaposition against sequential argument – *insistere in vicem nequeant*; and for *frusta*. All the characteristics described so far have been similar in kind – characteristics, that is, of a style which has deviated from the precepts of classicism. Quintilian's *frusta* belong to the same category, imaging the momentary hedonism of a style too limited to strive after a larger or more serious structure. The correctly prepared meal is abandoned for the tasty morsel,[2] the individual device cultivated to the detriment of the whole.[3]

Like Petronius and Fronto, Quintilian uses a particular kind of imagery for a particular kind of style. The food is no more than a mouthful; the ingredients for a full meal are missing. The style is the fragmented, anti-classical mode, best exemplified in the prose works of Seneca:[4] of the three *loci* under discussion, Fronto explicitly refers to Seneca, Petronius to the unclassical declamations, while Quintilian

---

[1] For Quintilian's criticisms of Seneca, *v.* A. D. Leeman, *Orationis Ratio* (Amsterdam 1963), pp. 278 ff.; on his critics as a whole, W. C. Summers, *Select Letters of Seneca*, introd. pp. xcvi ff.

[2] Cf. Mart. X. 59.3–4, of his own epigrams: *dives et ex omni posita est instructa macello/cena tibi, sed te mattea sola iuvat.*

[3] Excessive use of the *sententia* incurred much displeasure: e.g. Quint. VIII. 5.31, *nec multas plerique sententias dicunt, sed omnia tamquam sententias*; Sen. *Contr.* I *praef.* 23, on inorganic 'translaticiae sententiae', *quae nihil habent cum ipsa controversia implicitum*; Petron. 118.5, *curandum est ne sententiae emineant extra corpus orationis expressae, sed intexto vestibus colore niteant*; Tac. *Dial.* 20.4, on the desire for a detachable, take-away rhetoric, *iam vero iuvenes . . . non solum audire, sed etiam referre domum aliquid inlustre et dignum memoria volunt*; Epict. III. 23.26, on trivial phrases, ἔστι γὰρ τῷ ὄντι κομψὸν τὸ τεχνίον ἐκλέξαι ὀνομάτια καὶ ταῦτα συνθεῖναι καὶ παρελθόντα εὐφυῶς ἀναγνῶναι ἢ εἰπεῖν and 31, on the diminutive and useless νοημάτια and ἐπιφωνημάτια of the lecture hall. For literary *frusta*, *v.* further Quint. IV. 5.25, *nam et auctoritati plurimum detrahunt minuta illa nec iam membra, sed frusta* (cf. Plat. *Hipp. Mai.* 304a, κνίσματά τοί ἐστι καὶ περιτμήματα τῶν λόγων, ὅπερ ἄρτι ἔλεγον, κατὰ βραχὺ διῃρημένα); Sen. *Ep.* LXXXIX. 2, *philosophiam in partes, non in frusta dividam*; Sidon. Apoll. *Ep.* I. 11.3, *cumque frusta diversa carminis . . . per iocum effunderent.*

[4] We see from Quint. X. 1.125–7, on his battle against the imitators of Seneca, that the style was still active towards the end of the century.

exhibits antipathy towards the moderns. I submit that the titbits at Pers. I. 22 are similar types of food, and that they refer to a similar type of style. The reciter purveys tempting, but unnutritious dainties, the imagery implying that he is absorbed with the epideictic moment, and neglectful of the organic entity.

But in referring *escas* to Petronius' *mellitos verborum globulos*, to Fronto's *oleas* and *mollibus et febriculosis prunulis*, and to Quintilian's *frusta* – and to the kind of style suggested by those images – I would beware of chasing occult allusion to contemporaries, stressing that it is style, and style alone which is indicted through the metaphor.[1] Persius ranges far afield for his objects of criticism. The high style and epic, together with elegy and epyllion, lack of workmanship as well as too much workmanship[2] – all incur contempt. The link in this variety, as we have seen, is his moral concern. I would go no further than to say that at this point, and only at this point, Persius widens the focus of his attack to include a style lacking in cohesion, and abandoned to the sole purpose of the fleeting delectation of its audience.

EXCURSUS 3

'Cutis' at Persius I. 23

As in the case of *articulis* . . . *perditus*, *cute perditus* may correspond to something in the earlier description of the audience's reaction to erotic poetry. Interpreting the phrase as an allusion to impotence, we are possibly meant to look back to lines 20–1, *carmina lumbum/intrant*, where *membrum virile* might have been expected, instead of *carmina*. Once again, the insinuation, whether local – confined to 22–3 – or more general, is that the reciter is not equipped to deal with the reaction provoked by his poetry.

Parallels for *cutis* in the specific sense of 'prepuce' are problematic, since even in apposite contexts it may retain some, if not most, of its basic meaning, 'skin': so e.g. Celsus VII. 25.2–3,

---

[1] Persius was not impressed by Seneca, according to the *Vita*, 24–5: *sero cognovit et Senecam, sed non ut caperetur eius ingenio*; but this is no evidence for indirect allusion at I. 22. All we have is a classicist's case against the moderns.

[2] Cf. Pers. I. 90–1, *verum nec nocte paratum/plorabit qui me volet incurvasse querella*, a demand for unartful sincerity, with 106, *nec pluteum caedit nec demorsos sapit unguis*, a demand for careful composition.

si glans ita contecta est ut nudari non possit, quod vitium Graeci
phimosin appellant . . . subter a summa ora cutis inciditur recta linea
usque ad frenum . . . quod si parum sic profectum est, eius (infibu-
landi) haec ratio est: cutis, quae super glandem est, extenditur . . .
cutis acu filum ducente transuitur.

Even if we plead a case for a quasi-technical usage of the term in the
last passage, we meet difficulties with such incidences as Tert. *Nat.* I. 14,
solo detrimento cutis Iudaeus. But again, we might adduce Mart. VII.
30.5, *nec recutitorum fugis inguina Iudaeorum*, suggesting a technical
significance, as well as Porph. Hor. *Sat.* I. 9.69–70, *curtos Iudaeos dixit,
quia virile membrum velut decurtatum habeant* recisa *inde* pellicula, and
Schol. Juv. XIV. 104, *Iudaeos (dicit), qui sine* pellicula *sunt.*[1] In these
various passages, including Mart. VII. 35.4,[2] there seems to be a degree
of fluctuation between original meaning and technical transference.
Housman, who lists them along with *Corp. Gl. Lat.* II p. 206–49, does
not differentiate sufficiently.[3]

Korzeniewski, apparently ignorant of Housman's article,[4] interprets
much as I do: '*cutis* ist hier gleichbedeutend mit *praeputium* und somit
als pars pro toto mit *penis*'.[5] His best parallels are Ar. *Eq.* 29, where
δέρμα means *praeputium*,[6] and Archil. 72 D, καὶ πεσεῖν δρήστην ἐπ'
ἀσκὸν κἀπὶ γαστρὶ γαστέρα/προσβαλεῖν μηρούς τε μηροῖς, where he
explains δρήστην ἐπ' ἀσκόν with *patrantem in cutem*.[7] His other
citations are invalid.[8]

[1] Cf. Pers. v. 184, *recutita. . .sabbata.* Confinement to Jewish reference does
not invalidate potential technical status.

[2] Above, p. 89.

[3] *Hermes* LXVI (1931), 409–10.

[4] Like Dessen p. 36, he quotes, p. 394 n. 34, Mart. VII. 10.1–2, *pedicatur Eros,
fellat Linus: Ole, quid ad te/de cute quid faciant ille vel ille sua?* But Eros
is not 'a pederast' (Dessen), nor, as Housman pointed out (*op. cit.* p. 410),
is *ThLL* justified in interpreting *cutis* here as 'de . . . pene': the proverbial
de suo, or *alieno corio ludere* (cf. Otto, sv *corium*), suggested by Housman,
is the obvious explanation.

[5] P. 394; 'pars pro toto' is not necessary.

[6] He includes *Eq.* 27; Blaydes, only 29.

[7] Schol. Eur. *Med.* 679, citing this fragment, remarks ἀσκὸν τοίνυν λέγει
τὸν περὶ τὴν γαστέρα τόπον. But given γαστρὶ γαστέρα immediately
afterwards, *membrum virile* is more in place.

[8] Eur. *Med.* 679, ἀσκοῦ με τὸν προύχοντα μὴ λῦσαι πόδα (cf. Plut. *Thes.* 3
for similar language in an oracle) is wrongly interpreted: πόδα here
corresponds to *membrum virile*, ἀσκοῦ to τὸν περὶ τὴν γαστέρα τόπον.
Catalepton XIII. 39 is irrelevant, correctly interpreted by Westendorp-
Boerma as *podicem*, adducing *Priap.* LXXVII.

The evidence, then, is tenuous, but still, I submit, sufficient for my explanation. Given the sexual reference of *articulis . . . perditus*, where parallel material, though sparse, is unequivocal, the Roman reader would have been invited to delimit the area of meaning suggested by *cutis* to a similarly sexual level: either *praeputium*, or, after Korzeniewski, *pars pro toto* for *penis*. If the term had a technical medical signification, as perhaps implied by Celsus VII. 25.2–3, and the Jewish references, then all the more suitable for Persius, a moralist versed in medicine. A sexual explanation of *cute perditus*, a phrase in close conjunction with *articulis perditus*, makes sense. Other explanations, given context, do not.

EXCURSUS 4

'Pallor seniumque' at Persius I. 26 and *'scire'* at I. 27

First, I wish to pursue my argument that *pallor seniumque* at line 26 alludes to a condition which results from the exertions of lines 24–5, not a condition prior to the act there described, and directed at its achievement. The words refer to the reciter's physical appearance, as caused by the strain of attempting to achieve something for which he is not physically endowed.

Often the phrase is interpreted as meaning 'so this is the point of your studies, this is the thing at which you aim'. Both *pallor* and *senium* are taken as referring to poetic and scholarly study: for *pallor* thus, Jahn cites Pers. I. 124, III. 85, Juv. VII. 97, Quint. I. 2.18, VIII. 10.14, Mart. Cap. I. 13.3, to which could be added Pers. v. 62, *nocturnis . . . impallescere chartis*, and prol. 4, *pallidamque Pirenen*; for *senium* of literary study, Hor. *Ep.* I. 18.47, *inhumanae senium depone Camenae* is usually cited, to which add Hor. *Ep.* II. 2.82, *et studiis annos septem dedit insenuitque/libris et curis*,[1] and Casaubon's adduction of Aretaeus, *de Diuturnis Morbis* IV. 5.25, p. 73H., τοῖσδε ὧν τηκεδὼν μὲν τοῦ σκήνεος, ἄχροοι καὶ ἐν νεότητι γηραλέοι καὶ ὑπ' ἐννοίης κωφοί, ψυχὴν δὲ ἀμειδέες, ἀμείλιχοι, explained by the note 'comitatur hos corporis tabes; sunt pallidi, in *juventute senes*, ob cogitationem muti, animo a risu alieno, insuaves et incommodi' (my italics). But a problem immediately

---

[1] Perhaps add Callim. *Aetia praef.* 34–8, and cf. Hor. *Ep.* I. 7.85, *immoritur studiis et amore senescit habendi*, on love of gain.

faces us if we explain *en pallor seniumque* as a condition anterior to the lines 24–5. The exclamation, 'this is the point of your studies', most naturally refers to the reciter's objection at 24–5: if the imagery there is not given any particular slant, then the exact nature of the 'point' is obscure; hence, no doubt, unwarranted comments like Macleane's 'this is what you have studied for, to be flattered by such people as these'. Perhaps we could say that the exclamation refers only generally to 24–5, interpreting it as meaning 'you have studied in order to communicate your knowledge'. But this is manifestly weak – the topic of communication recurs, more explicitly, in 26–7 – and surely leads to the conclusion that the colour of 24–5 must be more closely defined. It is not communication in general which is the goal of literary study, but a particular kind of communication. This brings us back to the erotic cast of 24–5. If that objection is explained in sexual terms, then the exclamation, 'sexual enjoyment, derived from the act of communication, is the point of your studies' has slightly more force, but is still rather flat, since Persius has known for some time that the recital has an ulterior sexual motive. It would be rather odd if final realisation of the reciter's intentions only dawned at the last minute.

Hence my proposition that the exclamation *en pallor seniumque* arises from the act described at 24–5. Parallels for the two nouns can be found which present a Persius logically expressing detached expectation: 'no wonder you look as you do, given the strain of attempting the impossible'. Some form of pale decrepitude was generally regarded as the mark of one in love.[1] Here *pallor* and *senium* depict the diseased look of a *senex amans*, incapable of consummating the proposed act of 24–5, no matter how hard he tries. Read on a sexual level, Casaubon's note is pertinent: 'palloris huius duas causas affert Philo: laboris adsiduitatem et spem incertam finem optatum consequendi: ait in Allegoriis: ὠχροὶ οἱ ἐν ἀσκήσει διά τε τὸν τρύχοντα πόνον καὶ διὰ δέος τοῦ μὴ τυχεῖν ἂν ἴσως τοῦ κατ' εὐχὴν τέλους.' Uncertainty about attaining his desired goal is the reason for his complexion. A relatively neutral term from amatory vocabulary, *pallor*, is enlivened by the addition of *senium*, to allow momentary representation of the sickly appearance resulting from the reciter's futile erotic efforts. For *pallor* here, the nearest parallel is Juvenal's use of *pallere* at 1. 43, describing

---

[1] Cf. the symptoms of love-sickness at Theocr. II. 88 f., καί μευ χρὼς μὲν ὁμοῖος ἐγένετο πολλάκι θάψῳ,/ἔρρευν δ' ἐκ κεφαλᾶς πᾶσαι τρίχες, αὐτὰ δὲ λοιπά/ὀστί' ἔτ' ἦς καὶ δέρμα; Gow–Page 1099, ὀστέα σοι καὶ μοῦνον ἔτι τρίχες (Callimachus); Ov. *Her.* XI. 29, *fugerat ore color, macies adduxerat artus*; Nisbet and Hubbard on *macerer* at Hor. *Carm.* I. 13.8.

the aftermath of sexual indulgence. Except for some Senecan *loci*,[1] other material, including the various elegiac and comic incidences of the word and its cognates (adequately summarised by the Ovidian prescription, *palleat omnis amans: hic est color aptus amanti*)[2] is not quite so relevant.[3] For old age as a sign of love-sickness we can adduce Hor. *Epod.* XVII. 21, *fugit iuventus*, and, with *senium* of a state caused by sexual passion, *Ciris* 248–9, *tristibus istis/sordibus et senio patiar tabescere tali.*[4] Then, on the aging effect of lust, there is Cic. *Cat. Mai.* 9.29, *etsi ipsa ista defectio virium adulescentiae vitiis efficitur saepius quam senectutis; libidinosa enim et intemperans adulescentia effetum corpus tradit senectuti.* Line 26 describes an effect, not a cause, of 24–5.

Finally, there is the possible sexual innuendo in *scire*, which according to L & S, citing Treb. *Trig. Tyr.* 30.12, can mean 'of a woman, to know carnally a man'. Alternatively, of a man knowing a woman, there are the incidences of *cognoscere* at Ov. *Her.* VI. 133, Just. V. 2.5, XXII. 1.13, Cat. LXI. 147 (cf. 187), Tac. *Hist.* IV. 44, Colum. VI. 37.9, Papin. *Dig.* 34.9.14.[5] On *novimus* at Pers. IV. 43 (perhaps a dubious instance), Dessen remarks 'Plautus twice puns upon the double meaning of *noscere* in *Most.* 893–4, and *Pers.* 131.'[6] In general terms, the use of *scire* rather than *cognoscere* is apposite to a homosexual situation, though it does not exactly suit both reciter and audience: if he is a *paedicator*, only his audience is precisely accommodated by *scire–sciat alter*. A strain of ambivalence in the verb is perhaps sup-

---

[1] Sen. *Ben.* VII. 27.3, *senes pallidos*, probably with reference to debauchery; *Brev. Vit.* II. 4, *quam multi continuis voluptatibus pallent*, and *Vit. Beat.* VII. 3, *voluptatem . . . pallidam.*

[2] *A.A.* I. 729. *V.* Enk on Prop. I. 1.22.

[3] Given P.'s usage elsewhere of *pallidus, albus*, and their cognates, as indicative of disease and vice (III. 98, *albo ventre*; 115, *timor albus* (cf. III. 94 and 96); IV. 47, *viso si palles improbe nummo* (cf. Hor. *Sat.* II. 3.78, *argenti pallet amore*); V. 15, *pallentes radere mores*), there may be a medical nuance at I. 26, as in the more explicit Juv. II. 50, *morbo pallet utroque.*

[4] *senio* is the obvious correction of H, *seonia*; the corruption is explained by Haupt. Dr R. O. A. M. Lyne kindly informs me that the word is rare in poetry before the Silver Age (Enn. 1; Hor. 1; Sen. *trag.* 7; Luc. 4; Val. Fl. 1; Sil. 12; Stat. 16: no exx. in Lucr., Cat., Virg. (and *Virgiliana*), Prop., Tib., Ov., Juv. or Mart.) and tells me that 'rarely *senium* can denote "grief", "affliction", "trouble" *sim.* with little or no associations of, or reference to, old age itself', referring to Enk's note on Plaut. *Truc.* 466 (= 'maeror'); and Cic. *Mil.* 8.20, *luget senatus, maeret equester ordo, tota civitas confecta senio est.*

[5] *V.* ThLL sv IA 3aβ, 'speciatim de amore viri et mulieris, saepe i.q. concubitum facere, coire'.

[6] Pp. 69–70, and n. 33, on *cognoscere* and *noscere*.

ported by the specificatory *hoc* in 27: the most distinctive thing about the preceding lines has been their sexual colour. Given that a pronoun requires more than general reference, it is surely the sexual colour which is in question here, *hoc* conveying the previous tone into 27, to be picked up by the verbs. A neutral *scire* would isolate a loaded *hoc*.

EXCURSUS 5

Dogs and doorsteps at Persius I. 108–10

I have argued that at 108–10 the interlocutor represents Persius as a client, snarling like a dog before the houses of the great, and so running the risk of forfeiting their patronage. That the doorway – *limina* – is not the post of a guardian dog, but the place where the client queues to pay his respects and receive remuneration, has been seen by several commentators, including Némethy,[1] Villeneuve,[2] and Koenig. Persius' imagined situation is paralleled from several sources: e.g. Colum. VIII. *praef.* 9, *salutatoris mendacissimum aucupium circum-volitantis potentiorum limina*; Mart. XII. 18.4–5, *dum per limina te potentiorum/sudatrix toga ventilat*; Suet. *Tib.* 32, *hunc Romae salutandi causa pro foribus adstantem*; Juv. III. 124–5, *limine summoveor, perierunt tempora longi/servitii*; and Sen. *ad Marc.* 10.1, *ampla atria et exclusorum clientium turba referta vestibula*.[3] His personal social status has no bearing on the interlocutor's picture: the irony is that as satirist, he is totally self-sufficient and free-spoken, immune from the collusive bribery of the patron–client relationship. Once more the antagonist does himself a disservice, by attributing his own servile priorities about the *sportula* to the incorruptible Persius.

Next, the problem of *canina littera*[4] and *hic* at 109–10. Should the words be referred to the offended *maiores*, so depicting Persius, the would-be *cliens*, as kept at a distance from their homes by a watch-dog? Or is the *canina littera* an attribute of the snarling satirist, *hic* a reference to the criticisms aimed at society and letters during the course of the satire,

---

[1] 'ne maiores te frigidius excipiant, cum limen eorum *salutandi causa* transscendis': my italics.

[2] 'Il prend le seuil comme symbole de l'amitié des grands recevant, chaque matin, leurs clients et leurs protégés.'

[3] Also Mayor on Juv. I. 100 and 132.

[4] V. Fraenkel p. 25 n. 2, with refs., R. G. Austin on *canina eloquentia* at Quint. XII. 9.9.

not to the *limina* of the great? With Anderson[1] I believe that the dog is the discontented Persius, not a possession of the resentful *maiores*, and that *hic* in 109 means 'here in your satire', not 'in domo divitum', the misleading gloss of the scholiast. This argument is supported by the presence of *de nare*, the nose being elsewhere in this composition, except for 33, a symbol for the fastidious criticisms of the satirist. The specification of nostrils means that our dog is metaphoric, not real, and as such, more at home in satire than on the *limina maiorum*. Our only way of attributing the *canina littera* to the *maiores*, is to stress their contempt for Persius,[2] so that a metaphor for critical disdain attends upon a literal allusion, through *limina*, to the doorsteps of the great.

But we have another argument for awarding the *canina littera* to Persius, in that the dog was connected with the Cynic, and hence with the figure of the satirist. As we see from, e.g., Lucian *bis accus.* 33, the dog came to symbolise an ill-natured critical attitude: τελευταῖον δὲ καὶ Μένιππόν τινα τῶν παλαιῶν κυνῶν μάλα ὑλακτικὸν ὡς δοκεῖ καὶ κάρχαρον ἀνορύξας, καὶ τοῦτον ἐπεισήγαγέν μοι φοβερόν τινα ὡς ἀληθῶς κύνα καὶ τὸ δῆγμα λαθραῖον, ὅσῳ καὶ γελῶν ἅμα ἔδακνεν.[3] As Anderson notes, Lucilius and Horace represented the satirist as a dog: Hor. *Sat.* II. 1.85 is especially to the point, since that composition supplied Persius with his image of the cold *maiorum limina*. The general upshot of *sonat . . . littera* is the conventional accusation levelled at the satirist: *laedere gaudes*.[4]

[1] *CQ* ns VIII (1958), 195 ff.

[2] Cf. v. 91, *ira cadat naso*, for the possible application of *de nare* to the opponents of the satirist, rather than the usual reference of such allusions to the satirist himself.

[3] As early as Hom. *Od.* XX. 13, ὑλακτεῖν is used metaphorically of anger: cf. Sappho 158 L–P, σκιδναμένας ἐν στήθεσιν ὄργας/πεφύλαχθαι γλῶσσαν μαψυλάκαν.

[4] Canine imagery is perhaps continued at 114–15, where Lucilius is represented as breaking his teeth on his victims. For the troublesome *secuit* ('beissen'), Korzeniewski, p. 424 n. 107, quotes Celsus VIII. 1.9, *quaterni primi (dentes) quia secant, tomis a Graecis nominantur.* Etymology may have conditioned the use of *secare* here, but cf. also Plaut. *Most.* 825, of a worm, *ambo (postes) ab infumo tarmes secat*, cited by Conington on 114 and translated 'gnaws'; for *genuinum* (the strongest of the molars), Jahn cites Cic. *D.N.D.* II. 54.134, Juv. V. 69, and Sidon. Apoll. *Epp.* I. 11 and I. 1.

EXCURSUS 6

Attractive surface and internal corruption

The implication of *sacer est locus*, Pers. I. 113, is that society has erected a deceptive camouflage. This the satirist penetrates, to discover interior realities. Here, as often elsewhere in satire and diatribe, the imagery of false surface and inner corruption is employed: Persius sees through into the essence concealed from defective vision by specious decorative piety.

Seneca's one hundred and fifteenth letter illustrates the moralist's claim to see into the vices hidden by a thin veneer of ornamentation; e.g. §9,

> miramur parietes tenui marmore inductos, cum sciamus, quale sit quod absconditur. oculis nostris imponimus, et cum auro tecta perfudimus, quid aliud quam mendacio gaudemus? scimus enim sub illo auro foeda ligna latitare. nec tantum parietibus aut lacunaribus ornamentum tenue praetenditur; omnium istorum, quos incedere altos vides, bratteata felicitas est. inspice, et scies, sub ista tenui membrana dignitatis quantum mali iaceat.

Similar are *Ep.* CXX. 5, *suberant illis multa vitia, quae species conspicui alicuius facti fulgorque celabat; haec dissimulavimus*, and LIX. 10, *nemo nostrum in altum descendit; summa tantum decerpsimus*, instances of the imagery of exterior and interior, modified at XLIII. 3 f., where 'outside' is preferred to 'inside':

> tunc autem felicem esse te iudica cum poteris in publico vivere, cum te parietes tui tegent, non abscondent, quos plerumque circumdatos nobis iudicamus non ut tutius vivamus, sed ut peccemus occultius. rem dicam ex qua mores aestimes nostras: vix quemquam invenies qui possit aperto ostio vivere. ianitores conscientia nostra, non superbia opposuit.

From Persius, we might quote IV. 43–5, *ilia subter/caecum vulnus habes; sed lato balteus auro/protegit*, and V. 105–6, *et veri specimen dinoscere calles/ne qua subaerato mendosum tinniat auro?*, both examples of gold concealing inner truth. In a literary context, there is Hor. *Sat.* II. 7.41–2, *verbisque decoris/obvolvas vitium*, already cited with reference to *tectoria* at Pers. V. 25; in a sexual context, *Sat.* I. 2.83 ff.

Skin is especially common as a metaphor for attractive façade and related ideas of deception, often used in conjunction with *intus* or *introrsum*, pointers to disguised recesses. Horace writes of Lucilius, *detrahere et* pellem, *nitidus qua quisque per ora/cederet*, introrsum *turpis*, *Sat.* II. 1.64 f.; with this we can compare *Ep.* I. 16.4–5, introrsum *turpem, speciosum* pelle decora, and 2.29, *in* cute *curanda plus aequo* operata iuventus. Persius follows suit with III. 30, *ad populum phaleras!* ego te intus *et in* cute *novi*, IV. 14, summa *nequiquam* pelle decorus, 18, *adsiduo curata* cuticula *sole*, and V. 116, pelliculam *veterem retines et* fronte *politus*. Simply with *intus*,[1] we can quote Pers. I. 49–50, *nam 'belle' hoc excute totum:/quid non* intus *habet?*, of the connivance glossed over by promiscuous applause.

EXCURSUS 7

Structural techniques: the condemnation of the crowd

With relative consistency,[2] Persius underlines the importance of private values in opposition to the impercipience of the crowd, so asserting the ethical ramifications of his theoretical statement, *secrete loquimur*, V. 21. The interesting thing is that he tends to end his compositions with harsh words for the common man – the unthinking slave of desire who is beyond the pale of philosophy. In this way structure coincides with a fundamental theme.

Just as he concludes the first satire with rejection of the unfeeling mob, 127 ff., after several condemnatory references to the *populus*,[3] so he ends the sixth with a dismissal of the *profanum vulgus – vende animam lucro* . . . , 75 f. – as well as the fifth, *dixeris haec inter varicosos centuriones* . . . 189 ff. In the latter case he contrasts the true freedom bestowed by philosophy with the corruption of the lives of the majority, 52 ff., and with the false freedom of political franchise, 73 ff., finding that most men are slaves to their appetitive instincts.

Technique is varied somewhat in the second and fourth satires, their conclusions presenting a dismissal of the banal, accompanied by positive recommendations. In the second satire, the empty outward signs of conventional worship – *quin damus id superis, de magna quod dare*

---

[1] Cf. Lucr. VI. 17 ff., *intellegit ibi vitium vas efficere ipsum/omniaque illius vitio corrumpier* intus.

[2] Except for the recommendatory *plebeia . . . beta*, III. 114, and *plebeia . . . prandia*, V. 18.

[3] Note 15, 42 and 63. He takes Callimachean exclusiveness to an extreme, upholding a principle which the interlocutor does not even begin to understand.

lance/*non possit magni Messallae lippa propago,* 71–2, are set against the superiority of inner moral worth – *conpositum ius fasque animo sanctosque recessus*/*mentis,* 73 f. In the fourth, the worthlessness of the common man, with his idea of public repute, is stressed repeatedly through the body of the satire – e.g. *plebecula,* 6; *blando . . . popello,* 15; *discincto . . . vernae,* 22; *populo,* 36; *vicinia,* 46; *populo,* 50 – to end in a contrast between plebeian adulation[1] – *tollat sua munera Cerdo,* 51, and self-knowledge – *tecum habita,* 52.

In the third satire, on the other hand, where possessions and status – e.g. 24 ff. and 73 ff., are contrasted with education in ethics – e.g. 23–4 and 66 ff., criticism of the mindless crowd is concentrated in the middle, lines 77–87 condemning the *gens hircosa centurionum,* the *populus,* and the *multum . . . torosa iuventus* for their blindness. But discrepancy in technique should be no grounds for alarm.[2]

Horace is Persius' forerunner in contempt for the *iudicium vulgi.*[3] Anderson is worth quoting on the matter. Of Hor. *Sat.* I. 6 he writes (1960, p. 230), 'In this Satire Horace sets out to define the relation between high birth and personal value'; then, thanks to metaphors of slavery and sickness, 'politics emerge as a slave's existence: the mob both masters and serves the ambitions; the ambitious enslave themselves to the dubious goal of *gloria,* in the hope of becoming lords of Rome'; again, of Horatian emphasis on friendship, p. 231, 'Ironically, then, the son of a freedman has reached a position next to the great which the common herd regards as political honour and resents, but which in fact bears no real resemblance to the false criteria of political success, since it is ambitionless and informed by the ethical purposes underlying true friendship.' Finally, of *egregio . . . corpore,* 67, on the hypothesis of an etymological pun, we read, p. 233, 'Horace . . . suggests that his character, like the body, escapes the corruptions of the common slavish herd *(grex).*'

[1] I follow Bo's interpretation.
[2] As, e.g., in the case of G. L. Hendrickson, 'The Third Satire of Persius', *CPh* XXIII (1928), 332–42.
[3] *Sat.* I. 6.98.

CHAPTER 5

GRANDEUR AND HUMILITY: JUVENAL AND THE HIGH STYLE

Jahn's note on Pers. I. 20 correctly aligns physical hypertrophy with mental crassness: 'hoc vocat *ingentes*, ut v. 190, *ingentem centurionem*, III. 86, *multum torosam iuventutem*, v. 95, *calonem altum*, ut animum prae corpore neglectum significet.' He might have added II. 71 f., *quin damus id superis de magna quod dare lance/non possit magni Messallae lippa propago*,[1] where size, measured in terms of social importance, is a disqualification from acceptance by the gods, and v. 190, *ingens Pulfenius*, of an immense centurion amused by philosophy. As for the Horatian background to this fastidiousness about size, we can adduce the striking repetitions, *magno magnum* and *grandes . . . /grande* at *Sat.* II. 2.39 and 95–6, debunking the appetite for sheer quantity; *magni quo pueri magnis e centurionibus orti*, I. 6.72–3, an expression of scorn for his insensitive school-mates; the social satire of *magno prognatum . . . magno* at I. 2.70–2, and *magna . . . cena* at II. 6.104; then the philosophic irony of I. 3.136, *magnorum maxime regum*.[2] For *pinguis* in the ironic self-identification of *Ep.* I. 15.24–5:

> pinguis ut inde domum possim Phaeaxque reverti
> scribere te nobis, tibi nos accredere par est

where, with an eye to reformation, Horace allies himself with the materialism of Vala, his addressee,[3] Jahn can once again be invoked, with his comment on *pinguis aqualiculus* at Pers. I. 20:

---

[1] Cf. Ov. *Pont.* IV. 8.39 f., *nec quae de parva dis pauper libat acerra/tura minus grandi quam data lance valent.*

[2] Without *animus*, cf. the theme of small and great – *maioribus uti* – recurring in *Epp.* VII, XVII and XVIII.

[3] Vala and his like are at fault (*vos* at 45 is the clue to interpretation) not Horace, with his mask of the *inconstans*. The Epistle has three subdivisions: an ironic request for information about two places – *Velia* and *Salernum* – in which Horace himself has no real interest; from 26 ff., an implication that the moralist, momentarily pretending to the faults of Vala, has no right

'Eos autem minus sollertes, quibus obesissimus venter, e communi antiquorum sententia dicit Plinius *N.H.* 37.79. Similiter Graeci, Polemo *physiogn.* I. 22, γαστέρες λαγαραὶ καὶ σαρκώδεις, εἰ μαλθακαί εἰσι καὶ ἔξω κρέμανται, ἀνόητον, οἰνόφλυγα καὶ ἀκόλαστον δηλοῦσιν ἄνδρα. Adamant. *Martyr.* II. 12, γαστέρες μεγάλαι, σαρκώδεις, εἰ μὲν μαλθακαὶ εἶεν καὶ ἐκκρεμεῖς, ἀναισθησίαν, οἰνοφλυγίαν, ἀκολασίαν ἐμφαίνουσιν. Neque abludit quod de Catone narrat Plutarchus (*Cat. mai.* 9), τὸν δὲ ὑπέρπαχυν κακίζων 'ποῦ δ' ἄν' ἔφη 'σῶμα τοιοῦτον τῇ πόλει γένοιτο χρήσιμον, οὗ τὸ μεταξὺ λαιμοῦ καὶ βουβώνων πᾶν ὑπὸ τῆς γαστρὸς κατέχεται;'

We might add Alcaeus fr. 129.21, L–P, where Pittacus is reviled by the word φύσγων, and Gell. VI. 22.4, again of Cato, thinking it a disgrace if an *eques* had to be deprived of his horse by the censors, on grounds of excessive fatness: 'if we take the view of Cato, *id profecto existimandum est, non omnino inculpatum neque indesidem visum esse, cuius corpus in tam immodicum modum luxuriasset exuberassetque*'. Apart from general feeling on the subject, it clearly emerges that the satirist had qualms about the moral connotations of the physically gross or fat.

Take, for instance, the relative frequency of *ingens* in the different genres. As opposed to Virgil's 200 incidences – only 32 in the Georgics, never in the *Eclogues*, the usage of the *Aeneid* deriving from Ennius – Ovid's 74, 40 of which occur in the *Metamorphoses*, and even the attenuation of Virgilian precedent by Silius, 79 times, Valerius Flaccus, 69, and Lucan, 33, K. E. Ingvarson[1] counts only 18 incidences in Horace – 12 in the hexameters, 6 in the *Odes* – and 17 in Juvenal, coming to the conclusion '*ingens* est particulièrement un mot épique' (p. 66). I have not studied contexts closely, but would hazard a guess that satiric usage is mainly parodistic, as at Hor. *Sat.* II. 6.111, or disapprobatory, as at Juv. III. 240. At any rate, there is a case for

to pontificate, but nonetheless, in his editorial capacity, is well aware of his own faults and hence may be more virtuous than was apparent on first impressions; lastly, from 42 ff., a statement that Vala is right – Horace means wrong – in basing his values on Mammon.

[1] '*Ingens* dans la poésie et chez Tacite', *Eranos* XLVIII (1950), 66–70, following a hint from Kroll, *Studien zum Verständnis der Römischen Literatur* (Stuttgart 1924; repr. 1964), p. 272, who related the word to Virgil's predilection for hyperbole. From Ennius I. notes *Ann.* 132, 174, 211, 365, 479, 614, and *Scaen.* 367, 381. Lucr. uses *ingens* 20 times.

arguing stylistic aversion from the word in the lower genres, especially satire.

As we might expect, given the principle of correspondence between style and character, letters and βίος, the exponent of the lower forms correlates his attitude of scorn for physical enormity with abhorrence from the grandiose and inflated in literature. Anything *grande, magnum, pingue* or *tumidum* is automatically shunned. In addition to his contempt at I. 14 and 68, Persius spurns pretensions at V. 7, grande *locuturi nebulas Helicone legunto*: the term was apparently a fashionable, rather colloquial word for literary achievement, as we see from Sen. *Ep.* LXXIX. 7, of the Aetna theme, Sen. *Suas.* II. 17, of 'Seneca Grandio', *qui cupiebat* grandia *dicere*, and perhaps Ter. Maur. *de syllab.* 52 ff., *quia iam dicere* grandia/*maturum ingenium negat*/*nec spirant animas fibrae.*[1] As for *magnum* and cognates, we can add Lucil. 388 M, ⟨*illum ego*⟩ *in arce bovem descripsi magnifice* to J. K. Newman's citation of Horace's ironic depiction of the poet at *Sat.* I. 4.43, *ingenium cui sit, cui mens divinior atque os*/magna *sonaturum, des nominis huius honorem*, while discussing 'the non-Alexandrian *magnus*' at Prop. II. 10.11–12 and 19–20.[2] We have already studied examples of 'fatness' in literature, in particular the joke on the *pingue ingenium* transmitted by Callimachus to Virgil and Horace.[3] It might also be observed that at *Catalepton* IX. 64, the vulgar mob is in itself fat: *pingui nil mihi cum populo*. Finally, there is *tumidum*, not a target of the satirists in particular, but an affront to taste at Cat. XCV. 10, *at populus* tumido *gaudeat Antimacho*, and a fault at Quint. XII. 10.12, *M. Tullium suorum homines temporum incessere audebant, ut tumidiorem*, as at Gell. VII. 14.5, *plerumque sufflati atque tumidi fallunt pro uberibus.*[4]

---

[1] Cf. Quint. X. 2.16.

[2] *Augustus and the New Poetry* (*Coll. Latomus* LXXXVIII) (1967), p. 129: *surge, anima, ex* humili: *iam, carmina, sumite vires:*/*Pierides,* magni *nunc erit oris opus*, and *haec ego castra sequar: vates tua castra canendo*/magnus *ero*.

[3] Above, pp. 24 and 57–8.

[4] Cf. e.g. *ad Her.* IV. 10.15, using the body-analogy, *nam ita ut corporis bonam habitudinem* tumor *imitatur saepe, item gravis oratio saepe imperitis videtur ea quae* turget *et* inflata *est*; in a neater, more epigrammatic formulation, Longin. 3.4, κακοὶ δὲ ὄγκοι καὶ ἐπὶ σωμάτων καὶ λόγων οἱ χαῦνοι; Liv. XLV. 23.16, of Asian rhetoric, *tumidus*; Sen. *Contr.* IX. 2.27, *tumidus*,

Having expressed distaste for grossness on related moral and literary grounds, the moralist or satirist tended to take ethical refuge in self-preservation as poor, and small in stature, in an espousal of *parva*, and in the adaptation of a simple style to suit the humble *persona* created. Regarding poverty, the complaint, or boast, was conventional: Callim. *Epigr.* XXXII[1] is followed by e.g. Prop. I. 8 and 14, and Ov. *A.A.* III. 531 ff., with the poor poet/rich rival contrast, also by Horace, in e.g. *Sat.* I. 6, with its depiction of the modest satirist buying vegetables, and by Juvenal in *Sat.* VII, like Theocritus XVI treating the topic of patronage. Newman fairly assesses the ethical and literary aspects of the poverty motif in the smaller genres with, p. 375 n. 5:

> No doubt the poverty of which Callimachus complains had once been a reality. But long after the reality had ceased to exist he maintains the fiction, because poverty is also a stylistic and moral quality – stylistic, because the Callimachean poet rejects the luxury of the grand style, and moral, because in so doing he puts his conscience as an artist before the temptation to seek easy popularity with well-tried pieces.

Lucilius may have employed something like the motif of diminutive stature, depending on the weight we attach to *folliculo* at 622 M, *ego si, qui sum et quo folliculo nunc sum indutus,/non queo.*[2] Horace certainly did, so helping to create an impression of a man so unassuming and straightforward as to be infallible in his pronouncements: how could such a little man be partisan or self-righteous? In the self-portrait of the σφραγίς at *Ep.* I. 20.24, he is *corporis exigui*. Previously, at *Sat.* II. 3.308–11, he had characterised himself as a short man:

'longos imitaris ab imo
ad summum totus moduli bipedalis et idem

X *praef.* 9, *tumor*, X. 1.14, *tumidus*, *Suas.* I. 12, *tumidus*, and 16, *magnifice*; Plin. *Ep.* VII. 12.4, *tumidus, sonans, elatus*, against *pressus, exilis humilis*, IX. 26.5, *tumidus, plenus, immodicus, grandis, altus, enormis*; Quint. XII. 10.16, *inflatus* and *inanis*.

[1] *V.* Trypanis on Callim. *Ia.* III, wrongly including *Epigr.* XXXI and XXVIII, and referring to Wilamowitz, *Hellenistische Dichtung* (Berlin 1924), I, pp. 171 ff.

[2] Cf. the depreciation of *bulga* at 623 M, *ita uti quisque nostrum e bulga est matris in lucem editus.*

corpore maiorem rides Turbonis in armis
spiritum et incessum.'

He did not have to allude to his physique: even if he was short,
there must have been a reason why he chose this particular detail
for self-description. Like Epictetus, who similarly exploited his
lame and feeble constitution, Horace the moralist depicted himself
as the incarnation of humility and simplicity.[1]

Behind his *persona* we occasionally catch glimpses of a tradition
which seems to measure qualification for satirical or abusive
comment, or moral worth, in terms of size. As an example of the
former, there is the Homeric Thersites, probably the prototype
of the diminutive satirist. Many of the ingredients later contribut-
ing to the creation of this figure are found at the opening of *Iliad* II.
Reviling Achilles, Odysseus, and Agamemnon, the ugly bandy-
legged Thersites raises the voice of the simple man against the
motives behind heroic action: in this, not unlike Persius and
Juvenal on effete pretensions to 'Roman' morality. But the violent
treatment he receives from Odysseus casts him as an outsider,
dissociated from the uniformly accepted values of his society, not
a conservative calling the Achaeans back to traditional standards.
In this respect, he is closer to the patronised dwarf-fool than is
the independent reactionary satirist.[2] But his successors are not the
idiot-dwarfs of the Ptolemaic court, and the great houses of the
Empire – the 'moriones', 'stulti' or 'fatui', mentally deficient and
physically deformed creatures who answered a dubious call for
mindless entertainment. His progeny is the intelligent jester of
whom E. Welsford writes:[3]

[1] The low social status of his father, stressed throughout *Sat.* 1. 6 (*libertino
patre natum*) certainly helped. As Anderson, 1960, p. 231, remarks, 'he . . .
gives his father, the emancipated slave, the entire credit for the moral
character which he possesses'.

[2] E. Welsford, *The Fool, his social and literary history* (London 1935),
surprisingly overlooks Thersites. We tend to think of satire as a conflict
between revolution and orthodoxy, the individual looking to the future,
society to the origins of the *status quo*. With the exception of Thersites, the
opposite is true of ancient satire: the conservative moralist, even if reduced
to membership of a minority group, recalled fallen society to the ethical
archaism to which, *en masse*, it pretended to subscribe.

[3] *Ibid.* pp. 58–60, referring n. 3 to, *inter alia*, Suet. *Dom.* 4 and *Tib.* 61.

occasionally the dwarf-fools were quite sane and tickled their master's sense of humour as well as their degenerate curiosity. Suetonius tells us that when Domitian attended gladiatorial shows 'there always stood at his feet a small boy clad in scarlet, with an abnormally small head, with whom he used to talk a great deal, and sometimes seriously' . . . he records a daring rebuke offered to Tiberius by one of the dwarfs who stood among the jesters (*copreas*) at the Imperial dinner-table.

Though Catullus is hardly comparable, it might be worth recalling Caesar's clement attitude to the fifty-seventh poem, and possibly the twenty-ninth, as an instance of the acceptability of abuse at a higher social level.[1] For illustration of moral worth gauged by stature before the writings of Horace, supply seems almost deficient. But there is Archilochus fr. 60 D, where the iambist, not, admittedly, representing himself as a small man, employs an ethical antithesis based on the associations of physical size:

> οὐ φιλέω μέγαν στρατηγὸν οὐδὲ διαπεπλιγμένον
> οὐδὲ βοστρύχοισι γαῦρον οὐδ' ὑπεξυρημένον·
> ἀλλά μοι σμικρός τις εἴη καὶ περὶ κνήμας ἰδεῖν
> ῥοικός, ἀσφαλέως βεβηκὼς ποσσί, καρδίης πλέως.

The σμικρός here has some of the bodily characteristics of Thersites. But he has since acquired a degree of respect and social integration as a result of his creator's disregard for the heroic code. Later there is the Catullan *salaputium disertum*, LIII.

Perhaps partly contributory to Horace's self-portrait, certainly preparatory for correlation between βίος and style, is the principle, *parvum parva decent*.[2] Confining myself to Horatian material, I would draw attention to the way this principle receives immediate physical realisation in an opposition between humble Tibur and regal Rome, so substantiating professions of a modest life-style, *Ep.* I. 7.44–5:

> mihi iam non regia Roma,
> sed vacuum Tibur placet aut imbelle Tarentum.

Then, with the irony and didactic intent already mentioned with

---

[1] Suet. *Iul.* 73.   [2] Hor. *Ep.* I. 7.44.

regard to Vala, there is the mock inconstancy of *Ep.* I. 15.42–3 and 44–6, epitomising two attitudes to life, first, in terms of *parva*:

> nam tuta et *parvola* laudo,
> cum res deficiunt, satis inter vilia fortis;

then, in terms of *magna*:

> verum ubi quid melius contingit et unctius, idem
> vos[1] sapere et solos aio bene vivere, quorum
> conspicitur nitidis fundata pecunia villis.

Of course, Horace himself opts for *parvola*, which, in the form of *parvo . . . uti* at I. 10.41 in the fable of the stag and the horse, had been stipulated as a prerequisite of freedom.[2]

Next, there is the subject of *victus tenuis*,[3] treated by H. Mette '*genus tenue* und *mensa tenuis* bei Horaz',[4] which, as the title implies, pleads a case for correspondence between lowliness of style and sustenance. Mette is mainly concerned with the *Odes*, but their moralising trends should not be regarded as too disparate from those of the hexameter works. From the general precept, *vivitur parvo bene*, *Carm.* II. 16.13, which conjures up the earlier modesty of *Sat.* II. 6.1, *modus agri non ita magnus*, we pass on to *Carm.* I. 31.15 f., *me pascunt olivae,/me cichorea levesque malvae*, and thence to III. 29.11 ff., *omitte mirari beatae/fumum et opes strepitumque Romae./plerumque gratae divitibus vices/mundaeque parvo sub lare pauperum/cenae sine aulaeis et ostro/sollicitam explicuere frontem*. Finally, there is the ideal of eating a simple meal by a stream at *Ep.* I. 14.35, a composition structured round a

---

[1] Again, note the crucial pronoun, dissociating Horace from Vala and his kind.

[2] On occasions the normally scornful diminutive recommends simplicity, as at e.g. Hor. *Sat.* I. 1.33, *parvola*, 56, *fonticulo* (where the intended contempt turns against the speaker's stupid preference for the *magnum flumen*), and 59, *tantuli*.

[3] The phrase occurs at Cic. *T.D.* III. 20.49 and v. 32.89; cf. *tenuitas victus M'. Curii*, Cic. *Parad.* 1.12, also Lucian *Nigrinus* 26, where the eponym is endowed with the qualities of the Stoic moralist: τῆς τροφῆς τὸ ἀπέριττον (= *victus tenuis*) καὶ τῶν γυμνασίων τὸ σύμμετρον καὶ τοῦ προσώπου τὸ αἰδέσιμον καὶ τῆς ἐσθῆτος τὸ μέτριον, ἐφ' ἅπασι δὲ τούτοις τῆς διανοίας τὸ ἡρμοσμένον καὶ τὸ ἥμερον τοῦ τρόπου.

[4] *MH* XVIII (1961), 136 ff.

contrast between town and country: *cena brevis iuvat et prope rivum somnus in herba.*[1]

Stylistic ideology is now tailored to match βίος, most noticeably in Horace, whose *persona* borders on the facile, but also in Lucilius, despite, or perhaps because of, his gentlemanly status, and in Persius, whose life-style is more reserved than modest, an implied datum rather than a characteristic constantly presented for observation by an élite. Lucilius, whom we have already seen spurning grandiosity,[2] and perhaps subscribing to the motif of diminutive stature, not only made several assertions of stylistic humility – 590–1 M, *ego ubi quem ex praecordiis/ecfero versum*; 1279, *qui schedium fa⟨cio⟩*; 688–9, *... versibus Lucilius/quibus potest impertit* – but was also recognised as an exponent of the plain style by later critics, for whom he was variously *doctus, urbanus, comis, humilis* and *gracilis*.[3] That we need not allow for great bias in the archaising second-century *testimonia* is shown by the use of the word *humilitas* on the part of the classicistic Petronius.[4] Horace's usual self-depreciation is easily illustrated by such passages as *Sat.* I. 4.17–18, *di bene fecerunt, inopis me quodque pusilli/finxerunt animi, raro et perpauca loquentis*, and I. 10.88–9, *quibus haec, sint qualiacumque,/adridere velim*; then there is the *Musa pedestris* of II. 6.17, and the *sermones humi repentes* of *Ep.* II. 1.250. Lastly, the calculated but introverted diffidence of Persius finds expression in e.g. prol. 6, *semipaganus*, Sat. I. 45–6, *si forte quid aptius exit/(quando haec rara avis est)*, V. 14–15, *verba*

---

[1] Cf. Lucr. II. 20 ff., esp. 29 ff., *cum tamen inter se prostrati in gramine molli/ propter aquae rivum sub ramis arboris altae/non magnis opibus iucunde corpora curant*. In a military context, opposing pastoral and war, Corn. Sev. fr. 11 M, *stratique per herbam/' hic meus est' dixere ' dies'* (perhaps from Virg. *Georg.* II. 527 and *Aen.* IX. 164).

[2] 388 M above; below, pp. 174 n. 1, on his parodies of epic and tragedy.

[3] Cf. Cic. *de Or.* II. 6.25, *homo* doctus *et* perurbanus (*ibid.* I. 16.72 for the same adjectives), *Fin.* I. 7, on his *urbanitas*, Hor. *Sat.* I. 10.65, comis *et* urbanus; D'Alton, p. 56 n. 6, 'Several of the later critics lay stress on the plain and commonplace character of his satires', citing Gell. VI. 14.6, *vera autem et propria huiuscemodi formarum exempla* (the three styles) *in Latina lingua M. Varro esse dicit* ubertatis Pacuvium, gracilitatis Lucilium, mediocritatis Terentium, Petron. 4.5 (next note), and Fronto II p. 48, *in poetis autem quis ignorat ut* gracilis *sit Lucilius.*

[4] 4.5, *schedium Lucilianae humilitatis.*

togae sequeris . . . /ore teres modico and 18, *plebeiaque prandia noris.*
Then Juvenal deserted the standards of his three predecessors,
dropping their *sermo* style to create a new idiom in which epic
or tragic diction became a tool of satire.

JUVENAL AND THE HIGH STYLE

In his first satire, besides adopting the pose of street-corner
realism – *nonne libet medio ceras implere capaces/quadrivio?*, 63[1] –
and amidst reiterated statements of his calling for the genre,
Juvenal appropriates an imagery previously used by the adherents
of simplicity to condemn epic and tragedy, not only for description of his own manner, but also that of Lucilius. Open plain and
full canvas, symbols for the higher genres, replace the untrodden
path and small boat of the temperate. In addition, the military
vocabulary of epic is enlisted. Satire is no longer the self-consciously unpretentious form of Lucilius, Horace, and Persius.
Moral indictment of epic and tragedy is avoided, so leaving room
for usurping their techniques. Rejection takes place on grounds
of the irrelevance and unreality of myth, a tried topic;[2] theme is
dismissed, style retained.[3]

[1] Highet rightly notes the 'incoherence' of Juv. 1 as a facet of this realism;
but elsewhere confuses the contrived sound of sincerity with the actual
quality.
[2] Above, p. 12. Anderson, 'Venusina lucerna: the Horatian model for
Juvenal', *TAPA* xcii (1961), 8–9 correctly notes that Juvenal 'denies the
validity of epic in his time, in order to raise *Satura* up to the level of the
grand style and so replace the counterfeit topics and emotions of epic and
tragedy'. I dissent with amazement from his thesis that the Horace of the
Odes, not the *Satires*, is the model for Juvenal 1: 'high indignation' is a
dangerous guide in literary history.
[3] *V*. Anderson in *YCS* xv (1957), 34 ff., 'From the time of Lucilius, the
satirist regularly felt obliged to explain his concept of his genre in a
Program Satire which, in the writings of Horace and Persius, followed the
pattern set by Lucilius. Juvenal, too, faces the same problem and he answers the potential questions of his readers in *Satire* 1 by covering the
traditional themes: (1) The superiority of epic and the other genres of
great poetry to satire; (2) the style appropriate to satire; (3) the moral
responsibility of the satirist.' Categories (1) and (2) constitute the literary
justification for writing satire, (3) the social and moral. Where Horace and
Juvenal separate the two reasons for writing satire, Persius combines them.
I disagree with Anderson's contention that Juvenal blurs the distinction

The new conception has been noticed,[1] but without proper analysis of the clues in the first satire. Most frequently cited is VI. 634–6:

> fingimus haec, altum satura sumente cothurnum,
> scilicet, et finem egressi legemque priorum[2]
> grande Sophocleo carmen bacchamur hiatu.

The style of a previously alien genre has been adopted. Likewise, at XV. 29, *cunctis graviora cothurnis*, present crimes are worse than those of tragedy. Cross-reference between present and fictitious past is indicative of the hyperbole inherent in Juvenal's attitude to vice. Epic and tragic characters are revived to populate contemporary Rome: an Automedon at I. 61, an Achilles at III. 278, a Meleager at V. 115, a Medea at VI. 634 f., a spectacular, but ridiculous Neronian Orestes at VIII. 211 ff., and an Iphigeneia at XII. 119. Deflation through appeal to an ideal epic norm is the usual technique.

In his programme, Juvenal is warned from the dangers of composing through stolen military imagery, 168–70:

> tecum prius ergo voluta
> haec animo ante tubas: galeatum sero duelli
> paenitet.

After recommending the safety of conventional epic – *Aeneid* and *Iliad*, 162–3 – the interlocutor presents the satirist as a soldier on the point of joining battle: *galeatum, duelli*[3] and *ante*

---

between the two parts of the programme ('fuses them in his central theme, the nature of indignation') against Horatian separation (who 'carefully distinguishes'): the opposite is true, Horace's apologies a medley in arrangement, Juvenal's programme a tract dividing style from morals. Nor can I agree with his insistence on *indignatio*: the central theme of Juv. 1 is the prevalence of vice which leads to *indignatio*, not the nature of the mood itself.

[1] By e.g. I. G. Scott, *Juvenal's Grand Style*, Smith College Class. Studies 8 (Northampton, Mass. 1927), and Anderson, below, p. 169 n. 2.

[2] *V.* Brink on Hor. *A.P.* 135, esp. Hor. *Sat.* II. 1.1–2, *ultra/legem tendere opus*, and Juv. VII. 102, *sic ingens rerum numerus iubet atque operum lex*; add Sen. *Tranqu. An.* I. 14, *oblitus tum legis pressiorisque iudicii, sublimius feror, et ore non meo*, on adopting a higher style than normal, and Quint. X. 2.22, *sua cuique proposita lex, suus cuique decor est; nam nec comoedia in cothurnos assurgit nec contra tragoedia socculo ingreditur.*

[3] An archaism, like *induperator* (not *metri gratia*: other words were available) at IV. 29, a poem where the epic element is pronounced, and X. 138: noted by Mayor, also citing *defendier* (mainly, however, Plautus, Terence and inscriptions) in the same line as *tuba*, XV. 157, another epic piece.

tubas[1] convey a novel grandiosity. Previous satire, unlike elegy,[2] had mostly refrained from bellicose metaphor.[3]

Secondly, after saying that vice is now at its peak,[4] Juvenal illustrates his high ambitions with the nautical image of 149 f.:

> utere velis,
> totos pande sinus. dicas hic forsitan 'unde
> ingenium par materiae?'

The ship of poetry is to be launched under full sail. Originating in Pindar,[5] the metaphor came to symbolise the magnitude of an author's undertaking: open sea and full sail mirror the efforts of the higher genres, while a calm expanse of coastal water, sailed

---

[1] Similarly elevated, despite Friedländer's adoption of Otto's verdict, p. 322, 'sprichwörtlich', and Conington's comparable interpretation of Virg. *Aen.* XI. 424. Our only evidence for proverbial status is Petron. 44.9, *sic illius vox crescebat tamquam tuba*, probably a conscious vernacular derivation from the conventional military enhancement of unwarlike oratory, as at *Laus Pisonis* 27-8, *licet exercere togatae/munia militiae*, 58, *densaque vibrata iaculari fulmina lingua*; Tac. *Dial.* 5.4 f., answered by 12.2, *in locum teli*; 10.5, *in forum et ad causas et ad vera proelia voco*; 26.5, (Cassius Severus) *ipsis quibus utitur armis incompositus et studio feriendi plerumque deiectus, non pugnat, sed nixatur*; 34.5, *ferro, non rudibus dimicantes*; Mart. VIII. 3.21-2, the trumpet symbolising epic against the pipe of epigram, *angusta cantare licet videaris avena,/dum tua multorum vincat avena tubas*; Quint. X. 1.29-30; Van Hook, pp. 24 f. Mayor sees the point, 'The metaphor is kept up from 165 *ensis*', citing epic material on 169: *Aen.* XI. 424, *cur ante tubam tremor occupat artus?*; Sil. IX. 50-2, *nonne vides . . . / quamque fluant arma ante tubas?*; St. *Theb.* VI. 147, *ante tubas ferrumque*; Claud. *in Ruf.* I. 333 (imitating Statius); *Laud. Stil.* I. 192, *ante tubam*. Yet again in the epic context of XV (*v.* last note), *tuba* appears at 52, *animis ardentibus haec tuba rixae*.

[2] In conceits as widely varied as the banal *militat omnis amans*, Ov. *Am.* I. 9.1, and the subtle *tum vero longas condimus Iliadas*, Prop. II. 1.14.

[3] Scott, *Juvenal's Grand Style*, p. 32 n. 47 correctly notes Juv. I. 91 and II. 46 as examples of military metaphor: but VII. 10 does not qualify, nor do Hor. *Sat.* I. 4.30, 6.24 and II. 7.74, with the unwarranted comment, 'Such metaphors are common in Horace.'

[4] *V.* D. A. Kidd, *CQ* ns XIV (1964), 103 f., referring *in praecipiti . . . stetit* to Juvenal's other metaphors of fall from a dangerous height (but these are not private to J.: X. 103-7 is not necessary for interpretation), correctly translating 'every vice is now in a precarious position'.

[5] *Nem.* V. 51, ἀνὰ δ' ἱστία τεῖνον πρὸς ζυγὸν καρχασίου; *Pyth.* IV. 3, αὔξῃς οὖρον ὕμνων; XI. 39, ἄνεμος ἔξω πλόον ἔβαλε; *Nem.* VI. 28, εὔθυν' . . . Μοῖσα, οὖρον ἐπέων; III. 27, ἐμὸν πλόον (Wimmel, p. 228; cf. Kambylis, pp. 149 ff., 'Das Motiv der Selbstbescheidung im Bilde der Seefahrt').

by a small boat, images less energetic ventures.[1] In the relevant former case, Juvenal's imagery has several parallels: unafraid of the depths before him, the writer embarks under full canvas. For example, in the epic invocation of Maecenas towards the beginning of the second *Georgic*, Virgil writes, 41:

> pelagoque volans da vela patenti.[2]

Similar language measures the ambitions of Pythagoras' song at Ov. *Met.* xv. 176 f.:

> et quoniam magno feror aequore plenaque ventis
> vela dedi,

with which we can compare *Fasti* ii. 3–4:

> nunc primum velis, elegi, maioribus itis:
> exiguum, memini, nuper eratis opus

and iv. 729–30:

> navalibus exi
> puppis! habent ventos iam mea vela suos.

Then later, during an account of his various writings, there is *Tr.* ii. 547 f.:

> ne tamen omne meum credas opus esse remissum
> saepe dedi nostrae grandia vela rati

enumerating the *Fasti*, *Medea*, and *Metamorphoses* as examples of the higher poetry composed on his adventurous voyages. Except for the conventional self-disparagement of i. 79–80, Juvenal ignores prior theory on humility, to magnify satire by stealing imagery from the higher literary forms. Poetic analogues apart, indiscriminate citation of material[3] has caused confusion,

---

[1] For the latter cf. e.g. Prop. iii. 9.3–4, *quid me scribendi tam vastum mittis in aequor?/non sunt apta meae grandia vela rati*, and 35–6, with the pregnant epithets *tumidus* and *exiguus, non ego velifera tumidum mare findo carina:/tota sub exiguo flumine nostra mora est*; also, Apollo's Callimachean intervention at Hor. *Carm.* iv. 15.3–4, *ne parva Tyrrhenum per aequor/vela darem*.

[2] Cf. the excuse for not writing about horticulture, *Georg.* iv. 116 ff., *extremo ni iam sub fine laborum/vela traham et terris festinem advertere proram,/ forsitan … / … canerem*.

[3] Without regard for tone, Pind. *Pyth.* i. 91 and *Isthm.* ii. 40 (Mayor); Sen. *de Ira* ii. 31.5 (Friedländer), and Hor. *Carm.* ii. 10.22 (implied by Friedländer's reference to Otto).

submerging the most pertinent parallels – mainly from Pliny – which deal with the various manifestations of the *genus grande*. From the rather neutral Cic. *T.D.* IV. 9, *panderem vela orationis*, we progress to more extended formulations, such as Plin. *Ep.* VI. 33.10, *dedimus vela indignationi, dedimus irae, dedimus dolori, et in amplissima causa quasi magno mari pluribus ventis sumus vecti*; the nautical representation of *miseratio* at II. 11.3, *omniaque actionis suae vela vir movendarum lacrimarum peritissimus quodam velut vento miserationis implevit*; the elevated depiction of a *consolatio* at IV. 20.2, *est opus pulchrum validum acre sublime, varium elegans purum figuratum, spatiosum etiam et cum magna laude diffusum, in quo tu ingenii simul dolorisque velis latissime vectus es*; and finally, of historiography, VIII. 4.5, *proinde iure vatum invocatis dis, et inter deos ipso, cuius res opera consilia dicturus es, immitte rudentes, pande vela ac, siquando alias, toto ingenio vehere*. So Juvenal's *utere velis,/totos pande sinus*, though conventional, is an exhortation to aspire to ὕψος in the arraignment of vice. But where can a writer of sufficient gifts be found to treat the new grandeur arrogated by satire: *unde/ingenium par materiae?* We return to apologetics, where the poet pondered the adequacy of his *ingenium* or *vires* for his proposed *materia*. Horace epitomises the doctrine at *A.P.* 38 f.:

> sumite materiam vestris, qui scribitis, aequam
> viribus et versate diu, quid ferre recusent,[1]
> quid valeant umeri.

He who attempts the higher themes must be richly endowed, otherwise he is foiled by their magnitude, Ov. *Tr.* II. 335–6:

> divitis ingenii est immania Caesaris acta
> condere, materia ne superetur opus.

Juvenal's *materia* is the same, requiring a similarly powerful *ingenium*, except that Roman vice, not noble exploits, is the subject which now demands magniloquence.

---

[1] *V.* Brink *ad loc.*, citing *Ep.* II. 1.259, *Epict.* III. 15.9 for the motif, and referring to Otto, sv *umeri*. Add Hor. *Sat.* II. 1.12–13, *cupidum, pater optime, vires/deficiunt*, Ov. *Am.* III. 1.25, *materia premis ingenium; cane facta virorum*, and *Tr.* II. 531 f., *invida me spatio natura coercuit arto,/ingenio vires exiguasque dedit*; Wimmel, sv *vires* (fehlende), in his Stichwortindex.

There remains the representation of Lucilius. Twice during the first satire the prehistory of the genre is coloured in such a way as to imply that its *inventor* had similar inclinations towards epic. Horace begins the falsification of the Lucilian *persona*, and is followed by Persius.[1] Juvenal surpasses both, depicting the founder figure as a raging warrior, and as a grandiose charioteer.[2] Firstly, the warrior, at I. 165–6:

> ense velut stricto quotiens Lucilius ardens
> infremuit. . .

Admittedly, Horace had likened his satiric pen to a supposedly defensive sword at *Sat.* II. 1.40: but he made no consistent use of epic devices, nor did he depict Lucilius in military dress. After *ense*, there is *infremuit*, a verb belonging to the language of epic,[3] and *ardens*, descriptive of indignation (which required the high

---

[1] Though H. says Lucilius' admirers called him *comis et urbanus*, *Sat.* I. 10.65, he distorts the picture at II. 1.63, *cum est Lucilius ausus/primus in hunc operis componere carmina morem,/detrahere et pellem nitidus qua quisque per ora/cederet, introrsum turpis* (admittedly, preceded by e.g. *ad Fam.* XII. 16.3), as does P. at I. 114–15, *secuit Lucilius urbem,/te Lupe, te Muci, et genuinum fregit in illis*. I. Jack, *Augustan Satire* (Oxford 1952), shows, e.g. p. 137, that received opinion on Roman satire (add several other genres and authors) is to a large degree derived from Renaissance criticism.

[2] Anderson, *TAPA* XCII (1961), 12 n. 25, has noticed the epic colour of the portrait: 'Juvenal represents Lucilius in a manner quite different from his predecessors Horace and Persius. For Horace, he is many things, but most of all a delightful, outspoken type who belongs in the setting of a *convivium* [not true: *v.* last note]. Persius in I. 114–15 emphasises the invective in Lucilius' *Satires*. In doing so, he attributes no grandeur to the satirist, but develops an image of an animal biting people. When Juvenal describes Lucilius, he makes him into an epic hero, a portrayal which he can make only by ignoring those large portions of Lucilius' writings in which humorous confessions and good-natured jokes provide the dominant note. The chariot metaphor in I. 19–20 goes with an epic periphrasis, *magnus Auruncae alumnus*, which effectively exalts Lucilius into epic stature. Similarly, *Lucilius ardens* wearing armour and fighting his mighty battles against vice is a Lucilius created after Juvenal's image rather than a Lucilius corresponding to the great satirist of the second century B.C.' More weight should be attached to the original Lucilius, to the falsifications of Horace and Persius, and to the connexion of Juvenal's portrait with literary apologetics.

[3] *V.* Mayor *ad loc.*, 'A poetic and not common word, chiefly, if not always, used in the perfect', citing typically epic *loci*: Virg. *Aen.* VIII. 711, of a boar; Sil. XI. 245, of a lion; Val. Fl. I. 706–7, of a band of warriors.

style), and strong emotion, along with *gravis* and *acer*, at Cic. *Or.*
99; also of intensity, in Quintilian's verdict on Lucan, X. 1.90.[1]
Lucilius would have been surprised, given that he reserved
grandiosity for parody,[2] having himself professed a plain style,
the refined simplicity of which was recognised by later writers.[3]
Juvenal has deliberately reinterpreted the already prejudiced
satiric portrait of the Lucilian manner.

Next, the image of the charioteer, I. 19–20:

> cur tamen hoc potius libeat decurrere campo
> per quem magnus equos Auruncae flexit alumnus.

Satiric *humilitas* is betrayed outright by the epithet *magnus*: we
have observed the adjective, consorting with *ingens* and *grandis*,
as a vehicle for ridicule of pretence and bombast. Similarly out
of place in a description of a writer who had no time for the
ornamental is the large periphrasis *Auruncae ... alumnus*, a
collocation as heavy and unjustified as *magnus*.[4] With the
imagery of the plain and the chariot we are back in the realm of
poetics: as with the ship and its sails, the size of the chariot
and the terrain of the journey indicate the scope of an author's
aspirations. Callimachus wanted a light carriage and untrodden
paths, spurning the heavy wagon and the wide road, *Aetia* prol.
1.25 ff.:

> πρὸς δέ σε] καὶ τόδ' ἄνωγα, τὰ μὴ πατέουσιν ἅμαξαι
> τὰ στείβειν, ἑτέρων δ' ἴχνια μὴ καθ' ὁμὰ
> δίφρον ἐλ]ᾶν μηδ' οἶμον ἀνὰ πλατύν, ἀλλὰ κελεύθους
> ἀτρίπτο]υς, εἰ καὶ στεινοτέρην ἐλάσεις.

---

[1] *Lucanus ardens et concitatus et sententiis clarissimus.* Rudd p. 110, citing
Cic. *Or.* 99 above, surprisingly interprets J.'s picture of Lucilius as objective
evidence, adducing his representation as an *acer et violentus poeta* at Macrob.
III. 16.17 (cf. Scott, *Juvenal's Grand Style*, p. 114, 'Lucilius is Juvenal's
closer model, as he himself states in his introductory satire', again interpreting literally): both characterisations derive from the prejudiced Horatian tradition.

[2] Below, p. 174 n. 1. Note also his strictures on Albucius' Asianist oratory
and pretentious Graecisms, above, p. 24.

[3] Above, p. 163 and n. 3.

[4] Cf. e.g. the similar periphrasis, *incidit Hadriaci spatium admirabile rhombi*,
Juv. IV. 39, in a composition loaded with epic reminiscence.

While playing the part of self-appointed successor, Propertius placed similarly exclusive precepts in the mouth of Apollo, III. 3.18:

> mollia sunt parvis prata terenda rotis

after remarking that the highway is not the path to the Muses, III. 1.13–14:

> quid frustra missis in me certatis habenis?
> non datur ad Musas currere lata via.

Juvenal, however, replaces the light chariot and undiscovered path with open plain and horses; in this, like another but different Propertius, who, while toying with the idea of writing epic in obeisance to a social programme which did not favour undiluted Callimacheanism, spoke of his unintended project as follows, II. 10.1 ff.:

> sed tempus lustrare aliis Helicona choreis,
> et campum Haemonio iam dare tempus equo.
> iam libet et fortes memorare ad proelia turmas
> et Romana mei dicere castra ducis.

Finally resorting to quasi-Augustan themes, he spurs on a horse which would have languished in love-elegy, but was strenuous enough for his new undertaking, IV. 1.69–70:

> sacra diesque canam et cognomina prisca locorum:
> has meus ad metas sudet oportet equus.

Comparable are the tragic horses in Ovid's farewell to elegy, *Am.* III. 15.18:

> pulsanda est magnis area maior equis

or the earlier Virgilian representation of increasing ambitions through the image of a triumphal chariot, *Georg.* III. 18:

> centum quadriiugos agitabo ad flumina currus.

Juvenal's expansive *decurrere*,[1] his horses[2] and his plain – along

---

[1] The prefix suggests a sweeping movement across the whole of a plain, perhaps a military manoeuvre.

[2] Rudd p. 110, referring to *Or.* 128 on the high style, notes that Cicero has the image of a charging horse in mind: this bears on Juvenal, not Lucilius. For imagery from horse-riding cf. Quint. IX. 4.113; VIII *pr.* 27 (too much

with *magnus*, the periphrasis, and the nautical imagery – effect a break with tradition. Lucilius would have been taken aback,[1] both by the distortion of literary history, and by the new conception of genre, out of which Juvenal emerges as a satirist equipped with monumental resources.

How do we explain his decision to part with convention? The most plausible answer is discontent with the Lucilio-Horatian manner, perpetuated in compressed form by Persius. Perhaps he felt that his predecessors were somewhat ineffectual: vice is rampant, but how can the business of its castigation and correction be fulfilled by writers who pride themselves on humility and exclusiveness? As long as it maintained connexion with the apologetics of the small-scale genre, there was something too withdrawn, too refined about the form. How could an originally formalistic *jeu d'esprit*, self-conscious about its stylistic peculiarities, contain the moral purpose of the social malcontent? I do not mean to suggest that Juvenal dropped the normal pose, and its concomitant style, out of reformatory zeal, in order to reach a wider, less exclusive audience. But a semblance of pertinence mattered, apart from personal tenets and envisaged audience. Assuming superiority, and hence dispensing with the literary posturings – too often self-justificatory – which had deflected previous satirists from a primary concern with morality, epic style had a broader appeal, with its wide range of themes of general consequence. Or at least its themes ought to have been of general consequence. Noting the shortcomings of contemporary mythological epic, Juvenal substituted new material for old. Through the exchange, Roman vice became as monstrous and portentous as anything in the fictions of epic or tragedy. Juvenal's vision of its proportions was the decisive factor: the *materia* offered by life superseded that of myth in its horrific magnitude. It is only in the light of his predecessors' example that we can speak of a breach of decorum. Given his conception of his theme, Juvenal actually observed the dictates of literary propriety. His

care in the selection of words *cursum dicendi refrenat*); Scott, *Juvenal's Grand Style*, p. 32 n. 47, on racecourse metaphors in Juvenal.

[1] *V.* D'Alton, p. 56, 'He [*sc.* J.] regards himself as his lineal descendant, but it is doubtful if Lucilius would have shown much sympathy with Juvenal's grand manner.'

ψόγος deserved the high style.[1] Lucilius started off in the wrong direction.[2]

[1] *V.* D'Alton, p. 360, 'Invective is the proper weapon when one is dealing with great crimes', citing n. 9, Ar. *Rhet.* III. 7.3, Cic. *de Or.* II. 237–8 and *Or.* 88. On invective as opposed to *sermo* (Lucilius subscribed to the last), he cites p. 56 n. 2, Cic. *de Or.* III. 177, *Or.* 64, *de Off.* I. 132, II. 48; Fiske, pp. 114 ff., and M. A. Grant, *The Ancient Rhetorical Theories of the Laughable*, University of Wisconsin Studies XXI, pp. 131 ff.

[2] Scott's explanations of Juvenal's revolution, p. 113, are (i) that he was 'a true product of his age, an age when writing and speaking tended towards luxuriance and over-emphasis', and (ii) that it was 'due partly to lack of interest in nice distinctions of style'. But writers are as much the causes as effects of their ages: such determinism serves only to automate Latin literature, abandoning necessarily rhetorical quality for generalisations on quantity. That J. was aware of the *lex operis* is attested by VI. 635 ff. (p. 165 and n. 2): we cannot therefore create a first-century victim of promiscuity amongst the genres, manifested at a higher level by, e.g., blurred distinctions between prose and poetry (cf. H. Bardon, 'Poètes et prosateurs', *REA* XLIV (1942), 52–64). Scott's two proposals require a relentless internal evolution in Latin poetry, undirected by individual writers: which is not to say that I have any answer to the question raised by Pers. III. 53–5, *quaeque docet sapiens bracatis inlita medis/porticus, insomnis quibus et detonsa iuventus/invigilat, siliquis et grandi pasta polenta,* a bombastic periphrasis to the detriment of positive values. I see no reason for the circumlocution, but feel disinclined to resort to mechanistic explanation, invoking the unguided advance of 'rhetoric'.

ACCIUS AND PACUVIUS AT PERSIUS I. 76–8

The matter of the punctuation and ascription of 76–8 presents various difficulties:

> est nunc Brisaei quem venosus liber Acci,
> sunt quos Pacuviusque et verrucosa moretur
> Antiopa aerumnis cor luctificabile fulta.

If Persius speaks the words as a question, not as a statement, we have the anomaly of a satirist espousing the cause of an inflated and outmoded genre – this, in complete contradiction to the tradition bequeathed by Lucilius and Horace.[1] If the interlocutor speaks them as a question, the position is much the same: for scornful dismissal by the interlocutor implies that the satirist favours the awkward archaic cause.[2]

Another problem, concerning the *monitus* and *sartago loquendi* of the subsequent passage, arises from the assumption of an interrogative, 79 ff.:

> hos pueris monitus patres infundere lippos
> cum videas, quaerisne unde haec sartago loquendi
> venerit in linguas . . . ?

---

[1] For Lucilian parody of tragedy, *v.* Marx vol. I p. 100, 'Pacuvii imitatio', e.g. frs. 597–600, a travesty of his *Antiopa, perdita inluvie atque insomnia*, fr. 5 (9) R²; also 653–7, 794, 875 M; Hor. *Sat.* I. 10.53, for Lucilius and Accius. His attitude may have derived from Callimachus, who, despite the fact that he wrote tragedies (below, p. 183), assailed tragedians at *Iamb.* II. 12–13, οἱ δὲ τραγῳδοὶ τῶν θάλασσαν οἰ[κεύντων/ἔχουσι φωνήν. For epic parody, Marx *ibid.* 'Enni imitatio aut irrisio'; J. H. Waszink, 'The Proem of the Annales of Ennius', *Mnem.* ser. 4, XIII (1950), 215–40, on the reference to 1008 M, *quantum haurire animus Musarum fontibus gestit*, to Enn. *Ann.* fr. 215 and 217 V, and Hor. *Sat.* I. 10.54; also, e.g., 1190 M (Serv. ad *Aen.* XI. 602), then Hor. *Sat.* I. 2.37–8. Little can be gleaned from the allusions to Ennius at Hor. *Ep.* I. 19.7 and *A.P.* 259 f. But in general, note H.'s objections to the taste for archaic literature at *Ep.* II. 1.18 ff., esp. 50 ff.; also Juv. I. 4 ff.

[2] P. himself parodies Ennius at *Prol.* 1–3 (*v.* Witke, *Latin Satire*, p. 81 n. 3 for bibliography) and VI. 9–11 (*v.* J. H. Waszink, '*Varia et exegetica*', *Mnem.* ser. 3, XI (1943), pp. 68–71). When archaisms, e.g. *patranti* 18, are used in the first satire, the effect is contemptuous.

If Persius has lamented the neglect of archaic tragedy by terminating 76–8 with a question-mark, the topics of paternal advice and corruption of poetic diction are left suspended, devoid of acceptable relationship to the enquiry which immediately precedes their introduction: the sole, and exceptionally weak solution would be to suppose that Persius' question implies that the old men have warned the youth away from archaic literature. This harsh sequence of thought would follow with greater ease if the interlocutor had dismissed archaic tragedy with a contemptuous question. But since this involves a satirist in a very un-satirical attitude towards a traditionally abhorred genre – what the interlocutor rejects, Persius necessarily espouses – we must abandon this approach even though *monitus* and *sartago loquendi* would now be partly, though wrongly, explicable. The warnings of the old are to steer clear of archaic tragedy, and the degeneration of poetic diction is, in Persius' eyes, the result of the implementation of those very warn-ings: he is left to tell his interlocutor that the reason for the decadence of the contemporary literary scene is a misguided refusal to see the true worth of archaic tragedy. If the teachers of the young would only mend their ways, then poetic diction might be reinvigorated by the infusion of *sesquipedalia verba*.[1]

A question-mark after *fulta* is clearly impossible: Persius attacks the taste for Accius and Pacuvius. I therefore dissent from the punctuation of C. F. Hermann, S. G. Owen, and Clausen; also from Villeneuve,[2] who refuses to associate a liking for Accius and Pacuvius, since they have 'encore de la virilité', with 'l'élégance artificielle et énervée de la poésie moderne'; from H. J. Rose,[3] who seems to think there was no archaising school to attack in Persius' day, and states that the sense is 'when their masters and pastors tell the schoolboys that the classics are rubbish (poor blind leaders of the blind!) is it any wonder that our modern style is as the crackling of thorns under a pot?'; and from Dessen's interpretation, p. 28 n. 35, following Rose and R. Marache.[4]

The truth is seen by, amongst others, Fiske:[5] 'we find that Persius like Horace assails the fondness for archaic writers'; also by Jahn on

---

[1] Given the self-conscious, and often ironic assertions of humility made by the satirists in the Lucilian tradition, it is hardly possible to maintain that the immense *verrucosa . . . Antiopa aerumnis cor luctificabile fulta* is happily accommodated by normal stylistic precepts.

[2] *Essai*, p. 205.

[3] *CR* XXXVIII (1924), 64.

[4] *La critique littéraire de langue latine et le développement du goût archaïsant* (Rennes 1952), pp. 34–5.

[5] *HSCPh* XXIV (1913), 23.

75 ff.: 'ineptum studium antiquos auctores ita imitandi ut obsoleta atque situ squalida verba inde sumant, vituperat in scriptoribus sui temporis etiam Seneca'. Leaving aside the earlier periods,[1] there seems to have been an archaising trend throughout the first century A.D., culminating in the excesses of the second century. Jahn mentions Sen. *Ep.* CXIV. 13, *multi ex alieno saeculo petunt verba, duodecim tabulas locuntur. Gracchus illis et Crassus et Curio nimis culti et recentes sunt, ad Appium usque et Coruncanium redeunt.* Then there is Tac. *Dial.* 23.2, on *isti qui Lucilium pro Horatio et Lucretium pro Vergilio legunt,* foreshadowed by, e.g., Mart. XI. 90.3–4, on the vogue for Lucilius:

> et tibi Maeonio quoque carmine maius habetur,
> 'Lucili columella hic situ' Metrophanes'

where 'classical' is set against 'archaic' as Virgil against Accius and Pacuvius in Persius. We might also adduce Sen. *Ep.* LVIII. 5, on the *verborum situs* of Ennius and Accius, Martial v. 10.7, on the preference for Ennius over Virgil:

> Ennius est lectus salvo tibi, Roma, Marone[2]

and in particular, Quintilian's observations on archaic diction at VIII. 3.24 ff., esp. 30, *odiosa cura; nam et cuilibet facilis et hoc pessima, quod eius studiosus non verba rebus aptabit, sed res extrinsecus arcesset, quibus haec verba conveniant,* an accusation of verbalism without regard for content,[3] which, in view of his recent strictures on *aerumnosum* (or *aerumnas*) at VIII. 3.26,[4] might be taken as exemplifying the classically-minded Roman's response to Persius' monstrous *aerumnis cor luctificabile fulta,* I. 78.[5] Given that Hor. *A.P.* 102–3, *dolendum*

---

[1] *V.* W. D. Lebek, *Verba Prisca,* Hypomnemata, Heft XXV (Göttingen 1970).

[2] Cf. St. *Silv.* II. 7.75, showing that Ennius was still read; Appendix 2 for Virgil's own archaisms.

[3] Cf. Cic. *Or.* 68, *vocibus magis quam rebus inserviunt.*

[4] Cf. e.g. Enn. *Ann.* 54 V³, *Ilia, dia nepos quas* aerumnas *tetulisti;* Scaen. 61 V², *quantis cum* aerumnis *illum exanclavi diem.*

[5] Besides the above *testimonia* on archaism, cf. Sen. *Contr.* IV *pr.* 9, on the moderate archaist Haterius; Suet. *Aug.* 86.1, for Augustus' distaste for the movement, *cacozelos et antiquarios, ut diverso genere vitiosis, pari fastidio sprevit; ibid.* 86.2, for his criticisms of Tiberius, *nec Tiberio parcit et exoletas interdum et reconditas voces aucupanti* (Suet. *Tib.* 70.1, *adfectatione et morositate nimia obscurabat stilum*). Suet. *Gramm.* 24, which deals with Probus' proselytising on behalf of archaic authors read in the provinces (he wrote a *silva observationum sermonis antiqui*), notes that they were scorned in Rome: but the identity of these writers is obscure, and the rest of the evidence contradicts Suetonius.

est/primum ipsi tibi and especially 98, *si curat cor spectantis tetigisse querella* contribute to Pers. I. 90–1, *verum nec nocte paratum,/plorabit qui me volet incurvasse querella* (Brink on *A.P.* 102–3), the whole doctrine of *A.P.* 95 ff. is probably here recalled:

> et tragicus plerumque dolet sermone pedestri
> Telephus et Peleus, cum pauper et exsul uterque
> proicit ampullas et sesquipedalia verba,
>   si curat cor spectantis tetigisse querella.

For *sermone pedestri* Brink adduces Ar. *Rhet.* III. 7, 1408a, 18–19, ἐὰν δὲ ἐλεεινά, ταπεινῶς (λέγειν), and Demetr. *Interpr.* 28, ἁπλοῦν γὰρ εἶναι βούλεται καὶ ἀποίητον τὸ πάθος, ὁμοίως δὲ καὶ τὸ ἦθος, citing P. Shorey, *CPh* I (1906), 293–4. Add Russell on Longin. 8.2, on the need for low language when treating the low emotions of pity, grief and fear; Cic. *de Or.* III. 217 allows more elevation in the style appropriate to *miseratio* and *maeror*, which should be *flexibile plenum interruptum flebili voce*. Antiope, *aerumnis cor luctificabile fulta* – her sorrow couched in language which precludes sympathy – has not learnt the lesson of Telephus and Peleus, that bombast should be absent from the depiction of tragic grief.

Later, Gellius, and especially Lucian, can be enlisted to parallel the situation in Persius. Gellius I. 10 records the advice of Favorinus to a young man seduced by archaic diction, and at XI. 7 expresses distaste for obsolete words. In both cases the victim of criticism seems to have sprinkled normal Latin with old-fashioned glosses, much as Persius' opponents, with their penchant for an exotic poetic diction, have gathered *flosculi* from archaic tragedy. The pupil at Lucian *Rhet. Praec.* 16–17 is advised by his modernist preceptor to cull fifteen or twenty 'Attic' words for constant use,[1] to read only contemporary literature, and to despise the classics. This parallels the predilection of Persius' opponents for archaic diction at 76 ff., their claim to be modern (64, *nunc demum*; their examples of *decor* and *iunctura* at 93 ff., and of 'neoteric' *tenerum* at 99 ff.), and their rejection of the 'classical' *Aeneid* at 96–7, probably on the grounds of its containing less flamboyant, and therefore uninteresting and unacceptable, types of archaism. A further point is that just as the 'Atticisms' in Lucian are recognised to be out of line with the rest of the composition – 16, μελέτω δὲ μηδὲν τῶν ἄλλων, εἰ ἀνόμοια τούτοις καὶ ἀσύμφυλα καὶ ἀπῳδά – so in Persius tragic archaism helps to produce a *sartago loquendi*.

---

[1] Amongst the 'Attic' words recommended, μῶν, for instance, was obsolete in Lucian's day.

Most of the confusion about the passage seems to stem from a refusal to associate 'modernism' with any kind of archaistic tastes. Leaving aside the fact that Catullus, a 'modern' in his own day, employed archaisms,[1] we can quote as a corrective the comments of A. Guillemin on the *novi* of the first century A.D.,[2] 'Rien n'étant plus neuf que ce qui est très vieux, non seulement on recherchait le langage archaïque, mais on était à l'affût des sujets qui prêtaient à un grand déploiement de langage archaïque'; also A. N. Sherwin-White on Pliny I. 16.2, 'Quint. VIII. 3.24–30[3] criticises the excessive use of archaisms. They are not necessarily a mark of Atticism, since the new rhetoric of the Principate, which was mainly Asian in affiliation, searched them out for its own purposes.' Finally, unambiguous proof of the connexion between learned and effeminate 'modernism', and the cultivation of precious archaisms, is found in this same letter, §5: *praeterea facit versus, quales Catullus meus aut Calvus, re vera quales Catullus aut Calvus – quantum illis leporis dulcedinis amoris! inserit sane*, sed data opera, *mollibus levibusque* duriusculos quosdam; *et hoc quasi Catullus aut Calvus.*

So much, then, for the literary background. But who speaks lines 76–8 of the first satire? If it is the interlocutor, then they are probably an objection to some recent comment of Persius: the topic of archaism would not have been introduced unless context called for an answer to some previously expressed, or implied, accusation.[4] Previous argument has been that pupils attempt heroics, when their only experience consists of writing epigrams in Greek – young men so incompetent that they fail even in elementary descriptions of early Rome's agricultural virtues. So the interlocutor perhaps halts at an insinuation from Persius, that the moderns are not yet equipped for heroics and at a loss with primitivistic *loci communes*, his appeal to Accius and Pacuvius an apologetic rejoinder: 'Your gibes are unfair, because we are in fact acquainted with archaic literature, and therefore qualified to write heroics, also to describe the rural life of early Rome,[5] in which case

---

[1] *V.* H. Heusch, *Das Archaische in der Sprache Catulls* (Bonn 1954).

[2] 'La Critique Litteraire au 1er Siècle de l'Empire', *REL* VI (1928), 169.

[3] Quoted above, p. 176.

[4] An adversative is not necessary for the lines to convey an objection. We find *at* at 28 and *sed* at 92 and 107, but the substantial objection at 24 is introduced without an adversative: cf. 40 and 63.

[5] It does not matter if the interlocutor undermines his own argument by the choice of unfortunate phraseology: he does this on several occasions, e.g. 24–5, 28–30. We should recall his insubstantiality, proved by 44, *quisquis es, o modo quem ex adverso dicere feci.*

the satirist turns the tables on his adversary, remarking that this very acquaintance with Accius and Pacuvius, inculcated by an unsound education, has caused the corruption of diction, *monitus* and *sartago loquendi* now being directly dependent on the unfortunate plea of 76–8.

If Persius is responsible for the passage, it marks a new stage in his campaign against bad education: first, the teaching of heroics; then mismanagement of elementary exercises; now, the close reading of turgid time-ruined texts. The last criticism then has a loose associative connexion with the second, incongruous treatment of the *rus saturum*, an old-fashioned Roman theme, leading to the topic of archaism. Now *monitus* and *sartago loquendi* depend in the first place upon 76–8, but more generally upon the thesis that the whole of education is at fault. Originating in *docemus* at 69, *monitus* is a comprehensive reference to the pedagogic advice proferred to youth by the old, the last part of which is a recommendation of Accius and Pacuvius; *sartago loquendi* has similar origins, the corruption of poetic diction likewise caused by a quaint educational system.

If we accept a sequence of thought consisting of objection to criticism as adumbrated above, it is better to ascribe the lines to Persius' adversary, since *monitus* and *sartago loquendi* are then directly linked to the germs of self-incrimination inherent in 76–8. Otherwise Persius himself is our candidate, despite the fact that *monitus* and *sartago loquendi* are then less closely tied to 76–8. In apology for the lack of instant sequence, we might plead that his dissatisfaction with the whole of contemporary education allows him to soliloquise on one topic after another, starting with *docemus* at 69, and summing up his discontent at 79 ff.

VIRGIL AND THE MODERNS AT PERSIUS I. 96

I have recently touched on the attitude of the 'moderns' to Virgil. Who precisely were these moderns, and why did they scorn the *Aeneid*? The first question involves the history of mannerism in Rome. Firstly there is the problem of original Roman contact with Alexandrianism, and more specifically, Callimacheanism.[1] Ennius, Catulus and Lucilius seem to have been acquainted with Callimachus: Ennius with his dream at the beginning of the *Annales*,[2] and his claim to be a polished modern at 214–16 V,[3] Catulus with his adaptation of Callim. *Epigr.* XLI at fr. 1 M,[4] and Lucilius with his knowledge of Callimachean literary theory.[5] Next, there is the question of Ciceronian

---

[1] As will become clear, I part company from the views of W. V. Clausen, *GRBS* v (1964), 181 ff., followed by D. O. Ross, *Style and Tradition in Catullus* (Harvard 1969), pp. 137 ff., who dismiss the earlier evidence, to posit Parthenius as the herald of Callimachus in the middle of the first century. On the Roman background to Catullus, discussing its points of contact with Callimachus, *v.* N. B. Crowther *CPh* LXVI (1971), pp. 246 ff.

[2] Cf. the dream at the beginning of the *Aetia*. O. Skutsch, *Studia Enniana* (London 1968), pp. 7 ff. (apart from the Hesiodic nature of the dream, in which he meets Homer), states categorically 'he *must* have had Callimachus in mind', p. 8. It is perverse to suggest (Clausen p. 186) that Ennius' purpose here was 'polemical and anti-Callimachean: he designed to refute Callimachus, *alter Hesiodus*, in something like Callimachus' own oblique style'. Better to interpret Ennius' breaking of the ban on Homer as Skutsch, p. 9, 'Did he, in setting out to write a great epic poem, justify his venture by declaring that he was not an imitator of Homer but Homer reborn? It would be no small thing to see the great vision that opened the *Annales* as the result at once of admiration for the early literature of Greece and of respect for the theory and taste of a later age.'

[3] *quos olim Fauni vatesque canebant,/quom neque Musarum scopulos . . . / . . . nec dicti studiosus quisquam erat ante hunc*, Cic. *Brut.* 18.71.

[4] Because the repeated *dicit* at Cat. LXX reproduces the double ὤμοσε of Callim. *Epigr.* 26, Ross, pp. 152–3, argues for Catullan acquaintance with Callimachean theory, from which, following Clausen p. 187, he dubiously excludes Catulus, on the grounds of his epigram being too loose an adaptation. If Catulus knew the epigram, he surely knew the literary theory as well.

[5] *V.* Puelma Piwonka, *Lucilius und Kallimachos*.

poetic practice, and Ciceronian taste, both of them relative factors. He seems to have gravitated away from modernism towards conservatism: in poetry, away from (probably) the ἔπος τυτθόν[1] and Aratus,[2] towards a more grandiose hexameter manner;[3] in taste, towards antipathy against the *novi* of his later years, with concomitant admiration for the *veteres*. Of course, 'old' and 'new' have no absolute sense: the terms at this stage are entirely relative.[4] All we can say of the traditional '*poetae novi*' of the older literary histories, from Ciceronian evidence at least, is that a group of moderns shared certain metrical traits – the σπονδειάζοντες described in the reference to οἱ νεώτεροι at *ad Att.* VII. 2.1, in November 50 B.C., and the regard for final *s* in prosody, mentioned at *Or.* 161, six years later, in 44 B.C.[5] As for the *cantores Euphorionis*, upbraided for their contempt of Ennius at *T.D.* III. 45 in 45 B.C., what better candidate for membership than Gallus, the imitator of Euphorion?[6] We are now very close to Virgil's *Eclogues*

---

[1] So I interpret the titles 'Halcyones', 'Glaucus Pontius', and 'Thalia Maesta', after G. B. Townend p. 111, in *Cicero, Studies in Latin Literature and its Influence*, ed. D. R. Dudley and T. A. Dorey (London 1964). None of these compositions is mentioned in the prose works, perhaps, as Townend suggests, because Cicero suppressed them.

[2] Admired by Callimachus (*Epigr.* 27 Pf.), hence probably, at this period, aligning the translator with the Callimachean poetic: χαίρετε λεπταί/ῥήσιες, Ἀρήτου σύντονος ἀγρυπνίη.

[3] Not to say that the later works display no innovations: *v.* Townend, *op. cit.* pp. 118 ff.

[4] *V.* Curtius, 'The "Ancients" and the "Moderns"', pp. 251 ff., correctly interpreting the Ciceronian references to *novi* and νεώτεροι as purely relative; also E. J. Kenney's criticisms of E. Castorina, *Questioni neoteriche* (Florence 1968), *CR* ns XX (1970), 51 ff., for his 'assumption that "neoterism" was an absolute'. Apart from such early manifestations of the 'quarrel' as exhibited in Aristophanes' *Frogs* we can cite, e.g., Timotheus *Persae* 219 ff. D, ὁ γάρ μ' εὐγενέτας μακραίων Σπάρτας μέγας ἀγεμὼν/ βρύων ἄνθεσιν ἥβας/δονεῖ λαὸς ἐπιφλέγων/ἐλᾷ τε αἴθοπι μώμῳ,/ὅτι παλαιοτέραν νέοισ'/ὕμνοις μοῦσαν ἀτιμῶ, and fr. 7D, οὐκ ἀείδω τὰ παλαιά./καινὰ γὰρ ἀμὰ κρείσσω./νέος ὁ Ζεὺς βασιλεύει./τό πάλαι δ' ἦν Κρόνος ἄρχων./ἀπίτω μοῦσα παλαιά. Cf. the question 'who are the *veteres*?' asked by Cicero at *Brut.* 10.39, Horace at *Ep.* II. 1.34, Tacitus at *Dial.* 15 ff.; also D'Alton ch. v.

[5] N. B. Crowther, *CQ* ns XX (1970), 322 ff., pursues the metrical argument, relating to Catullus Cicero's references to σπονδειάζοντες and final *s*. Given the time gap after the death of Catullus, and our loss of so much material (a factor which throws doubt on statistics), this, like the addition of Cinna to the *cantores Euphorionis*, p. 326, seems to me a dubious proposition. More interesting is his contention that neither Ciceronian *locus* displays antagonism.

[6] Virg. *Ecl.* X. 50–1.

(traditionally, 42–39 B.C.),[1] and Catullus has not yet been mentioned. All we can do to accommodate him within a 'circle' is to relate him to other literary figures referred to in his works, who are known from Suet. *Gramm.* 11[2] to have been associated with Valerius Cato, poet and literary preceptor.[3] There are three of them: Ticidas, Bibaculus and Cinna. The first is of no use at all,[4] likewise the second, unless the Furius of Cat. XI is Bibaculus. Cinna, by virtue of Cat. XCV, provides the important point of access into a group, to which Calvus may be added, his name being linked with that of Catullus by Tibullus, Propertius and Horace.[5] Since Catullus, on the normal dating,[6] has been dead for six years before *ad Att.* VII. 2.1, and eleven or twelve years before *T.D.* III. 45 and *Or.* 161, it is hazardous to enlist the Ciceronian *loci* as evidence for a school, with Catullus somewhere near the centre. But Callimacheanism had now been incorporated into the Roman poetic, perhaps partly as a result of the infusion of new energy by Parthenius,[7] but more likely the product of a gradual dissemination of the imagery and theory of the master.[8] One is tempted to enquire about the extent of the distortion necessitated by the superimposition of a scheme evolved for third-century Alexandria on the realities of Republican literary-history: for example, *was* there an overwhelmingly large body of turgid epic? Or is this a false impression, resulting from extant theory, and lost practice? When we reach what might be called the neo-Callimacheanism of Virgil, we find an odd use of the adjective *novus* in the third *Eclogue*. Elsewhere, Virgil insinuates his adherence to the Callimachean poetic by the use of terms like *tenuis* and *gracilis*, in this, more orthodox than Catullus. But at *Ecl.* III. 86, presumably in

---

[1] Since the dates have no absolute validity, Virgil, like his friend Gallus, may have been in Cicero's mind at *T.D.* III. 45, even though he had no personal connexion with Euphorion's poetry. But to be a *cantor* (leaving aside derogatory overtones) is only to be an adherent (cf. Hor. *Sat.* I. 10.19, *cantare*), and Virgil could well have been this, esp. given his tributes to Gallus.

[2] Containing the relevant fragments, for which *v.* also Morel.

[3] On his relationship to Horace, *v.* Hendrickson, *CPh* XI (1916), 249 ff.; XII (1917), 77 ff. and 329 ff.

[4] Fr. 1 M is not sufficiently close to Cat. LXI. 107 to be of any assistance.

[5] *V.* Fordyce on Cat. XIV.   [6] 55 B.C., on argument from silence.

[7] So Clausen and Ross, with too much emphasis on the missionary work of a single Greek.

[8] Lucretius is not normally classed as a 'neoteric', yet, as E. J. Kenney demonstrates ('Doctus Lucretius', *Mnem.* ser. 4, XXIII[4] (1970), 366 ff.), he was acquainted with Callimachus. This does not make him a conscious 'modern': it merely shows the extent to which the Callimachean poetic had permeated the Roman literary scene.

relationship to an implied *vetus*, as in the Ciceronian *loci*, rather than as a quasi-technical term, we read the surprising

Pollio et ipse facit nova carmina.

Given the ensuing image of a bull, this surely applies to Pollio's tragedies, not his epigrams. According to Suidas, Callimachus wrote tragedies. But the genre as a whole tended to incur criticism from the 'thin' poets, because of its tumidity and bombast.[1] At any rate, tragedy is an unexpected addition to the repertoire of the late Republican *novi*.[2]

Finally, we arrive at the ornamental Callimacheanism of Propertius,[3] and the static Alexandrianism of Ovid. From these points of departure, we come across *poetae novi* in Seneca's *Apocolocyntosis*, 12 *vs* 29 (apparently a relative use of 'new': speculation about their style is impossible), and then the moderns of Persius' first satire. The impression given is that originally fluctuating and relative trends have now been stabilised somewhat – that 'new' is now more of a technical expression. Peculiar metrical phenomena, and grouping around a central figure – our only valid criteria for situating the Republican *novi* – seem to have been replaced by an all-purpose mannerism, less flexible and relative than its various predecessors. At last we seem to have found a homogeneous school, with shared style and theory: unless, of course, Persius has simplified the position, grouping together as *teneri* poets whose aims were rather more diverse. But if the term 'neoterism' is to be applied at all, I would award it first to the writers attacked by Persius – writers who seem to be uniformly culpable for roughly the same range of stylistic quirks; then, tentatively, I might extend it to a tradition of preciosity, running from Laevius, through the polymetrics of Catullus, the affectations of Maecenas and Nero, to Castorina's questionable *novelli*. Any other similarity between Republic and Empire I take to be general: Horace's obsession with Lucilius and his adherents could be said to parallel Persius' attacks on Neronian modernism, in that the *fautores Lucili* seem to have been a group of outmoded *novi* who constituted a threat to the 'true' modernist Horace – just as the aspiring classicist Persius was faced with a repressive fashionable orthodoxy which masqueraded as an *avant-garde*.

At Pers. I. 96 the interlocutor, with his taste for 'neoterism', which we have also seen to be inclusive of archaism, rejects 'classical' epic –

[1] For Callimachus' own criticisms, *v.* p. 174 n. I.

[2] Is Pollio *novus* in relationship to, e.g., Accius and Pacuvius; or in relationship to more recent writers; or as a result of employing a refined style?

[3] Esp. the opening poems of III.

the *Aeneid* – like the Sextus of Mart. x. 21, for whom Cinna was superior to Virgil,[1] line 4,

> iudice te maior Cinna Marone fuit.

The more complex, the better. Fiske[2] assesses the situation correctly with 'Horace's model for epic *decus* (*qui nil molitur inepte, A.P.* 140) is Homer, as Persius' in spite of his obscuring irony is the *Aeneid*.' There was obviously room for objection to the archaistic aspects of the *Aeneid*:[3] but not, as Persius implies, from the mouths of moderns enticed by the obsolete diction of works from the long-distant past. Like his preceptor Cornutus – *iamque exemplo tuo etiam principes civitatum, o poeta, incipient similia fingere*[4] – Persius takes the normal attitude of admiration for Virgil, while his opponent, convinced of the superiority of the moderns, by-passes the great Augustan, to glean what he can from archaic tragedy.[5]   The satirist objects to the phenomenon noted by Seneca the Elder, *Contr.* IV *praef.* 1: *acrior cupiditas ignota cognoscendi quam nota repetendi. hoc in histrionibus, in gladiatoribus, in oratoribus de quibus modo aliquid fama promisit, in omnibus denique rebus videmus accidere: ad nova homines concurrunt, ad nota non veniunt.* For the interlocutor, Virgil is *notum*, tragedy *ignotum* and *novum*.[6]

---

[1] Like Persius, Martial has the *Aeneid* in mind, not the Callimachean *Eclogues*.

[2] *HSCPh* XXIV (1913), 25.

[3] Cf. Sen. *ap.* Gell. XII. 2, for Virgil's insertion of archaisms into the *Aeneid* to please the conservative public: *Virgilius quoque noster non ex alia causa duros quosdam versus et enormes et aliquid supra mensuram trahentes interposuit, quam ut Ennianus populus agnosceret in novo carmine aliquid antiquitatis*; Quint. I. 7.16 and IX. 3.14, for Virgil as *amator vetustatis*; E. Norden, *Aen. VI*, pp. 365 ff., for Ennian reminiscences, also *Ennius und Vergilius* (Leipzig and Berlin 1915).

[4] Charis. p. 100 K. In general an admirer, Cornutus criticised *Aen.* VIII. 404 f.: cf. Gell. IX. 10.5.

[5] The fact that Virgil was now an established classic (an authority on 'grammar', *grammaticus futurus Vergilium scrutatur*, Sen. *Ep.* CVIII. 24; a school text book, Mayor on Juv. VII. 227, *cum totus decolor esset/Flaccus, et haereret nigro fuligo Maroni*) may partly account for the cavalier attitude of the interlocutor.

[6] Paratore's view, (above, p. 2 n. 2, esp. p. 167) that the first satire contains parody of Virgil (e.g. 28–30, 36) is absurd: 28–30 are a commonplace, and 36 need have no ulterior purpose. Persius admires, while his opponents detract: cf. E. J. Kenney, *CR* ns XIX (1969), 172–3.

THE IMAGE OF THE CHILD IN ANCIENT SATIRE AND
DIATRIBE

At Pers. I. 113 the satirist is represented as a small boy, whose intention is to befoul the dignified vices of Roman society. From the latter's point of view, such behaviour is culpable and irresponsible. But for Persius, the child's proposition is a justifiable comment on the adult world. Here we find in combination the two attitudes of ancient satire and diatribe, where the child is alternately irresponsible and innocent, the example of his behaviour sometimes negative, sometimes positive.

Antiquity offers nothing so complex as the figure of Alice in Wonderland, treated by W. Empson in *Some Versions of Pastoral*.[1] In the preface to Callimachus' *Aetia*, the child belongs to the symbolism illustrating simplicity of style; the image of a mere boy is enlisted, singing small epics, 5–6:

ἔπος δ' ἐπὶ τυτθὸν ἑλ[ίσσω
παῖς ἅτε, τῶν δ' ἐτέων ἡ δεκὰς οὐκ ὀλίγη.

As Snell notes, Callimachus 'often stresses the playful nature of his poetry by casting himself in the role of *ingénu*', or again, 'Ancient myths whose truth he finds it hard to credit, and stories invented by himself, he tells with the semblance of childish seriousness.'[2] He goes on to remark how Callimachus was 'the first among Greek poets to be able to picture the behaviour of children in its true colours, though, of course, with an admixture of irony which guarded him from losing himself entirely to the world of the child'.[3] Innocence, somewhat contrived, seems here to have been the dictating concept.

From Callimachus, we move on to Horace, Seneca, and Epictetus. As we shall see, there is a slight ambivalence in the representation of the child in Sen. *Ep.* cxv, and a dualism in Epictetus, where the child symbolises those who need correction, as well as innocence. But

[1] London 1935.
[2] *The Discovery of the Mind*, tr. Rosenmeyer (Harvard 1953), p. 271; also, 'he himself calls his poetry "childish play" (*paizein* and *paignion*)'
[3] In illustration, Artemis, depicted as a little girl in *Hymn* III. 6 ff.

Horace takes up what seems in origin to have been a Hellenistic phenomenon[1] – the sentimentalisation of the child – and invests it with a more stringent moral colour, opposing it to the materialism of the adult, *Ep.* 1. 1.52 ff.:

> vilius argentum est auro, virtutibus aurum.
> 'o cives, cives, quaerenda pecunia primum est;
> virtus post nummos!' haec Ianus summus ab imo
> prodocet, haec recinunt iuvenes dictata senesque,   55
> laevo suspensi loculos tabulamque lacerto.
> est animus tibi, sunt mores, est lingua fidesque,
> sed quadringentis sex septem milia desunt;
> plebs eris. at pueri ludentes, 'rex eris', aiunt,
> 'si recte facies.' hic murus aeneus esto,   60
> nil conscire sibi, nulla pallescere culpa.
> Roscia, dic sodes, melior lex an puerorum est
> nenia, quae regnum recte facientibus offert,
> et maribus Curiis et decantata Camillis?
> isne tibi melius suadet, qui 'rem facias, rem,   65
> si possis, recte, si non, quocumque modo, rem'?

Assuming that *virtus* is preferable to worldly possessions, Horace criticises contemporary education, especially for the way in which youth is infected by bad lessons from the old. Social status is decided by money: worthy inner qualities – *animus, mores, lingua, fides* – cannot save the impecunious from plebeian oblivion. A corollary to introducing the theme of status through the word *plebs* is the antithesis now set up between common people and king. Another antithesis follows – an etymological opposition of the recently introduced *rex*, against *res*, or *recte*. 'Children at play' – a symbol of innocence, unlike the *iuvenes* at school, warped by the old – are acquainted with the correct etymology: to be *rex*, one has to act *recte*, not to possess *res*. From 62 ff. there arises a question about the priority of modern social conventions, against those transmitted from antiquity. Suggesting a line of continuity from the respected names of mythologised history – *Curii* and *Camilli*, an alliance of virility with guilelessness – down to the simplicity of the contemporary child, Horace tacitly implies a Roman

---

[1] In Greek tragedy, it does not seem to be the innocence or simplicity of the child which matters: rather, he is the victim of war, or the scapegoat for the crimes of his forefathers. In the case of Astyanax, the important thing is not so much his innocence, as the fact that with his extinction, his father's line will die out.

origin, and a Roman prerogative, for the Stoic doctrine that only the wise man is king.[1]

At Sen. *Ep.* cxv. 8, the figure of the child begins a·brief literary career by typifying less than exemplary behaviour: *tunc intellegere nobis licebit quam contemnenda miremur, simillimi pueris, quibus omne ludicrum in pretio est; parentibus quippe nec minus fratribus praeferunt parvo aere empta monilia.* Like the little boys at Lucr. II. 55–8,[2] and the irresponsible child of Persius III, Seneca's figure is so far a creature deserving correction. But his complexion changes in what follows:

> quid ergo inter nos et illos interest, ut Ariston ait, nisi quod nos circa tabulas et statuas insanimus, carius inepti? illos reperti in litore calculi leves et aliquid habentes varietatis delectant, nos ingentium maculae columnarum, sive ex Aegyptiis harenis sive ex Africae solitudinibus advectae porticum aliquam vel capacem populi cenationem ferunt.

The earlier denigratory note, 'we are no better than mere children', now expresses approval: 'children have a naïve interest in nature, whereas we concern ourselves with objects torn from their proper place in the order of the world'. Significantly, the child is represented as closer to nature than the adult, his pebbles a source of innocuous delight, while we violate nature in search for materials to enhance our false sense of grandeur. Seneca's child has not yet entered the adult world and been misled. The idea had great potential: Tacitus, for instance, uses it in his representation of Britannicus and Octavia in *Ann.* XIII, where, as paradigms of Republican virtue, they provide a point of moral access into, and comment on, the decadence of the court.

Epictetus varies his technique when dealing with the figure of the child, sometimes delivering an approbatory verdict, more often, one of disapproval. On one occasion the child might exemplify the inexperience of the convert; on another, he might contribute to a contrast with adult behaviour. Again, there is sometimes the expression of direct affection.[3] Of the innocence which requires attention when

---

[1] The commentators refer to Dio Chrysostom, *de Regno* 4, οὐδὲ γὰρ τῶν παιδίων ὁ νικήσας, ὅταν παίζωσιν, ὡς αὐτόν φασι βασιλέα, τῷ ὄντι βασιλεύς ἐστιν; also *v.* Nisbet and Hubbard on Hor. *Carm.* I. 36.8, Hdt. I. I.114, Plato *Theaet.* 146a, Procop. *Anecdota* 14.14. But the Herodotean passage, e.g., is no way primitivistic.

[2] *V.* D. West, *The Imagery and Poetry of Lucretius* (Edinburgh 1969), pp. 82 ff., 'Light and little boys'.

[3] W. A. Oldfather, the Loeb editor, overestimates the positive side, writing (vol. I, p. xix) 'He is much more an angel of mercy than a messenger of

dealing with the philosophic *tiro*, he writes, I. 29.31 ff.: τοῖς γὰρ παιδίοις, ὅταν προσελθόντα κροτῇ καὶ λέγῃ 'σήμερον Σατορνάλια ἀγαθά,' λέγομεν 'οὐκ ἔστιν ἀγαθὰ ταῦτα'; οὐδαμῶς · ἀλλὰ καὶ αὐτοὶ ἐπικροτοῦμεν. καὶ σὺ τοίνυν, ὅταν μεταπεῖσαί τινα μὴ δύνῃ, γίγνωσκε ὅτι παιδίον ἐστὶ καὶ ἐπικρότει αὐτῷ. There is no brittle idealism, either here, or at II. 16.39 ff., where the convert is likened to a child, in need of more solid food. Progress in philosophy is the aim, hence the candid and sensible view-point; not far away is the sober notion of the child as the type of that which needs the civilising force of education. Once, like Seneca, with regard to the rift between young and old, Epictetus represents childish actions, though unconstructive, as better than those of the adult (III. 13.18). For children can always amuse themselves, unlike their elders. Then there is the unqualified admiration of II. 24.18, where affection, rather than innocence, is the writer's motivating force, who desires to imitate the ways of the very young.

Finally, there are the unsympathetic verdicts. Especially in the realm of education, the child leaves much to be desired, as at II. 1.16, τί γὰρ ἐστι παιδίον; ἄγνοια. τί ἐστι παιδίον; ἀμαθία. With this should be compared Pers. III. 44 ff., where he refuses instruction:

> saepe oculos, memini, tangebam parvus olivo,
> grandia si nollem morituri verba Catonis
> discere non sano multum laudanda magistro,
> quae pater adductis sudans audiret amicis.

As the satirist goes on to show, the child's main interest is in games: we are a long way distant from Hor. *Ep.* I. 1.52 ff. Epictetus' children also often epitomise habits which we, being adult, should not imitate. At II. 16.25 ff., we are told to avoid temptation of the palate, and to be motivated by true judgement – in this, unlike children; at I. 24.20, we are warned from resembling cowardly children with μὴ γίνου τῶν παιδίων δειλότερος, ἀλλ' ὡς ἐκεῖνα, ὅταν αὐτοῖς μὴ ἀρέσκῃ τὸ πρᾶγμα, λέγει 'οὐκέτι παίξω', καὶ σύ, ὅταν σοι φαίνηταί τινα εἶναι τοιαῦτα, εἰπὼν 'οὐκέτι παίξω', ἀπαλλάσσου, μένων δὲ μὴ θρήνει; then there is III. 24.53, οὕτως οὐδέποτε παύσει παιδίον ὢν νήπιον; οὐκ οἶσθ' ὅτι ὁ

vengeance ... this aspect of his character comes out most clearly perhaps in his attitude towards children, for with them a man can be more nearly himself than with his sophisticated associates. No ancient author speaks as frequently of them, or as sympathetically. They are one of his favourite parables, and though he is well aware that a child is only an incomplete man, he likes their straightforwardness in play, he claps his hands to them, and returns their "Merry Saturnalia" greetings, yearns to get down on hands and knees and talk baby talk with them.' I have not seen R. Renner, *Das Kind. Ein Gleichnissmittel des Epiktets* (Munich 1905).

τὰ παιδίου ποιῶν ὅσῳ πρεσβύτερος τοσούτῳ γελοιότερος;, a comment on undesirable behaviour, which, like III. 19.6, οὕτως καὶ αὐξηθέντες φαινόμεθα παιδία. παῖς γὰρ ἐν μουσικοῖς ὁ ἄμουσος, ἐν γραμματικοῖς ὁ ἀγράμματος, ἐν βίῳ ὁ ἀπαίδευτος, applying childish traits to adults, might be adduced to support the theory that *nucibus . . . relictis*, Pers. I. 10, intimates that we have not in fact grown up. Elsewhere Epictetus is utterly condemnatory: at III. 9.22, the child is an instance of selfishness and insatiability; at IV. 7.32, he is classed along with the fool. Innocence is by no means the whole story. Besides representing an ideal of simplicity, children are also regarded as unmoulded clay, ready for education, or vicious products of an uncultivated nature to be domesticated and civilised.

THE DISCLAIMER OF MALICE

The disclaimer of malicious intent is allied to the theory of the liberal jest. Iambists, epigrammatists, and satirists tend to disown malice, the product of illiberal humour, claiming to be free of gratuitous invective, and perhaps arrogating some reformatory mission. Care is taken over personal dissociation from the antics of the *scurra*, or βωμολόχος, who wounds his victims.

Plato seems to be the origin of a good deal of later theory. From his distinction between humour without anger, and ill-natured abuse or ridicule, at *Leg.* 935 ff., we arrive at Aristotle's generalised comments on the buffoon, envy and malice, at *Eth. Nic.* II. 7, 1108 a, then his statement of belief that the vices of the soul are voluntary and therefore blameworthy, and that bodily defects are so sometimes, when we ourselves are responsible for them, III. 5.15, 1114a, 24: οὐ μόνον δ' αἱ τῆς ψυχῆς κακίαι ἑκούσιοί εἰσιν, ἀλλ' ἐνίοις καὶ αἱ τοῦ σώματος, οἷς καὶ ἐπιτιμῶμεν. τοῖς μὲν γὰρ διὰ φύσιν αἰσχροῖς οὐδεὶς ἐπιτιμᾷ, τοῖς δὲ δι' ἀγυμνασίαν καὶ ἀμέλειαν. ὁμοίως δὲ καὶ περὶ ἀσθένειαν καὶ πήρωσιν. οὐδεὶς γὰρ ἂν ὀνειδίσειε τυφλῷ φύσει ἢ ἐκ νόσου, ἢ ἐκ πληγῆς, ἀλλὰ μᾶλλον ἐλεήσαι. τῷ δ' ἐξ οἰνοφλυγίας ἢ ἄλλης ἀκολασίας πᾶς ἂν ἐπιτιμήσαι. τῶν δὴ περὶ τὸ σῶμα κακιῶν αἱ ἐφ' ἡμῖν ἐπιτιμῶνται, αἱ δὲ μὴ ἐφ' ἡμῖν οὔ. Finally there are his pertinent remarks on gentlemanly humour, at IV. 8, 1128a ff., where he defines the jests appropriate to the ἐπιεικής and ἐλευθέριος, and warns against hurting the feelings of the victim, expressing distaste for the low activities of the βωμολόχος. Theophrastus continues the tradition of aversion from malignant humour with his picture of the κακολόγος at *Char.* XXVIII: καὶ συγκαθήμενος δεινὸς περὶ τοῦ ἀναστάντος εἰπεῖν ⟨κακά⟩, καὶ ἀρχήν γε εἰληφὼς μὴ ἀποσχέσθαι μηδὲ τοὺς οἰκείους αὐτοῦ λοιδορῆσαι, ἀλλὰ πλεῖστα περὶ τῶν φίλων καὶ οἰκείων κακὰ εἰπεῖν καὶ περὶ τῶν τετελευτηκότων, ⟨τὴν⟩ κακολογίαν ἀποκαλῶν παρρησίαν καὶ δημοκρατίαν καὶ ἐλευθερίαν, καὶ τῶν ἐν τῷ βίῳ ἥδιστα τοῦτο ποιῶν.

Cicero takes up the Platonic and Aristotelian distinction, defining it in roughly similar fashion. At *Or.* 88–9 improper scurrility is to be shunned, as well as jokes aimed at misfortune, and tasteless humour at the expense of friends:

illud admonemus tamen ridiculo sic usurum oratorem, ut nec nimis frequenti ne scurrile sit, nec subobsceno ne mimicum, nec petulanti ne improbum, nec in calamitatem ne inhumanum nec in facinus ne odi locum risus occupet, neque aut sua persona aut iudicum aut tempore alienum. haec enim ad illud indecorum referuntur. §89 vitabit etiam quaesita nec ex tempore ficta sed domo allata quae plerumque sunt frigida. parcet et amicitiis et dignitatibus, vitabit insanabiles contumelias, tantummodo adversarios figet nec eos tamen semper nec omnes nec omni modo.

Implied is an injunction to generosity. This large exposition is paralleled by the contrast at *de Off.* I. 104:

duplex omnino est iocandi genus, unum illiberale, petulans, flagitiosum, obscenum, alterum elegans, urbanum, ingeniosum, facetum. quo genere non modo Plautus noster[1] et Atticorum antiqua comoedia, sed etiam philosophorum Socraticorum libri referti sunt, multaque multorum facete dicta, ut ea, quae a sene Catone collecta sunt, quae vocant ἀποφθέγματα. facilis igitur est distinctio ingenui et inliberalis ioci. alter est, si tempore fit, ut si remisso animo, gravissimo homine dignus, alter ne libero quidem, si rerum turpitudini adhibetur verborum obscenitas.

His concern for avoidance of low humour reappears at *de Off.* I. 134, while discussing *sermo*:

in primisque provideat, ne sermo vitium aliquod indicet inesse in moribus; quod maxume tum solet evenire, cum studiose de absentibus detrahendi causa aut per ridiculum aut severe maledice contumelioseque dicitur.

People must not be hurt. Finally, there is *de Or.* II. 244, enjoining abstention from *scurrilis dicacitas*. It is against this background of ethical and rhetorical theory that the various disclaimers of malice – an offshoot of illiberal humour – should be weighed: not against fear of legislation for libel.[2]

[1] Apparently almost anyone qualified as a liberal humourist. Rudd, *Mnem.* ser. IV, vol. X (1957), 320 suggests a Panaetian origin (περὶ τοῦ καθήκοντος) for Cicero's 'liberal' Old Comedy, against Aristotle.

[2] Counter to the mainstream tradition, since apparently regardless of the individual's responsibility, is the statement that there is room for humour at the expense of physical, as well as moral, deformity, in the *Coislinian Tractate*, §5, ὁ σκώπτων ἐλέγχειν θέλει ἁμαρτήματα τῆς ψυχῆς καὶ τοῦ σώματος, also, even though advocating proper measure, Cic. *de Or.* II. 239, *est etiam deformitatis et corporis vitiorum satis bella materies ad iocandum*: *v.* Hendrickson, *AJPh* XXI (1900), 132 n. 3.

We have seen how, at lines 107–10, the interlocutor of Persius' first satire charges the author with spite:

> 'sed quid opus teneras mordaci radere vero
> auriculas? vide sis ne maiorum tibi forte
> limina frigescant: sonat hic de nare canina
> littera.'

Soon we see a similar accusation levelled by Persius at the *sordidus*, by implication a member of the interlocutor's party. After 107–10, indicted for snarling at his audience, the satirist pretends to disappear – *discedo*, 114 – but only after the further abuse of *euge*, 111, and the sarcasm of his temple image. Despite appearances, he is still the snarling dog. Remembering the precedent of Lucilius and Horace, 114–18, he publishes his secret, 119–21, appropriately accompanied by a swipe at bad literature. For his own audience he wants a reader tried by Old Comedy, blasted through by its emotional force: *adflate*, 123. The *et* of 125 places Persius in the same tradition of scathing satire, leading us to expect that he no longer regards his work as trivial – *tam nil*, 122 – and that he will now venture to proclaim affiliation with the strenuous violence of Cratinus, Eupolis, and Aristophanes. But he deceives us, deflecting our attention to style: *si forte aliquid decoctius audis*, 125. Perhaps this tactic is momentarily to imply acquaintance with Aristotle's objections to Old Comedy. But the subject of stylistic compression immediately gives way to renewed allusion to Comedy, 126. His reader must cleanse his ears by listening to the Old Masters, coming hot – *ferveat* – to his own works. Yet Persius will not commit himself, refusing to liken the impact of his satire to the emotive power of Comedy: perhaps, again, because he knew Aristotelian doctrine. What he does, though, stems from knowledge of the mainstream distinction between the two kinds of humour: those whose idea of the amusing is pitiless and malign are excluded from his audience. His own works will not provide scurrilous amusement, their humour not being to the taste of the *sordidus* – Aristotle's βωμολόχος – but consisting of constructive assaults on vice.

From the first satire, which through the accusations of the interlocutor, and then Persius, twice makes contact with the theory of humour, and hence with the subject of malice, I move on to the fifth satire, which contains positive assertion of adherence to the doctrine of the liberal jest, 15–16:

> pallentes radere mores
> doctus et *ingenuo* culpam defigere *ludo*.

As Fiske notes,[1] 'In thispassage we have clear evidence of Aristotle's distinction between βωμολοχία or scurrility, and εὐτραπελία or refined humour.' Through *ingenuo ... ludo*, a personal variation on the claim to gentlemanly wit, Persius disowns bitterness and malevolence, assuming instead a broad and dignified attitude to his mission.[2] In doing so, he subscribes to a long, and somewhat various literary tradition.

We have seen rhetorical theory. What of poetic practice? The fragments show that Archilochus was abrasive enough, shaming his victims through abuse.[3] As yet there is no theory, no ban on malice. For later antiquity, Archilochus, along with Hipponax, was synonymous with that vitriolic invective from which the ἐπιεικής should dissociate himself. But his hounding of Neobule to suicide is as legendary as Hipponax' effect on Bupalus, and Semonides' on Orodeicides: popular tradition supplied all three with victims, presumably in the belief that invective was as powerful as a curse.[4] Just as the curse became domiciled as a literary gehre,[5] so iambic invective, once torn from its initial place in society, opened itself to the modifications of theory. Of course, later writers can still be savage, sometimes in contra-

---

[1] P. 118.

[2] Cf. Ar. *Eth. Nic.* IV. 8, 1128a 20, καὶ ἡ τοῦ ἐλευθερίου παιδιὰ διαφέρει τῆς τοῦ ἀνδραποδώδους, cited by Hendrickson, *AJPh* XXI (1900), 139: 'the *ingenuus ludus*...is the Aristotelian mean of εὐτραπελία removed from boorishness (ἀγροικία), which is the ἔλλειψις, and from scurrility (βωμολοχία) which is the ὑπερβολή'.

[3] For defamation in Archil. fr. 88 D and Cat. XL, *v.* Hendrickson, *CPh* XX (1925), 155–7. Public derision leading to death is more apposite in a primitive shame-culture than a literate society. But see next note.

[4] *V.* Hendrickson, 'Archilochus and the Victims of his Iambics', *AJPh* XLVI (1925), 101 ff.; Cic. *D.N.D.* III. 91, for a rationalised ascription of the fates of the victims of Archilochus and Hipponax to sympathetic magic rather than external causation, also Plin. *N.H.* XXXVI. 12, on the fictitious nature of Bupalus. But there was real fear of curses: Plin. *N.H.* XXVIII. 19, *defigi diris precationibus nemo non metuit.* Earlier, the 'Ερινύες are personified as 'Αραί; allied is the tragic curse (e.g. Cic. *T.D.* III. 26, on Thyestes: but cf. *D.N.D.* III. 90 ridiculing the same); then there are the curses of the Bouzygai at the Athenian Bouphonia: *CIA* III. 294, Eupolis fr. 97 K, of an habitual curser, τί κέκραγας ὥσπερ βουζύγης ἀδικούμενος;, *Paroem. Gr.* I p. 388 (61), βουζύγης. ἐπὶ τῶν πολλὰ ἀρωμένων; also, the *devotiones* and *carmina* surrounding the death of Germanicus, Tac. *Ann.* II. 69; cf. VI. 23, of Drusus.

[5] E.g. the 'Αραί of Moiro (cf. Parthen. *Erot. Path.* 27 for her *Alcinoe*); the Χιλιάδες of Euphorion (the 'Αραί ἢ ποτηριοκλέπτης may have been a separate work); the *Ibis* of Callimachus and Ovid; and the *Dirae* of the *Appendix Vergiliana.*

---

diction of supposedly private beliefs. But when we reach Callimachus, even though invective has a future career, literary theory, as exemplified in Plato and Aristotle, has drawn the teeth of the iambist.

Following Callimachus, Roman satirists, iambists and epigrammatists profess innocence, inhibited more by the ethical and rhetorical dictation of charity and humanity in matters appertaining to the comic, than by legal considerations. R. E. Smith[1] concludes that the law of the Twelve Tables which 'made the singers and authors of slanderous songs liable to the death penalty' was irrelevant for the first and second centuries B.C., apart from the possible exception of Naevius. Further, the lex Cornelia de iniuriis, which he postulates as the influence on Hor. *Sat.* II. 1, was a law 'to which in the last disintegrating years of the Republic there had been little or no recourse'. One could also argue for the dissociation of recognised literary genres from libellous pamphlets, and against the exaggerated importance awarded to the related questions of 'naming names' and legal sanctions, as both resulting from the invention of Old Comedy as a source for Roman satire.[2] An ideological, not a legal, explanation is required for the various disclaimers.

Partly with a view to epideictic demonstration of the ἰαμβικὸν εἶδος, partly to parade his ποικιλία[3] in a series of experiments, Callimachus turned to iambics, in which, like Lucilius and Horace at a later date, he devoted a good deal of space to literary disputes.[4] From the first, he renounces the polemical spirit hitherto proper to the genre. As *Hipponax redivivus* he comes, *Iamb.* I. 3 f.,

[1] 'The Law of Libel at Rome', *CQ* XLV (1951), 169 ff., following Fraenkel, *Gnomon* (1925), 185 ff. on Cic. *de Rep.* IV. 11, our source for the law. Plato, above, ideally recommends legal sanctions.

[2] *V.* Leo, *Hermes* XXIV (1889), 71, detecting Varro as the culprit. The intention was no doubt to parallel Roman literary history with Greek. Fraenkel follows suit with slight modification, p. 126, 'In Horace's time it was taken for granted, probably on the authority of Varro, that Lucilius with his ὀνομαστὶ κωμῳδεῖν was walking in the footsteps of Old Comedy'; cf. Brink on Hor. *A.P.* 283–4, with regard to Roman emulation of restriction on censure in Old Comedy, 'Instigated by these Greek models, Roman grammarians, perhaps Varro, seem to have brought some legal provisions against *Fescennina licentia* into connexion with the development of Roman comedy: H. makes reference to this connexion at *Ep.* II. 1.145 ff.'

[3] C. Dawson, 'The Iambi of Callimachus', *YCS* XI (1950), 1–169, esp. 137 ff., traces the principle of diversity back to Isocr. *Pan.* 5, asking writers to desert areas where perfection has been achieved; *ibid.* 8, advocating variety of expression. Roman *variatio* is the later equivalent.

[4] Dawson, *YCS* XI (1950), 139 for links between the *Iamboi* and Roman satire, including Ennius.

φέρων ἴαμβον οὐ μάχην [ἀείδ]οντα
τὴν Βο]υπ[άλ]ειον.

In theory there is no rancour; but in practice he retains a degree of expected truculence, an inconsistency which we shall see again in the case of Horace.

Like Archilochus, Lucilius gained an unwarranted reputation for acerbity. True, there is invective, enough to inspire a loaded passage like *ad Fam.* XII. 16.3, where Trebonius vindicates his *libertas* in attacking Antony by appeal to satiric precedent:[1]

In quibus versiculis si tibi quibusdam verbis εὐθυρρημονέστερος videbor, turpitudo personae eius, in quam liberius invehimur, nos vindicabit. ignosces etiam *iracundiae* nostrae, quae iusta est in eiusmodi et homines et cives. deinde, qui magis hoc Lucilio licuerit assumere *libertatis*, quam nobis? cum, etiamsi *odio* pari fuerit in eos, quos *laesit*, tamen certe non magis dignos habuerit, in quos tanta *libertate* verborum incurreret.

The key words are *iracundia*, *libertas*, and *odium*, more components of iambic than satire.[2] *Testimonia* for his style apart – he seems in fact to have been a *tenuis poeta*, not an impassioned rhetorician – his representations in Horace, Persius, and Juvenal give a general impression of free-spoken violence as his main characteristic.[3] At Quint. x. 1.94, *nam eruditio in eo mira et* libertas *atque inde* acerbitas *et abunde salis*, his invective is again depicted as free and unrestrained. Some of this no doubt squares with practice, the '*Lucilianus character*' (Varro *R.R.* III. 2.17) being a real combination of invective and scurrility. But in theory he followed the lead of Callimachus, perhaps encouraged by Panaetius' naturalisation of Aristotelian theory,[4] to disown, like a

---

[1] *V.* C. A. Van Rooy, *Studies in Classical Satire and related Literary Theory* (Leiden 1966), p. 59, 'Personal or political pamphlets of the above nature, including the invectives which passed between Antony and Octavian, may have been colloquially classified as "*saturae*", "satires", or "invectives", but strictly speaking they fell outside the genre.'

[2] *Ibid.* p. 59, 'These *versiculi* were presumably not hexameters.'

[3] Some writers did see that he possessed the qualities described at Cic. *de Off.* I. 104, *elegans, urbanum, ingeniosum, facetum*; above, p. 163 and n. 3.

[4] Fiske, p. 90, 'Since it can be shown that in a satire in book thirty, ... Lucilius develops a ... discussion as to the types of humour appropriate for the *sermones* and rebuts charges of backbiting or invective, the question arises whether Panaetius was not one of the most important intermediaries, in naturalising ... the Aristotelian theory of liberal humour in the critical satires of Lucilius.'

13-2

true gentleman, acrimony and spite. From book XXX Puelma Piwonka, p. 68, extracts the following fragments as probably bearing on the repudiation of malevolence: 1015 M, *gaudes, cum de me ista foris sermonibus differs* (cf. *laedere gaudes*, Hor. *Sat.* I. 4.78); 1016, *et maledicendo in multis sermonibus differs*;[1] 1014, *idque tuis factis saevis et tristibus dictis* (cf. *tristi laedere versu*, Hor. *Sat.* II. 1.21); 1021, *quod t⟨u nunc⟩ laedes culpes, non proficis hilum*; 1013, '*et sola ex multis nunc nostra poemata ferri*' (sc. *per omnium ora*); 1035, *nunc, Gai* [sc. *Lucili*] *quoniam incilans nos laedis vicissim*; 1022, *hic ut muscipulae tentae atque ut scorpios cauda/sublata*. Other related fragments are 1030, *nolito tibi me male dicere posse putare* (Lucilius is not a slanderer; but is he a social reformer?); 1095–6, *inde canino rictu oculisque/involvem*; 1027, *summatim tamen experiar rescribere paucis* (the satirist answers criticisms).[2] Even if we discount the violence attributed by later portraits, it is probably fair to say that Lucilian practice was divorced from theory – but not to the degree of malignancy attributed by received opinion.

Likewise Horatian iambics are divided against themselves. At *Epod.* VI. 13–14, Horace likens himself to the savage Archilochus and Hipponax – *qualis Lycambae spretus infido gener/aut acer hostis Bupalo*[3] – yet later, in the theoretical *Ep.* I. 19.23 ff., he follows Lucilius and Callimachus in disowning malevolence:

> Parios ego primus iambos
> ostendi Latio, numeros animosque secutus

[1] Fiske p. 92, 'Lucilius in fragments 1015, 1016, seems to put into the mouth of an *adversarius* a charge of βωμολοχία levelled against himself. He too is charged with having disseminated scurrilous attacks in many discourses'; cf. Van Rooy, *Studies in Classical Satire*, p. 54, 'The Lucilian manner is here described by his opponents as defamatory.' I cannot assent to Fiske's hypothesis of a 'sharp distinction ... between ... humour and ... invective', p. 90. True, Archilochus, Hipponax, Catullus, and Horace's practice in the *Epodes* (v. Rudd, above p. 191 n. 1, p. 325 for personal abuse in the iambists: note also the relentless *Catalepton* XIII) seem to face in an opposite direction from *sermo* ('The conversation, whether written or spoken should not reveal the venom or censoriousness of the writer or real defects in his character. Hence Horace is extremely careful in the third satire of the first book to differentiate mere censoriousness from the light, but reforming humour of the free satirist'): but Callimachus, Horace in *Ep.* I. 19, Phaedrus, Babrius, and Martial, like the writers of *sermo*, disown scurrility.

[2] Van Rooy p. 54 rightly notes that Lucilius 'refused to subscribe to such a charge ⟨of harming people⟩': cf. D'Alton, p. 55.

[3] *V.* Fraenkel, pp. 56–7, esp. on the dog image. We cannot gloss over the inconsistency, dismissing the Epode as an 'exercise': no names are mentioned, but this is insignificant given allusion to Archilochus and Hipponax.

Archilochi, non res et agentia verba Lycamben.
ac ne me foliis ideo brevioribus ornes
quod timui mutare modos et carminis artem
temperat Archilochi Musam pede mascula Sapphu,
temperat Alcaeus, sed rebus et ordine dispar,
nec socerum quaerit, quem versibus oblinat atris,
nec sponsae laqueum famoso carmine nectit.[1]

He has imitated Archilochus, but has avoided personal acrimony: subscription to the theory of liberal humour – now apparently a necessity, at least notionally – has involved abstinence from the injury of insult. In *Sat.* I. 3 we come across further traces of adherence to the concept of liberal humour and the rejection of malice. As Hendrickson[2] remarks, 'In this work he begins ... in the censorious manner of satire, with a review of the character of Tigellius, but passes at once to a sharp censure of such ill-natured criticism.' Then, of I. 4, 'The charges of an imaginary critic describing Horace as an envenomed and unsparing satirist – in terms such as literary criticism employed concerning Lucilius or Aristophanes – gives the poet opportunity to utter his protest against this character which tradition had attributed to satire.' Quite correctly, he emphasises the literary status of *Sat.* I. 4: 'It is ... a criticism of literary theory put concretely', not an answer to 'the harsh criticisms of a public which felt aggrieved and injured by his attacks'.[3] At I. 4.34 ff., he represents himself as someone publicly regarded as a dangerous animal, who will not even spare his friends:

'faenum habet in cornu: longe fuge! dummodo risum
excutiat sibi, non hic cuiquam parcet amico;
et quodcumque semel chartis illeverit, omnes
gestiet a furno redeuntes scire lacuque
et pueros et anus.'

We can parallel the animal imagery from *Epod.* VI. 11, *namque in malos asperrimus/parata tollo cornua*, and *Sat.* II. 1.52, *dente lupus,*[4] *cornu taurus*[5] *petit*; the reference to friends, from Ar. *Eth. Nic.* IV. 14, 1128a, 36, of the βωμολόχος, οὔτε ἑαυτοῦ οὔτε τῶν ἄλλων ἀπεχόμενος,

---

[1] For the problems, *v. ibid.* pp. 341 ff.
[2] *AJPh* XXI (1900), 122.
[3] *Loc. cit.* p. 124; contrast Rudd, *CQ* ns v (1955), 142 ff., who conceives of the piece as an answer to criticisms levelled at the 'malicious spirit' and 'prosaic form' of satire.
[4] Cf. *Epod.* VI. 15, *atro dente.*
[5] Cf. Ovid's image of a bull at *Tr.* IV. 9.27 ff.

εἰ γέλωτα ποιήσει, and Cic. *Or.* 89, *parcet amicitiis.* Charged with βωμολοχία[1] Horace sidesteps the moral issue of personal injury with a formalistic statement, lines 65 ff., to the effect that he is not much read because his works are too good for the crowd – an elusive literary tactic which further implies that his audience has forfeited all rights to deliver such charges, since they are like the robbers of 69. More positive is the motif of friendship: against 35, *non hic cuiquam parcet amico,* 81, *absentem qui rodit amicum,* 86 ff., of the man who is too *liber* in his gibes (note the pun, 89), and 96 ff., '*me Capitolinus convictore usus amicoque/a puero est, causaque mea permulta rogatus/fecit, et incolumis laetor quod vivit in urbe;/sed tamen admiror quo pacto iudicium illud/fugerit*', four *loci* which call into doubt the most basic human relationship, we can set 73, *nec recito cuiquam nisi amicis idque coactus,* and 135 f., *sic dulcis amicis/occurram* (cf. 132, *liber amicus*), passages which depict a liberal moralist, concerned about his intercourse with others. Here lies his answer to the allegation of βωμολοχία: what matters is not his lack of publicity, but his regard for the finer points of human fellowship. Scurrility is proclaimed to be far from his manner, 101–3; he is neither *lividus* nor *mordax,* 93. Yet he does not boast about the humane nature of his satire. It is merely one of his frailties, 139 f., *hoc est mediocribus illis ex vitiis unum.*

In *Sat.* II. 1 he adopts an ambiguous stance, at one moment a pacifist, at another, an aggressor. Like Juvenal, he will not attack the living, 39 ff.:

> sed hic stilus haud petet ultro
> *quemquam animantem* et me veluti custodiet ensis
> vagina tectus.

Nor will he injure anyone, unless provoked, 41 ff.:

> quem cur destringere coner
> tutus ab infestis latronibus? o pater et rex
> Iuppiter, ut pereat positum robigine telum,
> nec quisquam noceat cupido mihi pacis! at ille,
> qui me commorit (melius non tangere, clamo),
> flebit et insignis tota cantabitur urbe.

In fact, he does draw the sword briefly, at 47 ff., while purporting to describe the defensive tactics of Cervius, Canidia, and Turius – also,

---

[1] Hendrickson, p. 197 n. 2 above, p. 128, 'the picture which Horace draws of the satirist, as people think of him, corresponds to Aristotle's characterisation of the βωμολοχία which he found exemplified by the Old Comedy, and to such terms as are used to describe iambic and satirical poets generally'.

more gratuitously, the crimes of Scaeva. Trebatius introduced the topic of danger at 21–3. After the threat of 44–6, Horace responds with an oblique exemplification of aggressive malevolence, even though he has inveigled us into believing that this weapon will serve only for self-defence. Vindictiveness, therefore, the child of a propensity for ill-natured humour, has a potential function in Horatian satire. Lucilian virulence is duly invoked to illustrate the contention, but then, with a more explicit version of the technique employed in *Sat.* I. 4, the moral question is ironically resolved in terms of style. For a brief period Horace has exploited the rhetorical theory of humour, at one moment representing himself as illiberal, with his threats, and indirect illus-trations of a capacity for libel, at another, as ingenuously pacific.[1] Somewhat different, and closer to Persius' first satire, is *Ep.* I. 1.94 ff., where barren and potentially constructive humour are opposed:

> si curatus inaequali tonsore capillos
> occurri *rides*; si forte subucula pexae
> trita subest tunicae, vel si toga dissidet impar,
> *rides*: quid, mea cum pugnat sententia secum,
> quod petiit spernit, repetit quod nuper omisit,
> aestuat et vitae disconvenit ordine toto,
> diruit, aedificat, mutat quadrata rotundis?
> insanire putas sollemnia me neque *rides*,
> nec medici credis nec curatoris egere
> a praetore dati, rerum tutela mearum
> cum sis et prave sectum stomacheris ob unguem
> de te pendentis, te respicientis amici.

Appearances provoke laughter. But such humour is shallow and lacks direction, reformation not being one of its aims. Morals, on the other hand, elicit no response. Where laughter in the form of the liberal

---

[1] Cf. Hendrickson, 'Are the Letters of Horace Satires?', *AJPh* XVIII (1897), 313, 'for the purposes of the situation which he has created ... he plays with the traditional doctrine of the acerbity of satire, and threatens ven-geance on his enemies with a vehemence which is un-Horatian in all but its sly fun'. On the legal aspect at 80 ff., I agree with Rudd, *CQ* ns X (1960), 173, 'It has to be remembered that when Horace spoke of *mala carmina* in II. 1.82, he probably had the other seven poems of the book in front of him and knew perfectly well that they contained no defamatory material. The more one thinks about II. 1.80 ff., the less inclined one feels to take the passage as anything but a joke. The libel law existed to be sure, otherwise the play on the requirements of law and satire would have been pointless ... but Horace was in no danger of infringing it.'

jest could be remedial, there is resignation to the disease of inconstancy.

By denying prior ill will at *Tr.* II. 563, *non ego* mordaci *destrinxi carmine quemquam*, and 565, *candidus* a salibus suffusis felle *refugi:/nulla* venenato *littera mixta ioco est*, Ovid implies continuity in the conventional theory of humour. More statements than disclaimers – if anything, iambic is envisaged rather than satire – these passages nonetheless derive from the sanctioned contrast between venomous and humane wit. With his reference to the viciousness of satire at *Silv.* I. 3.103, *sive/*liventem *saturam* nigra *rubigine turbes*, Statius shows that the theory was still alive in the later first century, while Quintilian's discussion of humour at VI. 3 proves the survival of the rules (note §11), in particular the ban on hurtful jests, §28, *laedere numquam velimus*. But now, though of some importance before, the question of 'naming names' assumes greater sometimes too great, proportions.[1] Phaedrus, for instance, claims to represent life in a general sense, not to brand specific individuals, III prol. 49–50:

> neque enim *notare singulos* mens est mihi,
> verum *ipsam vitam et mores hominum* ostendere.

To mention names in a spiteful and polemical spirit is illiberal – and

---

[1] A distinction should be drawn between the interpretation of Athenian ὀνομαστὶ κωμῳδεῖν in terms of the *nota censoria* (Fraenkel, p. 126 n. 2, with Ciceronian references; Van Rooy, *Studies in Classical Satire*, p. 148, citing Hor. *Sat.* I. 3.24, 4.3–5, and 106: 'he gives the Peripatetic-Alexandrian tradition concerning the ὀνομαστὶ κωμῳδεῖν a Roman colour by his use of the word "*notabant*")', and the law of libel, which seems to have become more stringent in later Augustan times, and in the reign of Tiberius (Smith, *CQ* XLV (1951), 179). The latter – along with the theory of humour – could explain some aspects of post-Augustan discretion, while the former, a purely literary figment, could support a qualified addition of Lucilius, his ὀνομαστὶ κωμῳδεῖν as much a Varronian invention as an observable trait in his works, to Kenney's assertion, *PCPhS* ns VIII (1962), 37, that 'neither Horace nor Persius nor Juvenal ever attacked an eminent contemporary, either by name or by unmistakeable innuendo'. Rather, Lucilius, like Accius, 'brought cases for damages against mime-writers who had criticised them by name' (Smith, p. 171, citing, n. 3, *ad Her.* II. 13.19). For names in the three post-Lucilian satirists, *v.* Rudd pp. 132–59; Jahn, *prolegomena* pp. lxvii f., finding that Persius' names are mainly fictitious; Highet pp. 289 ff. The problem has been abnormally exaggerated by those who feel that integrity – a condition behind a composition – depends on the real or fictitious nature of the personalities mentioned. Better to take the disclaimers on a level with, e.g., the historiographical formula, *sine ira et studio* (for which *v.* O. Weinreich (Berlin 1923), on Seneca's *Apocol.*), and abandon the search for 'real' individuals.

perhaps dangerous – while the topic of life allows the fabulist to retain the desirable qualities of candour and humanity.[1] Babrius, by way of contrast, perpetuates the mainstream tradition of domesticating the acrimonious iambic, prol. I. 19:

πικρῶν ἰάμβων σκληρὰ κῶλα θηλύσας.

This amounts to no more than disowning the precedent of Archilochus and Hipponax, after the fashion of Callimachus and Horace.

Martial, like Phaedrus, denies enmity against personalities, professing general moral concern, presumably with designs on praise for liberality, X. 33.10:

parcere personis, dicere de vitiis.

It is the Muse who has commanded him to depict life in this catholic fashion, VIII. 3.19–20:

at tu Romanos lepido sale tingue libellos:
adgnoscat mores vita legatque suos.

Anonymity is to be one of his guiding principles, II. 23:

non dicam, licet usque me rogetis,
qui sit Postumus in meo libello.

Then again, at IX. 95 b, he disavows knowledge of the realities, or unrealities, behind his pseudonyms, incidentally proving public interest, probably futile, in tracking down the individual:

nomen Athenagorae quaeris, Callistrate, verum.
si scio, dispeream, qui sit Athenagoras.

Taken singly, none of these passages has immediately apparent bearing on the theory of humour, even though they are implicit denials of wilful intention. Perhaps with an eye on the partly unwarranted later reputation of Lucilius, and on the deserved notoriety of Catullus, Martial says in the preface to his first book that only the guilty need fear him. Other writers might be less discriminating. The guilt theme had occurred earlier, in Theocritus' nineteenth epigram:

ὁ μουσοποιὸς ἐνθάδ' Ἱππῶναξ κεῖται.
εἰ μὲν πονηρός, μὴ προσέρχευ τῷ τύμβῳ·
εἰ δ' ἐσσὶ κρήγυός τε καὶ παρὰ χρηστῶν,
θαρσέων καθίζευ, κἢν θέλῃς ἀπόβριξον.[2]

---

[1] V. C. E. Lutz, 'Any Resemblance ... is Purely Coincidental', CJ XLVI (1950), 115 ff., esp. p. 118, with dubious speculation about disguised allusion.

[2] Cf. Anth. Pal. VII. 405, ὦ ξεῖνε φεῦγε τὸν χαλαζεπῆ τάφον/τὸν φρικτὸν Ἱππώνακτος.

Martial's work is a *ludus poeticus*,[1] different from that of earlier writers in so far as it spares the names of contemporaries, whatever their social status, I *praef.*:

> spero me secutum in libellis meis tale temperamentum ut de illis queri non possit *quisquis de se bene senserit,* cum *salva infimarum quoque personarum reverentia ludant,* quae adeo antiquis auctoribus defuit ut *nominibus* non tantum *veris* abusi sint sed et *magnis.*

Again, there is no apparent connexion with the theory of humour, though, as before, Martial immunises himself from possible charges of spite.

We can, however, bridge the gap between the question of names,[2] and the theory of humour, by examining the poetic extension of a motif which occurs in this same preface: *absit a iocorum nostrorum simplicitate malignus interpres nec epigrammata mea scribat.* For in several epigrams on the subject of malicious forgery and interpretation, theoretical vocabulary makes a vestigial appearance. In order, there is the black venom of the wrongly attributed compositions at VII. 72.12–16:

> si quisquam mea dixerit malignus
> *atro* carmina quae madent *veneno,*
> ut vocem mihi commodes patronam
> et quantum poteris, sed usque, clames
> 'non scripsit meus ista Martialis'.

Again, he rejects the lower forms of wit at X. 3.9–10, this time with the image of *nigra fama*:[3]

> procul a libellis *nigra* sit meis *fama,*
> quos rumor *alba* gemmeus vehit pinna.

Finally, the traditional motif of *laedere versu* crops up at X. 5.1 ff.:

> quisquis stolaeve purpuraeve contemptor
> quos colere debet *laesit impio versu*
> erret per urbem pontis exul et clivi,
> interque raucos ultimus rogatores
> oret caninas panis improbi buccas.

---

[1] H. Wagenvoort, on *ludus poeticus*, in *Studies in Roman Literature, Culture and Religion* (Leyden 1956), pp. 30–42, is disappointing. From satire, cf. Lucil. 1039 M, ludo *ac sermonibus nostris*, Pers. I. 117, of Horace, *circum praecordia* ludit, v. 18, *doctus et ingenuo culpam defigere* ludo.

[2] On names in Martial, *v.* J. W. Spaeth *CJ* XXIV (1929), 381; A. Cartault, *Mélanges Boissier* (Paris 1903), p. 103.

[3] For *niger* of tasteless wit, cf. Hor. *Sat.* I. 4.85, 91, 100–1, *hic nigrae sucus lolliginis, haec est/aerugo mera*; perhaps *Ep.* II. 2.60, of Bion's diatribes, *sale nigro.*

Since the poem continues in this rancorous vein for another fourteen lines, an irony may be intended, Martial 'harming' the 'harmful' forger. Now it seems we are back in the realm of illiberal humour, via the application of conventional imagery to the related, but in itself unadorned subject of 'naming names'.

In Mart. VII. 12 the position is clarified. A recently observed formula – *laedere versu* – links the business of specifying individual names with the denial of commonplace Archilochean malevolence:

> sic me fronte legat dominus, Faustine, serena
> excipiatque meos qua solet aure *iocos*
> ut mea *nec* iuste quos odit pagina *laesit*
> et mihi de *nullo* fama *rubore* placet.
> quid prodest, cupiant cum quidam nostra videri,
> si qua *Lycambeo sanguine* tela madent,[1]
> *vipereumque* vomat nostro sub nomine *virus*,
> qui Phoebi radios ferre diemque negat?
> *ludimus innocui*: scis hoc bene: iuro potentis
> per genium Famae Castaliumque gregem
> perque tuas aures, magni mihi numinis instar,
> lector *inhumana* liber ab invidia.

The two kinds of humour meet in the persons of Martial and his forger. Martial credits his reader with humanity, to which he aligns himself through his profession of benign and playful innocence: having no desire to hurt people, even when he has cause, he emerges as the kind and tolerant humanist of which theory would approve. The forger, on the other hand, is the scurrilous and inhuman wit, who infects his victims *nominatim* with poisonous libel.

Finally, an instance of self-conscious Juvenalian tastelessness. Ideally, as we have seen, the humorist should not wish to harm individuals, being concerned instead with the generic: as Pliny says of the philosopher Euphrates, *Ep.* I. 10.7, *insectatur vitia, non homines*, a principle similar to Martial's *parcere personis, dicere de vitiis*. Living as he did near the end of a tradition, Juvenal must have been saturated with rhetorical and ethical teaching on humour. Told by theory that he must spare the individual, his perverse inclination is to attack, I. 153–4:

> cuius non audeo dicere nomen?
> quid refert, dictis ignoscat Mucius an non?

[1] Imitated from Ov. *Ibis* 54.

Like that of the *scurra*, or βωμολόχος, his immediate reaction is, theoretically speaking, ill-considered and violent. But in context it seems brave. Warned against the dangers of *ad hominem* invective, he again attempts to claim the prerogative of personal reference, 158–9:

> qui dedit ergo tribus patruis aconita, vehatur
> pensilibus plumis atque illinc despiciat nos?

Once more he is silenced, advised of the safety of mythological themes: in sum, enjoined to forgo scurrilous gibes at the expense of contemporaries.[1] Even as far as 169, the reader must have been aware of his tinkerings with the subject of βωμολοχία: instead of orthodox concern with the generic, he has been faced with an experimental programme of designs against the individual. Under a skilful disguise of justifiable sincerity, the satirist has aspired to the status of vicious βωμολόχος. But none of this has been intended to elicit surprise. The tone of innocence only disappears at 170–1, where he shows that compulsion to dispense with one kind of βωμολοχία – disrespectful assaults on living individuals – involves another kind, that described by Theophrastus at *Char.* XVIII. 4, on κακολογία, consisting of ill-natured criticisms of the dead:

> experiar quid concedatur in illos,
> quorum Flaminia tegitur cinis atque Latina.

Denied the opportunity for scurrilous behaviour in one sphere, he adopts it in another, perhaps with Horace's ambiguous *quemquam animantem*, *Sat.* II. 1.40, in mind, also perhaps with the intention of substituting *mala carmina* for his predecessor's *bona carmina*, but certainly with a desire to shock the reader versed in rhetorical theory. Where conventions should be preserved, with regard to the living, and, in particular, the dead, he reverses standard procedure, so representing himself as a literary iconoclast. Instead of subscribing to the thesis 'no offence, either to living or dead', he displays a desire to attack the living, which, when thwarted, becomes a desire to libel the dead. Within the framework offered by the theory of liberal humour, Juvenal makes two departures: least important, and perhaps not meant to be obtrusive, an enthusiasm for the criticism of contemporaries; then, with obvious irony, an intention to malign the dead. This is not a case of illiberal humour applied, but one of liberal humour traduced. Unlike Horace, Juvenal will write *mala*, not *bona*, *carmina*.

---

[1] Mucius and Tigellinus, 154–5, though literally 'dead', symbolise contemporaries.

O curas hominum! o quantum est in rebus inane!
'quis leget haec?' min tu istud ais? nemo hercule. 'nemo?'
vel duo vel nemo. 'turpe et miserabile.' quare?
ne mihi Polydamas et Troiades Labeonem
praetulerint? nugae. non, si quid turbida Roma   5
elevet, accedas examenve inprobum in illa
castiges trutina nec te quaesiveris extra.
nam Romae quis non – a, si fas dicere – sed fas
tum cum ad canitiem et nostrum istud vivere triste
aspexi ac nucibus facimus quaecumque relictis,   10
cum sapimus patruos. tunc tunc – ignoscite (nolo,
quid faciam?) – sed (sum petulanti splene) cachinno.
    scribimus inclusi, numeros ille, hic pede liber,
grande aliquid quod pulmo animae praelargus anhelet.
scilicet haec populo pexusque togaque recenti   15
et natalicia tandem cum sardonyche albus
sede leges celsa, liquido cum plasmate guttur
mobile conlueris, patranti fractus ocello.
tunc neque more probo videas nec voce serena
ingentes trepidare Titos, cum carmina lumbum   20
intrant et tremulo scalpuntur ubi intima versu.
tun, vetule, auriculis alienis colligis escas,
articulis quibus et dicas cute perditus 'ohe'?
'quo didicisse, nisi hoc fermentum et quae semel intus
innata est rupto iecore exierit caprificus?'   25
en pallor seniumque! o mores, usque adeone
scire tuum nihil est nisi te scire hoc sciat alter?

6 ve *CGLNS et ud vid. P*: que α*XMRW*   8 romae *Leid. Voss.* 13, *Bern.*
398: roma est α: romae est *PXΦS*   ha *Leid. Voss.* 13: ac *PαΦ*: *om. XW.*
cf. III. 16, *Iuv.* XIV. 45   9 tum α*XMR*: tunc *PΦS*   11–12 *dist. Housman*
14 quod *PΦS*: quo α*XM*   17 leges Σ(*LU*): legens *PαXΦΣ*(*M*). *cf. Iuv.*
VII. 177   19 tunc *PG²M²*: hic α*XΦS*   nec *PαCXMNR*: neque
GLWS(*LU*)   23 articulis *Madvig, Advers. crit.* II. 128: auriculis *PαXΦSΣ*
24 quo *PGLMRS*(*M*): quod α*XNS*(*LU*): quid *CW*

'at pulchrum est digito monstrari et dicier "hic est."
ten cirratorum centum dictata fuisse
pro nihilo pendes?' ecce inter pocula quaerunt   30
Romulidae saturi quid dia poemata narrent.
hic aliquis, cui circum umeros hyacinthina laena est,
rancidulum quiddam balba de nare locutus
Phyllidas, Hypsipylas, vatum et plorabile siquid,
eliquat ac tenero subplantat verba palato.   35
adsensere viri: nunc non cinis ille poetae
felix? non levior cippus nunc inprimit ossa?
laudant convivae: nunc non e manibus illis,
nunc non e tumulo fortunataque favilla
nascentur violae? 'rides' ait 'et nimis uncis   40
naribus indulges. an erit qui velle recuset
os populi meruisse et cedro digna locutus
linquere nec scombros metuentia carmina nec tus?'
    quisquis es, o modo quem ex adverso dicere feci,
non ego cum scribo, si forte quid aptius exit,   45
quando haec rara avis est, si quid tamen aptius exit,
laudari metuam; neque enim mihi cornea fibra est.
sed recti finemque extremumque esse recuso
'euge' tuum et 'belle.' nam 'belle' hoc excute totum:
quid non intus habet? non hic est Ilias Atti   50
ebria veratro? non siqua eligidia crudi
dictarunt proceres? non quidquid denique lectis
scribitur in citreis? calidum scis ponere sumen,
scis comitem horridulum trita donare lacerna,
et 'verum' inquis 'amo, verum mihi dicite de me.'   55
qui pote? vis dicam? nugaris, cum tibi, calve,
pinguis aqualiculus propenso sesquipede extet.
o Iane, a tergo quem nulla ciconia pinsit
nec manus auriculas imitari mobilis albas
nec linguae quantum sitiat canis Apula tantae.   60
vos, o patricius sanguis, quos vivere fas est

30 pendes *PGR*: pendas α*X*Φ   32 circum *PCGLWS(LU)*: circa
α*XMNR Sang. S(M) Hieron. Epist.* LIV. 5   44 feci *P*Φ*S*: fas est α*XMR*
46 47 *hoc ordine PCLNWS*Σ: 46 *om. sed. add. in marg. inf.* G: 47 46 α*XMR*
46 haec α*X*Φ*S(L)*Σ*(LU)*: hoc *PGNS(MU)*Σ*(M)*   53–104 *exhibet Bob.*
57 propenso *PX*Φ *Bob.*: protenso α: protento *Prisc. G.L.K.* II. 251.
cf. Hieron. Adv. Iovin. II. 21, *In Hierem.* III. 15.3   58 pinsit] '*apud
Persium ambiguum* a tergo ciconia pisat *an* pisit *legendum sit*' *Diomed.
G.L.K.* I. 373   59 imitari *PGL Bob. S*: imitata est α*X*Φ   61 fas α*X*Φ
*Bob. S(M)*Σ: ius *PGWS(LU)*

occipiti caeco, posticae occurrite sannae.
  'quis populi sermo est'? quis enim nisi carmina molli
nunc demum numero fluere, ut per leve severos
effundat iunctura ungues? scit tendere versum   65
non secus ac si oculo rubricam derigat uno.
sive opus in mores, in luxum, in prandia regum
dicere, res grandes nostro dat Musa poetae.
ecce modo heroas sensus adferre docemus
nugari solitos Graece, nec ponere lucum   70
artifices nec rus saturum laudare, ubi corbes
et focus et porci et fumosa Palilia faeno,
unde Remus sulcoque terens dentalia, Quinti,
cum trepida ante boves dictatorem induit uxor
et tua aratra domum lictor tulit – euge poeta!   75
est nunc Brisaei quem venosus liber Acci,
sunt quos Pacuviusque et verrucosa moretur
Antiopa 'aerumnis cor luctificabile fulta'.
hos pueris monitus patres infundere lippos
cum videas, quaerisne unde haec sartago loquendi   80
venerit in linguas, unde istud dedecus in quo
trossulus exultat tibi per subsellia levis?
nilne pudet capiti non posse pericula cano
pellere quin tepidum hoc optes audire 'decenter'?
'fur es' ait Pedio. Pedius quid? crimina rasis   85
librat in antithetis, doctas posuisse figuras
laudatur: 'bellum hoc.' hoc bellum? an, Romule, ceves?
men moveat? quippe, et, cantet si naufragus, assem
protulerim? cantas, cum fracta te in trabe pictum
ex umero portes? verum nec nocte paratum   90
plorabit qui me volet incurvasse querella.
  'sed numeris decor est et iunctura addita crudis.
cludere sic versum didicit "Berecyntius Attis"
et "qui caeruleum dirimebat Nerea delphin,"
sic "costam longo subduximus Appennino."   95

69 docemus *PGL Bob. Sang. S(M)*: videmus α*XΦS(LU)Σ*   74 cum
PGMNWSΣ: quem α*XCLR Bob. fortasse subest* quom. *cf. Iuv.* III.
37 dictatorem *PαXGMR Bob. Σ(L)*: dictaturam *CLNWS*   81 istud
XΦS: istut *P*: istuc α*MRBob*.   86 doctus *Scaliger*   87 laudatur
CNRWΣ: laudatus *GLBob.*: laudatu *P*: laudatis α*XM*   hoc hoc bellum
PBob.: hoc bellum α*XGLMS(LU)*: hoc bellum hoc *CN*: hoc bellum est
RWS(M). cf. III, ii.19   92–97 *adversario*, 98–106 *Persio tribuerunt
Marcilius et Heinrich*

"Arma virum", nonne hoc spumosum et cortice pingui
ut ramale vetus vegrandi subere coctum?'
quidnam igitur tenerum et laxa cervice legendum?
'torva Mimalloneis inplerunt cornua bombis,
et raptum vitulo caput ablatura superbo   100
Bassaris et lyncem Maenas flexura corymbis
euhion ingeminat, reparabilis adsonat echo.'
haec fierent si testiculi vena ulla paterni
viveret in nobis? summa delumbe saliva
hoc natat in labris et in udo est Maenas et Attis   105
nec pluteum caedit nec demorsos sapit ungues.
    'sed quid opus teneras mordaci radere vero
auriculas? vide sis ne maiorum tibi forte
limina frigescant: sonat hic de nare canina
littera.' per me equidem sint omnia protinus alba;   110
nil moror. euge omnes, omnes bene, mirae eritis res.
hoc iuvat? 'hic' inquis 'veto quisquam faxit oletum.'
pinge duos anguis: 'pueri, sacer est locus, extra
meiite.' discedo. secuit Lucilius urbem,
te Lupe, te Muci, et genuinum fregit in illis.   115
omne vafer vitium ridenti Flaccus amico
tangit et admissus circum praecordia ludit,
callidus excusso populum suspendere naso.
me muttire nefas? nec clam? nec cum scrobe? nusquam?
hic tamen infodiam. vidi, vidi ipse, libelle: 120
auriculas asini quis non habet? hoc ego opertum,
hoc ridere meum, tam nil, nulla tibi vendo
Iliade. audaci quicumque adflate Cratino
iratum Eupolidem praegrandi cum sene palles,
aspice et haec, si forte aliquid decoctius audis.   125
inde vaporata lector mihi ferveat aure,
non hic qui in crepidas Graiorum ludere gestit
sordidus et lusco qui possit dicere 'lusce',
sese aliquem credens Italo quod honore supinus
fregerit heminas Arreti aedilis iniquas,   130

96–ii. 48 *deficit* G   97 vegrandi *Porph. in Hor. Serm.* I. 2.129, *Serv. in
Aen.* XI.553: praegrandi *PαXΦS*   107 vero αXΦS(*LU*)Σ: verbo *PR*.
cf. *Iuv.* I. 161   111 omnes omnes *LN et ut vid. W*: omnes *PαXMS*:
omnes etenim *CR. cf.* 87   *post* bene *dist. Buecheler*   119 me αXMR:
me∗ *P*: men ΦS   121 quis non] *Persium prius scripsisse* Mida rex *et* Σ *et
vita testantur*   129 sese XΦS: seque *P*

nec qui abaco numeros et secto in pulvere metas
scit risisse vafer, multum gaudere paratus
si cynico barbam petulans nonaria vellat.
his mane edictum, post prandia Callirhoen do.

The following translation is based on the rendering by Professor Niall
Rudd in *The Satires of Horace and Persius* published by Penguin
Books in 1973:

Ah, the obsessions of men! What an empty world we live in!
  'Who will read this?'
                   Are you asking me? Why, no one.
                                   'No one?'
Well, perhaps one or two.
                'Disgraceful! Pathetic!'
                         But why?
Are you worried in case 'Polydamas and the Trojan ladies' prefer
Labeo to me? What the hell. If woolly old Rome attaches
no weight to a piece of work, don't you step in to correct
the faulty tongue on her balance. Ask no one's view but your own.
Is there any Roman who hasn't – if only I could say it – but I can,
when I look at our venerable hair and that austere demeanour
and all we've been at since we gave up marbles and assumed the wisdom 10
of disapproving uncles, then – sorry, I don't want to –
I can't help it – it's just my irreverent humour – I guffaw!

  Behind our study doors we write in regular metre,
or else foot-loose, a prodigious work which will leave the strongest
lungs out of breath. On your birthday you will finally read this stuff
from a public platform, carefully combed, in a new white toga,
flashing a gem on your finger, rinsing your supple throat
with a clear preparatory warble, your eyes swooning in ecstasy.
Then, what a sight! The mighty sons of Rome in a dither,
losing control of voice and movement as the quivering strains   20
steal under the spine and scratch the secret passage.
Dirty old man, cooking erotica for other men's ears,
passive, demanding, which your gouty impotence can no longer please.

  'What's the point of study if that frothy yeast, that fig-tree
which has once struck root inside never exits, liver burst?'
  So that's why you're pale and peevish! My god, what have we
                              [come to?

Repression of urges, to know things without being known to know?'

'But it's nice to be pointed out, and for people to say "that's him!"
Isn't it something to be a set book for a mob of long-haired
schoolboys?'   30
      Look, the Roman élite with full stomach
are enquiring over the port 'What has deathless verse to say?'
Then a creature with a hyacinth mantle draped around his shoulders
mumbles some putrid stuff through his nose, filtering out
a Phyllis or Hypsipyle or some other tear-jerking bardic rot,
prettily wrestling the words against his tender palate.
The great men murmur approval. Now surely the poet's ashes
are happy; surely the gravestone presses more lightly on his bones!
The humbler guests applaud. Now surely violets will spring
from those remains, from his tomb, and from his blessed dust!

'You're making fun,' he says, 'and curling your nostrils unfairly.   40
Who would deny that he hoped to earn a place on the lips
of the nation, to utter words that called for cedar oil,
and to leave behind pages that feared neither mackerel nor incense?'

You, whoever you are, my fictitious debating opponent,
if in the course of my writing something special emerges
(a rare bird, I admit), but *if* something special emerges,
I'm not the man to shrink from applause; my skin's not *that* tough.
But I do say your 'Bravo' and 'Lovely' are not the final
and ultimate test of what's good. For just shake out that 'Lovely'.
What does it not contain? Why Attius' *Iliad*'s there,   50
dotty with hellebore. Yes, and all the dear little elegies
improvised by crapulous grandees, all the stuff in fact
that is scribbled on citrus couches. You know the trick – you serve
hot sow's udders, give a threadbare coat to a shivering dependant,
then say 'I'm a lover of truth; tell me the truth about myself.'
How can he? Would you like it from me? You're an airy doodler, baldy,
with your fat pot protruding at least a foot and a half!
Janus, *you* have no noisy stork pecking you from behind,
no hands held up to wag like white ears, no tongues
stuck out like a thirsty dog's when his star is parching Apulia.   60
My noble lords, who must live with a blind rear wall in your skull,
run and confront the jeering grimace at your back door!
  'Well what does the public say?'

               What you'd expect – that poems

at last have a smooth-flowing rhythm; where the joint occurs, it sends
the critical nail skidding across the polished surface.
He *rules* each line, as if stretching a cord with one eye shut.
Our poet's Muse always provides him with great themes –
the royal way of life, perhaps, or its splendours, or its dinners!

Just look, we are teaching them to voice heroic sentiments –
[amateurs
who used to doodle in Greek! They haven't the skill to depict   70
a clump of trees or the well-fed land with its baskets and hearths
and pigs, and the hay smoking on Pales' holiday, from which
came Remus and Cincinnatus, who was polishing his share in the furrow
when his flustered wife, with a quorum of oxen, invested him Dictator,
and the sergeant took home the plough. Bravo my noble bard!

Nowadays one man pores over the shrivelled tome of Accius
the old Bacchanal, others over Pacuvius and his warty Antiopa
'who has nought but woe itself to brace her dolorous heart'.
When you see myopic fathers brainwashing their sons like this,
is there any need to ask who's to blame for putting this sizzling 80
mish-mash into their mouths, and for that degrading rubbish
which makes our pumiced knights of the realm jitter on their seats?
You should be ashamed! Why you can't defend that venerable head
in court without eagerly listening for a murmur of 'Very nice!'
'You, Pedius, are a thief!' In answer Pedius weighs
the charges in shaved antitheses, winning praise for his clever figures.
'How lovely!' Well *is* it lovely? Or is Romulus wagging his tail?
If I heard a shipwrecked man singing, would I offer him a coin
out of sympathy? Do you sing as you exhibit on your back a painting
[of yourself
in the flotsam? Anyone who wants to bowl me over will need   90
to weep genuine tears, not rehearsed the night before.

'But the crude old verses have been given a new smoothness and grace.
A metrical rôle has now been assigned to "Berecyntian Attis"
and to "The dolphin who was slicing his way through dark blue
[Nereus",
and to "We stole a rib from the long spine of the Apennines."
"Arms and the man" – what desiccated antiquated stuff that is,
like the branch of an old cork tree enveloped in cakey bark!'

Well what would be fresh, and suitable for reciting with a languid
[neck?

'They filled their frightening horns with Bacchanalian brays.
The Bassarid carrying the head torn from a frisky calf   100
and the Maenad ready to guide the lynx with reins of ivy
cry Euhoe! Euhoe! The shout's taken up by restorative Echo.'
Could such things happen if we cherished a spark of our fathers' spunk?
This emasculated stuff, this Maenad and Attis, floats on the spit,
always on the tip of the tongue, ready to come drooling out.
It doesn't pummel the back-rest or taste of bitten nails.

   'Why do you feel you must rub biting truthful vinegar
into sensitive ears? Better watch it. You may get a chilly reception
from those baronial porches. The cynical sound of your satire
has been heard as it curls down your nose.' From this moment, then
                                        [everything's white   110
I don't care. Bravo! Superb! You're all just marvellous.
How's that? You erect a notice which says 'Refrain from shitting.'
Paint two holy snakes: 'This is sacred ground, my lads;
find somewhere else to piss.' I'm going. Lucilius bit into
the city – Lupus and Mucius and all – and smashed his molar on them.
While his friend is laughing, that rascal Horace puts his finger on all
his faults; gaining admission, he plays on the conscience – so clever
at holding the public up to ridicule on that well-blown nose.
Am I forbidden to whisper – to myself – to a ditch – anywhere?
Never mind; I'll bury it here in my book. I've seen it myself: 120
EVERY MAN JACK HAS AN ASS'S EARS! That's my secret;
that's my joke. Slight as it is, I wouldn't sell it
for all your *Iliads*.
   If you've caught the spirit of brave Cratinus
or are pale from devotion to angry Eupolis and the Grand Old Man,
if you've an ear for a concentrated brew, then have a look at this.
I want a reader with ears well steamed by that comic cure,
not the lout who jeers delightedly at the Greek style of sandal,
and is low enough to shout 'Hey one-eye!' at a man with that affliction,
who think's he's somebody just because as Aedile at Arezzo
he has smashed a few short measures with full municipal pomp,   130
nor the witty fellow who sniggers when he sees numbers and cones
traced in the sand of the abacus, and is vastly amused if a Nones-girl
has the impudence to pull a philosopher's beard. For them I suggest
the law reports in the morning and *Calliroë* after lunch.

INDEXES

1: INDEX OF MODERN AUTHORS

2: INDEX LOCORUM POTIORUM

3: INDEX OF IMAGES, TOPICS AND WORDS

INDEX OF IMAGES, TOPICS AND WORDS